Peter Brook: A BIOGRAPHY

Also by J. C. Trewin

Peter Brook
A BIOGRAPHY

J C Trewin

MACDONALD·LONDON

First published in Great Britain in 1971 by
Macdonald & Co. (Publishers) Ltd,
St Giles House, 49 Poland Street, London, W.1

Copyright © J. C. Trewin, 1971

Made and Printed in Great Britain by
Tonbridge Printers Ltd,
Peach Hall Works, Tonbridge, Kent

SBN 356 03855 6

In memory of
SIMON BROOK
and in deep gratitude

Contents

List of Illustrations

King Lear tour, 1964
Mrs Simon Brook

The Marat/Sade, 1964
Morris Newcombe and Royal Shakespeare Company

US, 1966
Morris Newcombe and David Farrell

Oedipus, 1968
Zoe Dominic and National Theatre

A Midsummer Night's Dream, 1970
David Farrell

King Lear, 1971
David Farrell

Peter Brook, 1971
David Farrell

Author's Note

EARLY in Peter Brook's career Sir Barry Jackson called him 'the youngest earthquake'. No director in the international theatre is more applauded, more debated, or so articulate: no listener to him during a BBC interview on New Year's Day 1971 is likely to forget his unflurried eloquence. This is the first full description of his career, with its sharp changes of key (*Titus Andronicus* to *Irma la Douce*), its achievements in theatre, cinema, opera house, experimental workshop. Theories fade; Peter Brook's progress is seen plainly in his acts. Now, after celebrating the arts of the theatre in a famous Stratford production of *A Midsummer Night's Dream*, he has turned again to the future – still, in Eliot's phrase, 'moving into another intensity – as director, in Paris, of an international centre of research, 'not a theatre, not an academy, not an institution'.

Though I have known so much of his work, this book could hardly have been contemplated without the extreme patience and understanding of his father, the late Simon Brook, whose records were a biographer's joy. No one could have been kinder and readier; I regret most deeply that, after his unwavering aid, he was unable to see a finished copy.

As always, Wendy, my wife, has been the wisest and most reassuring of collaborators from first to last.

I am grateful indeed to Paul Scofield, whose name has been linked with Brook's for a quarter of a century; to John Harrison, who was in five of the early productions; to John Kane for the charming passages I have quoted from his essay on *A Midsummer Night's Dream* at Stratford; to my former colleague, Charles Reid, for his expertise as a music critic; and to Mrs Christine Brook, Herbert van Thal, John Goodwin, Jonathan Griffin, Robert Marsden, Vincent Pearmain, Eileen Robinson, and the late Denys Blakelock. Susan Hodgart's generosity, as my editor, has been inexhaustible.

9

I am obliged to all from whom I have quoted (as acknowledged in footnotes and bibliography), and particularly to Patricia Louise Ryan for the opportunity to read her valuably detailed thesis for Wayne State University, Detroit. The last word should be to Peter Brook himself: he has added to my indebtedness across the years by reading through a complicated typescript. But, in the end, I am solely responsible for a biographer's resolute dogmatism.

J. C. T.

Hampstead, 1971

As this biography was going to press, Brook's film of *King Lear* (see pages 171–2) began a season at the Prince Charles Theatre, London: July 1971. Cut to a version of 137 minutes, the tragedy reached us from a primeval world, timeless, winter-bound. Through the snowscapes, through the dark castles – Child Rowland to these dark towers came – and through the pelting of the pitiless storm, there moved Paul Scofield's Lear, his voice like a 'slow thunderbolt' (as someone said of Macready), and his command, at all seasons, absolute. Again Brook had avoided explicit pity. The effect had to be less startling than upon the stage. Cutting could worry us; compression had to blur the secondary narrative; midway, the elements were distractingly in charge. But Scofield, as before, was magnificent in buffeted age, a man cut to the brains; Irene Worth was a searing Goneril; the face of the Fool (Jack MacGowran) belonged to a primitive woodcut; and Alan Webb's blinded Gloucester shared potently in the last meeting with Lear, set now upon the sea-shore. Two early lines stayed with me: the King's division of the realm that, 'unburden'd', he might 'crawl toward death', and Goneril's 'I love you dearer than eyesight', first mention of the sense insisted on throughout the tragedy. At the last the dead Lear sank slowly from our view: it was the world's end: men must endure their going hence even as their coming hither.

I

First Words: 1925-1945

I

I MUST have written Peter Brook's name first in a compressed
Observer notice of *The Infernal Machine*, Jean Cocteau's odd re-casting
of the Oedipus myth, at what was then a theatre club called the
Chanticleer, in a crevice of South Kensington. It was the damp late
spring of 1945, the war not yet over; London remained a place of
feverish discomfort hardly noticed after so many years. Moonless
nights could seem bitumen-black; I remember stumbling on one of
them into a small theatre club in Gloucester Road, with a chasm
between the audience and the actors, and a stage that looked like a
poised tea-tray, two-by-four; it was rather bigger. Still, even if the
cast was loyal to Cocteau, one thought less of the play than its
production, the calculated heightening of a text that needed this
steady sense of adventure. Peter Brook, in charge of the adventure,
was nineteen; then about five foot four and stockily built, with
prickling light brown hair that would get thinner, deep-set blue
eyes, a voice high-pitched and urgent, and a repertory of gestures
that reminded Penelope Gilliatt, in later years, of a polar bear using
its paws.

Twenty-three years after this, rather taller but not much changed
physically, the same Peter Brook was directing the *Oedipus* of
Seneca on the National Theatre stage at the Old Vic. No English-
speaking director was more regarded. Beginning as a young romantic in a world recovering from the war and needing the voice of
'bright Apollo's lute, strung with his hair', he brought Shakespeare
and Watteau together in *Love's Labour's Lost*. Within weeks he
proved that he had also the kind of merciless imagination to match
Sartre in the theatre; and he went on just as suddenly to alarm
conservative musicians by refreshing the production of opera at
Covent Garden. ('Upon my soul,' said Dickens's Barnacle Junior,
'you mustn't come into the place saying you want to know, you

know.') There was no chance to pigeon-hole him. Critics followed, panting, as he moved from the decorative to the austere, resurrecting at length the apparently unplayable *Titus Andronicus* and wringing from an older critic the cry: 'Give Peter Brook the impossible, and he will solve your problem. But it would be unwise, I fancy, to trust him with safe jobs.' He had a habit of designing his own sets and composing his own music, doing in fact all that Gordon Craig thought a complete man of the theatre ought to do. As a director of every kind of play, high tragedy to near-farce and light musical, as a director of opera and of the film, and as a writer for television, he discovered that all things in entertainment 'feed into each other reciprocally'. Presently, he grew into the stage's master-theorist, with the difference that he believed in practice. He was a zealot of the theatre, an innovator of the screen, an advocate of the stage polemic. In 1968 he began an exposition of his beliefs with the words, 'I can take any empty space and call it a bare stage'; we knew that nobody in his time had filled the space more diversely. Now, at the age of forty-six, he is still seeking the heart of experiment. 'All work,' he says, 'involves thinking. This means comparing, brooding, making mistakes, going back, hesitating, starting again. . . . The living material of actors is talking, feeling, and exploring all the time – rehearsing is a visible thinking-aloud.'

Peter Brook's career has been a visible thinking-aloud. Nobody has described it yet in its chronological, factual detail. From the facts emerge the reasons for his work; the ceaseless cogitation that has taken him from the revival of a romantic theatre in a war-weary land to those cerebral exercises that, like Claribel of Tunis, are ten leagues beyond man's life. 'Truth is always on the move. In life new leaves never turn, clocks never go back, we can never have a second chance. In the theatre the slate is wiped clean all the time.'

His true theatre story, the ceaseless wiping of the slate, begins at a Birmingham theatre one morning in the late summer of 1945. Barry Jackson, unsure whether he had been right to commit *Man and Superman* to the care of a boy of twenty, was hovering outside the door of the Repertory Theatre rehearsal room when a veteran actress came out and saw him. 'It's all right, Barry,' she said; 'that young man knows what he wants and he is going to get it.' He would go on getting it. We are all heirs of our own youth, and it will become plain enough in Brook's life how early influences persist.

II

Though his surname sounds British – 'Good Master Brook,' said Falstaff in Windsor, 'I desire more acquaintance of you' – he is of Russian descent. His father Simon Brook, fifth child of liberal-minded parents, was born at Dvinsk in 1888. By thirteen or so he was making about two roubles a month as 'Our Own Correspondent' of a new local paper. On leaving school he joined in the revolutionary (Menshevik) cause against Tsarism; for two months he was detained as a political prisoner before securing his bail by family influence and escaping abroad. Then, after two years studying languages – in Berlin briefly, and for much longer in Paris – he entered the Belgian University of Liège to read physics, mathematics, and electrical engineering. At this time a girl named Ida Janson, whom he had met in Russia, also came to study in Liège; her subject was chemistry. Daughter of progressive parents, and an excellent linguist, she had gone to a Russian school, and to the University of St Petersburg. During the spring of 1914 she and Simon were married while on holiday in Germany; that summer, when she became a Doctor of Science, he received his own diploma in electrical engineering.

War, long dreaded, flared violently. Advised to get out of Liège, where students were trench-digging, they just caught the last train to Brussels. The Germans were approaching fast; so hastening on to Ostend they took the only way and crossed as refugees to England with twenty-five Belgian francs, or about one English pound, between them. Greeted hospitably in London, and taken to a Russell Square hotel, they had difficulties at first, until Ida Brook got a post in an East End laboratory at Stratford as a research chemist in poison gases. Simon received a year's free postgraduate course at the Imperial College of Science; moreover, he went on writing popular scientific articles for Russian magazines. He gained his degree and joined a firm that made telephones for the Army under government control. They now had a family house in Bedford Park, Chiswick; during 1920 a first son, Alexis, distinguished later as a consultant psychiatrist, was born. A second son, Peter Stephen Paul, was born in the same house on 21 March 1925.

Peter Brook came into a world of what one day he would call the 'Deadly Theatre', though 'deadliness' for him had a wider meaning. On the night of his birth Gladys Cooper and Henry Ainley acted in an Adelphi revival of *Iris,* Pinero's robust *pièce bien faite* from thirty years before. On the previous night, the musical play, *Rose Marie,* 'a romance of the Canadian Rockies', had captured Drury Lane; its Totem Tom-Tom dance might have celebrated the abject surrender of a historic stage that one day Peter Brook would return transiently to Shakespeare. The year would have better things; Peter arrived at an unlucky hour.

Not that it worried him. It was some years before he went to the theatre, though he was theatrical enough to enjoy a circus procession on the wallpaper of his nursery, and, at the chemist's, what Kipling knew as 'tun-bellied Rosamund jars that flung inward their monstrous daubs of red, blue, and green'. He saw his first professional plays at Chiswick Empire in the autumn of 1933. There the Irish actor, Anew McMaster, battered flamboyantly through an old-style Richard III and Macbeth. A sweeping, egocentric artist who, in aspect, might have walked from a Florentine canvas of the high Renaissance, McMaster needed discipline; when he combined acting with direction as at Chiswick, he offered the kind of fustian Shakespeare Peter Brook would do his best to demolish. Peter's first cinema was calmer, *Tambi,* a jungle film at the Polytechnic; before he was ten he had his own 9.5 mm cine-camera, suggesting logically that if the family made its own films, it would save by not going to cinemas to see films made by other people.

It was a happy childhood in a close family circle. Inevitably, he disliked a variety of preparatory schools, where it was said that he had a habit of treating his teachers with 'detached compassion'; he had been only a short time at his first public school, Westminster, before he had to spend two years in Switzerland, recuperating from a glandular disease. When he returned he had two uneasy years at Gresham's which was transferred during the war from Holt in Norfolk to Newquay in Cornwall. The maturing youth, with his cosmopolitan background ('An apple doesn't fall far from the tree' says a Russian proverb) was never obvious public-school material: 'I am a romantic,' he proclaimed; 'everything new and unusual interests me.' In the circumstances it was not surprising that he left school at sixteen. By then the authorities more used to him, had asked him to stay ('Schoolmasters, I hope, are always willing to learn,' murmured the Head resignedly), but he preferred to join a unit engaged on commercial and industrial films in suburban London.

Wisely, his father persuaded him that there could be other occasions for script-writing, cutting, and directing; and in 1942, at the dark heart of the war, he went up to Oxford, one of the youngest undergraduates Magdalen College had known. A contemporary, Kenneth Tynan, said of him: 'It was as if he had come up by public request, like a high-pressure executive arriving to take over a dying business.' Early in October 1942, before his second term, he completed a personal vacation task, the production of Marlowe's *Dr Faustus*, acted by undergraduates from Oxford and London upon the tiny stage of the Torch Theatre Club, on behalf of the Aid to Russia Fund. In those days, to get to the Torch, you groped up a turning off Knightsbridge, climbed a fairly steep stair, and emerged under the roof in what looked like the top deck of an omnibus except that the gangway ran down one side. Brook, who had to make an immediate payment for hire of the theatre, raised it only towards the twelfth hour by sending out his cast to sell tickets. Visitors, either voluntary or press-ganged, found a two-hour version of the tragedy, its Chorus omitted and – the coming Brook here – all seven Deadly Sins played by Mephistophilis. Going as ever to the best sources, the director had invited Aleister Crowley to advise on the play's black magic; and Crowley, on considering the ritual, had replied simply, 'My dear boy, this would raise the devil even at a matinee.' The devil-raising, which cost £63 to put on, showed in the end a gratifying £17 profit.

In the following spring a Medical Board considered Brook's history and would not grade him. Romantically, he had tried to enter the Secret Service. At the end of an interview at headquarters somewhere under Whitehall, a colonel said, 'Keep in touch', but as he did not add how Brook could do this, British Intelligence lost a recruit. Not prepared at Oxford to waste himself too lavishly on work, he cast himself instead – he was now President of the University Film Society – as Britain's youngest film director; Magdalen authorities believed meanwhile that he was enmeshed in medieval French.

He had chosen a full-length treatment of Laurence Sterne's 'travelling fancy', *A Sentimental Journey Through France and Italy*. Sacha Guitry's mimeodramatic technique in *Le Roman de Tricheur* had impressed him, so the script had no dialogue, merely a commentary extracted from the book and spoken by Sterne himself, with a background of eighteenth-century music. Character parts, as in Russian films, were played by ordinary folk recruited from Oxford pubs and haunts. Improvising gallantly on a budget of £250 – the unit had to take a garden truck as a trolley – Brook shot his exteriors in Oxford and the country round, at Abingdon, and at Woodstock in Blenheim Park. The problem of interiors he solved after going to see John Gielgud's Haymarket revival of *Love for Love*. Calling at Gielgud's dressing-room, he asked tentatively if he might use the sets for his film; Gielgud agreed, and the unit came into the theatre for some rapid work. Unhappily, because the film was made on short lengths of raw 16-mm stock, each roll of which reacted to printing in a different way, *A Sentimental Journey* could not be shown in an ordinary cinema, and when it had its première at the Oxford Union, the hall was the wrong size, diminishing the images while disconcertingly magnifying the sound; further, a strange projector threw both sight and sound out of synchronization. Still, within two months, the film had a London showing at the Torch, for Brook a second home; I was first aware of his name when C. A. Lejeune's weekly film article arrived at the *Observer* in a Friday morning post: 'It is an odd experience watching *A Sentimental Journey*. It requires the patient cultivation of a mood of thirty years back when all that flickered was a film. . . . But it is all to the good that these young people have tried to do an honest job of work instead of largely criticising the work of others.'

There had been a crisis in the previous autumn. Brook had only just escaped being sent down from Magdalen where College authorities, holding that he should have more urgent business, complained of his obsession with cinematography; it was remarkable that they did not call it the bioscope. Because he had kept his unit in College after hours to wait for its first day's filming to arrive from the London laboratory, irritation turned to anger and he was fined five pounds. When the cheque he had sent to pay the fine failed to reach the authorities, they told him he would be sent down. His father averted this by a long interview with the Vice-President of Magdalen. Authority was arrogant; but years afterwards, when everybody in the theatre knew Peter Brook's name, an Oxford Professor, a Fellow of Magdalen, happened to sit by Simon Brook at a Guildhall banquet for an international congress on Gastro-Enterology. In this strange setting the old story came up. Magdalen dons, the Professor admitted, had often discussed 'the Brook case'. He added, practically in the words used by the Head of Gresham's, 'Teachers are always willing to learn.'

During the late spring of 1944, Peter Brook, now with his Oxford degree and willing to learn, joined the staff of another London film company. He chafed at a war-bound England. 'I want,' he wrote, 'to be a vampire of the outside world and at intervals to give back the blood I have drawn out, in some creative form. I want to change and develop, and dread the thought of standing still.' He stood still for less than a year; then in February 1945 he asked for a month's leave of absence – it would be a very long vacation – for his production of Cocteau's *The Infernal Machine* at the Chanticleer where Greta Douglas had a semi-permanent company. He arrived with everything worked out on paper to the ultimate moves; a lighting plot as well, fixed so absolutely that the players had to accommodate themselves to it. Loyally they did, and undeniably 'Peter Brook's Production', as advance leaflets announced it, did everything it could with bold lighting and bolder punctuation to strengthen an indifferent play on the Oedipus theme and the inexorable working of destiny. The ebullient journalist, Beverley Baxter, writing for the *Evening Standard,* thought Brook was 'a sensitive artist and something of a thruster'.

Encouraged, the young director stuck to the theatre. In the uncompromising barn of the Q at Kew Bridge, he directed for Jack de Leon *The Barretts of Wimpole Street,* a work of more than professional craft that did not deserve its later resurrection as a musical play. If *The Barretts* did nothing else for Peter Brook, it introduced him to the complexities of a full theatre switchboard and he had an experienced cast to light. Immediately after this, on the advice of the actress Mary Grew, ENSA – shortened from the Entertainments National Service Association – asked him to do *Pygmalion* for a Forces tour in England and Germany. He responded with a straight production, Mary Grew as Eliza, that kept faithfully to Shaw and had some amusing teacup business at the Eynsford-Hill party. That gentle spirit, William Armstrong, with his snuff and silver-knobbed stick, saw the dress rehearsal on the vast stage of the Theatre Royal, Drury Lane, and came from it strongly appreciative. 'Have you heard of the new boy?' he asked his friend, Barry Jackson. Jackson had invited Armstrong to open the post-war season at the Birmingham Repertory with *Man and Superman.* Why not get Brook instead? It was a far tougher piece than *Pygmalion,* and it had not been acted at the Repertory which had done twenty-eight of Shaw's plays, some more than once. Still, ever ready to experiment, Jackson agreed. Nearly a quarter of a century later, Peter Brook would write of him with affection as 'a very extraordinary old gentleman'. Extraordinary, yes, but only sixty-five, though to a director just turned twenty he must have been a benevolent Nestor. B.J.'s father, a wealthy Birmingham merchant, had let him indulge his own passion for the stage, and he was prepared as a rule, while keeping unobtrusive watch, to let other young people have the freedom of his theatre – an astonishing place that, in what became a city backwater, survived for fifty-eight years. Never interfering with his producers when a play was in rehearsal, he said once, as his last administrator, Nancy Burman, recorded: 'His view was that if there were to be mistakes, let one person make them – then they would at least be consistent.'

II

Master Brook: 1945-1948

I

DURING the dazed post-war summer of 1945, Barry Jackson's
Birmingham Repertory Theatre stood inconspicuously behind a
few acres of railway station as it had done since the spring of 1913.
It was in line with a small hotel, a clutch of modest shops, and a
cinema. The swiftest approach to it was under the echoing arch of
New Street Station; strangers, aware of its fame and expecting
something in key, were startled by so austere, so reserved a façade.
Within, the auditorium dropped sternly between its brownish walls
towards a stage deeper than one would have imagined. Holding
fewer than five hundred, this had been the English home of the
Shavian pentateuch, *Back to Methuselah:* Shaw, who enjoyed Jackie
Coogan, used to wander into the cinema after, and sometimes during,
rehearsal. The 'Rep' had been a professional university for Laurence
Olivier, Ralph Richardson, Cedric Hardwicke, Gwen Ffrangcon-
Davies, and dozens of others on the way to renown. Sir Barry
Jackson, civilized and fastidious, had always held to his claim 'to
serve an art instead of making that art serve a commercial purpose';
though the city was ungrateful (once he put on *Timon of Athens* in
modern dress because he said it reminded him of Birmingham) he
kept the theatre excitingly alive and preserved his independence.

This August he told a friend that he had one actor 'with the
future in his eyes'. That was Paul Scofield, then twenty-three, who
joined to a shaggy grace a sierra-voice, all peaks and valleys, that
could be taut or huskily caressing at need. He had, too, a generous
humour; Sir Barry said he had never genuinely seen the young
Shepherd in *The Winter's Tale* until Scofield played it in the previous
season, simplicity from the depths of Bohemia-by-Arden.

Though he trusted Scofield and was not prone to worry, especially in Station Street, Sir Barry did ask for a moment what might
happen when rehearsals opened for Shaw's *Man and Superman*. He

had given this to William Armstrong's nominee, Peter Brook, who looked rather like a cherub ready to be gilded and to blow a long, trumpet above a theatre proscenium. Willie Armstrong was not a man for facile praise. It was unthinkable that he would land the Repertory with a problem-child; and Sir Barry, a shrewd interviewer, had liked the assurance in Brook's hooded blue eyes and the good sense uttered in an unexpectedly high mezzo voice that was inclined to skid. Yet to put a boy of this age in charge of such a terror as *Man and Superman,* and a cast with some professionals who might be his grandparents – could anybody, even at the Rep, call this a reasonable risk? On the first morning Barry Jackson, behind his long cigarette-holder, sat nervously – for him – on the top floor of his theatre: a room filled with books, programmes, and old Malvern Festival photographs from a golden primeval decade. Windows stared at the dingy limbo of New Street Station, a prospect so familiar that he hardly noticed it. Progressively worried, he left his office and loitered outside the shut door of the rehearsal room where Peter Brook, who was wearing that day a tomato-coloured (some said ox-blood) suit, had begun to lead his company through the Shaw. Presently Mabel France, an actress of redoubtable experience, came out and saw her manager hovering. There he was, Jackson wrote to me later, wondering what might have blown up. Mabel France reassured him: 'It's all right, Barry, that young man knows what he wants, and he is going to get it.'

True; no one argued. The players accepted Brook and responded to his precisely-formed ideas, taking the text slower than usual, thinking carefully about it, keeping the argument in flow, dodging nothing. They were prepared to work all day on Sundays to get things straight, and they did get things straight: the performance was lucidity itself, and if Scofield's Tanner had to depend now and then upon the charm that can be a bloom on Shavian actors as well as Barrie heroines, it was clear that he and Brook understood each other. They were almost telepathically in rapport, and the autumn's partnership remained unbroken a quarter of a century later when Brook directed Scofield's film Lear in the winter snows of northern Jutland in 1969.

Shaw went well, and (G.B.S. would have agreed on the order) Shakespeare followed: *King John,* seldom profitable on the stage. Jackson had engaged Brook for three productions, each running for three weeks or a month and ending with Ibsen's *The Lady of the Sea.* No tyro had been asked to walk in so fierce a furnace; a natural salamander, he came out unscorched. I met his *King John*, play of drum-and-trumpet verse and sudden beauties, on the way back from Liverpool and an O'Casey première, a play by a dramatist who could have done with a Brook to match him in the theatre. Birmingham that October afternoon sulked under a smoky drift, but the theatre was crowded and eager: Brook enforced attention by opening with a bacchanal instead of the usual tableau in uncertain wax. Paul Scofield, as the Bastard, head but not heart of oak, a performance grandly attacking, looked Elizabethan as if the face gazed out at us from a miniature by Isaac Oliver. His voice, lighter than we should know it one day, stayed on the upper slopes, rarely slipping to a crevasse. These were inventive hours, though I gathered years afterwards that J. F. Waterhouse, at the time an English don at Birmingham University, was more doubtful than I had been. 'Many,' he wrote in the *Birmingham Post* – of which he had become music critic – 'will remember at the outset of Mr Brook's rise to fame a remarkable *King John* when the scenes teemed with mysterious black monks, little Arthur spoke his dying words* before his attempted leap to safety, and the King, far from dying in the miserably abrupt way indicated by the text, fainted in coils all over the stage.' The actor, David Read, did it ably; Brook saved the play from sagging into a monotony of booming barons, even if he was puzzled at the last – as his older self would not have been – by the peripatetic trinity of Pembroke, Salisbury and Bigot. I did miss Prince Henry's 'I am the cygnet to this pale faint swan': a speech, among Shakespeare's bounties to the lesser people, that hardly ever gets an actor with the voice or a director to worry over it.

Nevertheless, *King John* was a cygnet's hour at the Repertory. No London papers except the *Observer* reviewed it, but Midland critics were jealously proud of Brook's gift, and word went round Birmingham. Scarcely anyone pounced on an inserted phrase that bothered Barry Jackson, a Shakespearian faithful to the received text. Now, when directors add, link, and arrange as they please, it would be even less apparent. Brook explained himself two or three months after the production was over. In a letter to the *Sunday Times* (13 January 1946) about tampering with Shakespeare, he said:

It was obvious from the first that the audience would miss the meaning, and thus the force, of the whole of the great soliloquy about 'commodity'

---

* O me! My uncle's spirit is in these stones:
  Heaven take my soul, and England keep my bones!
                                        King John, IV, iii.

because of the complete change of sense this word has undergone. Yet to substitute another word throughout would have been unpardonably irritating to those who knew the speech. Consequently, we introduced an extra phrase on the first appearance of the word to 'plant' its meaning:

> That smooth-fac'd gentleman, *expediency*,
> Or, *as they say*, tickling commodity,
> Commodity, the bias of the world. . . .

Dr Dover Wilson, writing in the *Guardian* on the morning of Shakespeare's Quatercentenary, 23 April 1964, and repeating it in his posthumously-published autobiography, *Milestones on the Dover Road,* recalled a night at *King John* between Barry Jackson and 'one of his young geniuses', Peter Brook. At the Bastard's addition, 'Barry and Brook gave me a quick, timid glance; but I laughed in their faces . . . and so passed as a man and a brother. For without some explanation of the word commodity, no audience can really understand what the soliloquy is about.' More than twenty years after his *King John*, Brook would say: 'I do not for one moment question the principle of re-writing Shakespeare – after all, the texts do not get burned – each person can do what he thinks necessary with a text and still no one suffers.'

James Agate, quoting Brook's *Sunday Times* letter in his diary, *Ego 9* (1948), had agreed with the contention: 'I am for rather than against, when strictly necessary.' Brook had interfered neither with great poetry nor a familiar passage. But Agate added typically that in another play a director might not be pardoned if he said:

> Thus conscience – *meaning thereby consciousness*,
> *Awareness* – does make cowards of us all . . .

Agate, who died in 1947 before the last volume of his diary was published, saw little of Brook's work. A metropolitan, who spoke of Kew and Barnes as 'Asia Minor', he rejected Birmingham, even if he stabled his trotting ponies at Sutton Coldfield next door. He seldom went to the Stratford theatre which he loathed for no better reason than it was not in London; and elsewhere Brook had no chances to bring him to the boil. The critic might have said much about the young man's final production at the Repertory in the autumn of 1945. It was *The Lady from the Sea*. Eileen Beldon played the woman, sea-obsessed, in atavistic kinship with it, and obliged to choose between the Stranger who personifies the spell and the husband (Scofield, more anxious than normally, in a confining primness) who breaks it by granting her freedom of choice, freedom with responsibility. After Wangel's 'Now you can choose your own path in perfect freedom,' Ellida held a protracted silence before she asked, 'Is it true – true what you say?' Ten seconds in stage time can drift towards eternity; Brook's pause seemed to leave eternity behind. The Choice, as people would speak of it in capitals, crowned a production in which he insisted once more upon discovering what his author meant. He was the director-interpreter conscious of a duty to his audience. In another two years he would be told that he ignored this duty.

II

By the ebb of 1945 Brook had a fresh challenge: to put on *Love's Labour's Lost* as the youngest director in the history of the Stratford-upon-Avon festival. Barry Jackson, who had agreed to control the Shakespeare Memorial Theatre, had known the festivals since his youth, since Frank Benson's meridian with the 'band of brothers', when playgoing was an intimate town affair, a family ritual with only Miss Corelli disapproving from Mason Croft. Often he had sat in the old plum-cake, sham-Gothic structure, destroyed by fire; in the temporary quarters, a borrowed cinema; and in the huge brick building (1932) that had housed little to please the critics, though audiences multiplied. Ensuing festivals had been static and smug. Technically a Governor, Jackson had had no part in them, even if none could recognize better the infrequent flash – as when Theodore Komisarjevsky saw half a dozen plays with a sharp and irreverent eye, or when in 1936 and 1937 Donald Wolfit fumed like a sudden djinn from an unlikely bottle. Actors were cleft from the audience by a gulf hard to span: Baliol ('Bay') Holloway agreed that if you came downstage on a fine night, you could sometimes see the front stalls, but visibility had to be clear.

Stratford had just kept going during the war. Now 1946 must be the new spring. Everything was in a comfortable trench of tradition, little showed above the parapet, and Jackson realized that he must freshen the festival, lead the visitors to the theatre as well as to the tomb. There must be a largely young company, more rehearsals, no return to a log-jam of six premières in six nights. The strongly practical Robert Atkins, director for two years in a milieu that hardly suited him, had seen what could be done. Jackson, with new and ampler authority, began to do it. A few recognized principals such as Robert Harris and Valerie Taylor, led his cast, and he waited for the impact of Paul Scofield and Peter Brook (who had just come of age). 'The boy,' he said, 'is the youngest earthquake I've known.' The boy would say of him: 'Every conceivable value [at Stratford] was buried in deadly sentimentality and complacent worthiness – a traditionalism approved largely by town, scholar and press. It needed the boldness of . . . Sir Barry Jackson to throw all this out of the window and so make a search for true values possible once more.'

It would be a few nights before any sort of earthquake. Jackson, employing for each play a different director, chose to open with *The Tempest*, the great poem, epithalamic spectacle, that on the stage can stiffen, as it did now, to a diversion obstinately machine-bound. The second play, a much-clipped *Cymbeline,* collision between Snow White and the Decameron, is remembered for Scofield's enjoyment of the blockish Cloten, an astonishment to critics who did not know him. Brook's turn next: his treatment of *Love's Labour's Lost,* a comedy that had been Jackson's favourite child. Often Sir Barry would quote a passage from David Lindsay's fantasy, *A Voyage to Arcturus,* 'It looked as if life-forms were being coined so fast by nature that there was not physical room for all,' and refer it to *Love's Labour's Lost:* there a young dramatist, inventive beyond belief, was seeking while he could to express everything as elegantly as he could, and as if there could be no theatre after the morrow. Picked, spruce, peregrinate, the comedy is a festival of words. Armado has a mint of phrases in his brain; Costard is overwhelmed by the marvel of 'remuneration'; Holofernes loves the 'elegancy, facility and golden cadence of poesy'; Sir Nathaniel speaks of 'a singular and choice epithet'; Berowne, in love with language, may be Shakespeare's self-portrait, set in a speech by Rosaline, 'His eye begets occasion for his wit, For every object that the one doth catch The other turns to a mirth-moving jest.'

Peter Brook, as naturally at home in Paris as in London, had been to Paris that spring where he met Cocteau, Duvivier, and Louis Jouvet, and saw the first Parisian *Love's Labour's Lost* for thirty years, a French translation that seemed to anticipate much of Molière, Marivaux, and Musset, with certain scenes changed and rewritten, and Moth allowed to utter an epigram of Voltaire. It pleased Brook who by now had fixed his own treatment in his mind. When he met his players he knew what he required to a comma, though – prepared for trial and error – he would often transfer the comma to another place. From previous experience he believed that actors and, especially, stage managers were contemptuous of anyone unable to make up his mind. Anxiously he had marshalled his production, deliberating with cardboard players and a model of his set, going over and over his moves, and blackening the pages of his prompt book. On the rehearsal morning he discovered very soon that his plan did not work in practice. No matter. While it was going awry, another plan had begun to unfold, 'full of personal variations, shaped by individual enthusiasms and lazinesses, promising such different rhythms, opening so many unexpected possibilities'. It was Brook's personal point of deviation. He walked away from his book, in among the actors, and he never looked at a written plan again.

There are pictures of him, wearing overcoat and muffler in the frigid North London rehearsal rooms, and smiling benignly as he coaxes his first Stratford company through the text. The director John Harrison, who was with him as an actor both in Birmingham and Stratford, has said in a letter to me: 'Those of us who were at Birmingham felt an affectionate proprietary interest in the Boy Wonder. I remember defending him vigorously against the criticism of leading players at rehearsals for *Love's Labour's Lost*.' Nobody outside the theatre had heard much about the production; there had been little publicity for Brook, and the audience assembled in noticeable calm. Three hours later, anyone late on the Bancroft meadow would have guessed at something uncommon. From a Stratford failure the mourners file out quietly, but any success is talked volubly through the streets, as *Love's Labour's Lost* would be all that summer. Audiences a year after the war needed colour and light; Brook did himself. Aware of what a newspaper kept calling 'the mood of the moment', he had directed for eye and ear, dismissing period accuracy ('of supremely little importance') and dres'ing the comedy after Watteau. Swiftly he had persuaded Barry Jackson that there was some affinity between the play and the painting of the '*Voyage à Cythère*', itself inspired by theatre productions Watteau had seen. Nobody quoted the words of an English critic from a quarter of a century before. Then Agate, reviewing the Old Vic production of 1923, had described the play as 'a Watteau . . . of that significance in ordered beauty which unity alone can give'.*

Brook explained that the style of the dresses, with their broad, undecorated expanses of billowing satin, appeared to be 'the ideal visual correlative of the play's essential sweet-sad mood.' If rela-

* *The Contemporary Theatre, 1923*, London, 1924.

tively few people would have put it in these terms, most of them were ready to cheer a production, often reminiscent in mood of the *Fêtes Vénitiennes,* that was pictorial, witty and rhythmical, and never cast out the verse. Stray decorations might trouble the academics: a dumb-show prologue in which Navarre's tearful women read the King's ungallant proclamation; Brook's gift to the Princess of a mute zany, chalk-faced and white-clothed, forlorn and drooping, to symbolize the atmosphere of the court scenes, 'in period as much Schumann as Shakespeare'; and the aspect, deliberately Toy Town and anachronistic – more people worried about this than Brook knew – of Constable Dull with truncheon, Victorian helmet, light blue uniform and string of sausages. When the night was over, few dwelt peevishly on the telescope, the zany, Costard's water-pistol, and the harlequinade comedy. Rather they remembered one imaginative mind's response to another. As Siriol Hugh-Jones said in *Vogue,* 'A young producer is as rare as a young Prime Minister. Peter Brook is a born producer who rose straight to his profession.'

For him it was a director's task – 'producer' and 'director' were still interchangeable – to restore to a work of art what it had lost in its passage from author's dream to author's manuscript. The critics did not argue. A. V. Cookman of *The Times,* never led into three-piled hyperbole about a classical revival – and certainly not at Stratford – greeted 'something of a triumph'. None denied it. The comedy stayed at the festival's heart, carrying with it the other triumphant re-creation, Paul Scofield as Armado, embodiment of 'tawny Spain', looking (said Philip Hope-Wallace) 'faintly reminiscent of an over-bred and beautiful old borzoi'. He stood there, meditatively detached, his fingers poised about a black cane, and generations of grandees speaking in his resolute, fragile tones while he told the King, 'The schoolmaster is exceeding fantastical'. The closing scenes linger. Brook had continued to study a long silence. When conceits and silken terms were over, and the French lord Mercade had brought with his tidings of death the realities of life, the company remained stricken into absolute stillness, a fall of frost in the summer night, in the context both daring and just. One last surprise remained. With the songs of Owl and Cuckoo ended, and torchlight quivering above the singers, Brook gave to the Princess* the farewell speech that is usually Armado's: 'The words of Mercury

---

* Valerie Taylor was the Princess; her attendant ladies, *l'escadron volant,* were Joy Parker, Muriel Davidson, and Ruth Lodge (Rosaline). David King-Wood played Berowne.

gal, on a visit to Verona, and through a busy autumn, he was pondering on it. He grew sure that, in directing *Romeo*, he must 'capture the violent passion of two children lost among the Southern fury of the warring houses', a sentence, repeated in various forms, that critics would denounce as unwarrantable simplification. Writing (22 September 1946) to John Harrison, of the Stratford company, who shared many of his interests, he said: 'Have got hold of Variorum which includes complete reprint of Q1 and also a translation of Lope de Vega's *Monteschi e Capolleta* in which J. wakes up when R. enters tomb, so they emerge, make friends with Papa Capulet, and live happily ever after. Rather a better end, I think! Curiously, Lope's play has a certain beauty of its own.' Innumerable players, professional and amateur, coveted the two lost children; Brook faced a blizzard of hopeful inquiries. A farm-hand wrote to him: 'I am sixteen and an ideal Romeo. I don't like farm-work and feel that I am a born actor. If you don't let me know at once, I shall appear in a school play in the village.' Presumably he did. Brook wrote to Harrison on 16 November: 'No R and J settled but thousands seen. . . . Interested to hear that Nugent Monck had produced Esmé Percy as Romeo in 1904, but would have been much more delighted had you discovered that in 1903 Esmé Percy had produced Nugent Monck as Romeo.' Then on 29 December: 'As for *Romeo* there are a mass of things I would like you to read, but none of them is written yet.'

He had for a while a second occupation, a steady footnote. A great deal of ballet was in London performance; the *Observer,* then finely edited by Ivor Brown, needed a critic to cover the premières in those concentrated paragraphs, 100 to 150 words, that were as much as an arts page, still war-constricted, could take. Being responsible for the page, and worried about ballet, I telephoned to Brook. No call could have been richer. The invitation, he said in a debate years later, was irresistible. When he added that the *Observer* went on inviting him because nobody bothered much, he was wrong; we wanted him because he was expert, swift, and had no trouble with a style that defeated so many writers. Horace Horsnell called it the decalogue on a threepenny-bit. Ideally, each sentence, in the Hazlitt manner, had to smoulder like touchwood and the next to catch fire by attrition.

Peter Brook did far better than most. Nobody had yet begun, peevishly, to talk of his theatre work as 'balletic'. Covent Garden fascinated him. He discovered in ballet an elegance and finesse

B

unknown to him in a war-time world. Twenty years on he would think of the late Forties for its 'theatre of colour and movement, of fine fabrics . . . of all forms of mystery and surprise. It was the theatre of a battered Europe that seemed to share one aim – a reaching back towards a memory of lost grace.' Nowhere so surely as at Covent Garden where ballet offered the romantic past he had never experienced; here, when the red curtain rose, was a form through which certain ideas could be expressed more subtly than in words; here, pictorially, were dresses 'like blown ashes' (*The Haunted Ballroom*), or others (*Les Sirènes*) that 'filled the stage with pistache, marzipan and Turkish delight'. One production repelled him as 'a visually offensive piece of cubism, angular and percussive', but little could vitiate his new excitement.

Plans for *Romeo and Juliet* grew. In Portugal that summer, where, he wrote, he was 'staying at a wonderful lonely spot in the mountains, twenty miles from the nearest house,' he had studied the play intensely, concentrating upon his chosen key-line, 'In these hot days is the mad blood stirring'. At home he asked Bernard Shaw's advice; and G.B.S., who was just ninety, counselled him from Ayot St Lawrence to insist upon the youth of the lovers and the vigour of the fights, also to have a Romeo who could weep. In 1895 Shaw had written about 'the murderous excitement of the duel'; he did not repeat what he had said then, that the play should have 'an irresistibly impetuous march of music'. Brook had begun to think of enclosing his stage within the circlet of a city wall, miniature and crenellated; at luncheon with him about this time, the table inside a moment was walled with forks and salt-cellars. The production must have a morning freshness; it must escape from smudged Italian back-drops, limp cypresses, marble-tub balconies. Without trying to be perverse, he wanted to offer the shock of a new experience. Ideas foamed. Speaking of *Titus Andronicus,* the Shakespeare tragedy it was the custom to deride* – no one had attempted a professional revival since Robert Atkins at the Old Vic in 1923 – he thought at once of décor by Epstein. Brook on *Titus* (without Epstein) was only eight years ahead; but he had now to devote himself to *Romeo and Juliet* and his resolve to give to it a 'passionate Elizabethan-Italianate background'. In London his ballet nights continued. He was the *Observer's* recognized critic,

---

* Ben Jonson wrote in 1614: 'He that will swear *Ieronimo* [this was Kyd's *The Spanish Tragedy*] and *Andronicus* are the best plays . . . hath stood still these five and twenty or thirty years.'

though never formally appointed. After *La Boutique Fantasque* at Covent Garden he wrote: 'To slip back from that pool of civilization into the encircling gloom is to realize not only the function of ballet but its present necessity.' *The Sleeping Beauty* delighted him, its transparent gauze forests, the tinsel stairways that swept giddily into a Poussin heaven, and the fountains and cascades caught in endless immobility. At another theatre that spring he admired, in Cocteau's ballet *Le Jeune Homme et la Mort*, the effect of Wakhevitch's décor, the attic with 'an iron bed that expresses the horror of all the iron beds of all the top floors of the world'.

He was writing longer articles elsewhere. He claimed in *New Theatre* magazine, early in 1947, that a producer had so to co-ordinate every sensation – sound, word, movement, colour – that an audience would know what had urged a dramatist to 'the imperfect expression of pen and paper'. He added: 'Everything that gives meaning and quality to a producer's work he learns outside the theatre from the people he meets, the music he hears, the pictures he sees, and from his own travels, troubles and excitements.'

All was moving towards April in Stratford-upon-Avon, Sir Barry's second year, and the production designed to transmit true Elizabethan romanticism. It had been prematurely debated more than any other stage event: perilous publicity, for Brook had not yet had a failure and the swing must be near. Whereas no one had heard of his *Love's Labour's Lost* before it opened, *Romeo* suffered from too many puffs preliminary. Unaware, he rehearsed as strenuously as ever in one of the less inviting halls, up at Holloway in what somebody called London's Arctic Circle and owned at the time by Donald Wolfit. The spring of 1947 was frigid: the *Romeo and Juliet* company gathered, shivering. Diana Mahony (later Mrs Donald Sinden) remembers that when Peter Brook assembled the players and told them, in effect, 'You are in a hot, dusty street in Verona', she glanced up to see a trickle of snow through the roof. But within a few minutes Verona had displaced Holloway; Brook knew where he wanted to be. Peter Bull, then briefly involved with old Montague, admired 'a short genius who stands bolt upright through a production, so that there is never any question of the actors having an excuse for feeling tired'.* Walter Hudd, the Capulet, told me years later: 'He could illuminate, you know, astonishingly – but he could also flash the light into your eyes with a flick of the mind.'

* *I Know the Face, But . . .*, Davies, 1959.

Brook said: '*Romeo and Juliet* is not a play for ageing prima donnas. Juliet should be played by a girl of fourteen.' Though he was only half-serious about wanting a child-Juliet, he was delighted when next morning his telephone rang, and a breathless voice said: 'My name is Claire Bloom. I am fourteen!' Brook asked her to come to see him. Gravely, he explained to the child – who looked considerably older than her years – that what he really needed was an experienced player who might possibly suggest Juliet's age. Some time afterwards he admitted: 'Little did I realize I was talking to exactly the girl I wanted, but just a few years too soon.'

At the time he made an admirable choice in nineteen-year-old Daphne Slater, a gold medallist from RADA and a Chiswick girl, old Brook country. She was blue-eyed and ash-blonde. Her Romeo was the Italianate Laurence Payne, aged twenty-seven. Old friends, Beatrix Lehmann and Paul Scofield, played the Nurse and Mercutio. The revival sought to remove from its speaking, sets and music (the Spanish Roberto Gerhard's with 'the fierceness and violence of a bullfight') any hint at all of the moonlight and rambler roses of sentimentality. Brook experimented with anything. Thus a certain colour, a pure vermilion, had not been seen at Stratford for so long that it could be used in itself as a sharp dramatic emphasis. (Later other directors used it until its impact dulled.) 'I tried,' Brook explained, 'to make the production essentially 1947 in its approach to the staging and essentially Elizabethan in atmosphere.' Scenery and decoration could be irrelevant; one tree on a bare stage could suggest loneliness of a place of exile; one wall, as in Giotto, an entire house. He would be told, even so, that his own scenery and decoration were too obtrusive, and that though he had summoned the Veronese noon he had obscured the sound of the verse. Wryly, he recalled this after twenty years:*

Scenery is irresistibly fascinating. For me the theatre always begins with an image. If I find the image through the design, I know how to continue with the production. If I go into rehearsal with a nagging sense that the set is not right, I know I will never find my way out again. My most cherished theatre-going memories are of Bérard; Bérard the man, the gentle, bearded genius, always searching, always starting anew, and Bérard the designer, the greatest of stage magicians. . . . In human terms, my closest relationships have been with designers. Nothing makes me happier than to take a piece of cardboard and begin to fold and tear it into a set myself.

* Foreword to Michel Warre's *Designing and Making Stage Scenery*, Studio Vista, 1968.

Yet over the years I have worked always against the scenery – in reaction away from scenery. When Rolf Gérard and I did *Romeo and Juliet* at Stratford we began throwing out our own scenery at the dress rehearsal. Gradually we came down to an empty orange arena, a few sticks – and the wings were full of elaborate and expensive discarded units. We were very proud of ourselves, but the management was furious. . . . Nothing is so beautiful as a bare stage: yet its loneliness and its openness is often too strong a statement and it must be enclosed. How? What objects should be put into this great void? The problem is always agonizing. Not too little, not too much. What is appropriate . . .?

He was asking the question at the Stratford dress rehearsal, held on a glum night in a fretful, gusty April of swollen cloud. This year a close-knit company seemed to be, as in Benson's day, a part of Stratford life: townsfolk waited for news. The première was on a Saturday, an inauspicious evening, windy and wet, the river turbid and its willows blown aslant. Inside the theatre it was the kind of production unknown since the Russian, Komisarjevsky. To muted French horns the play began hauntingly with John Harrison's voice, grave and gentle, speaking the sonnet for Chorus, 'Two households both alike in dignity', as the actor in silhouette made a slow progress through the dark. His voice faded, and light blazed upon the stage, bare of scenery except the toy cincture of crenellated wall and backed by the indigo expanse that Brook called 'a great tent of Mediterranean blue'. In a few seconds all was alive, Capulets and Montagues among a polychromatic crowd stirred from a midday torpor. A magnificent opening; slowly disappointment supervened. For all its inspiration – the wit-cracking pointed with a flickering of rapiers, the appearance of the Nurse and Lady Capulet beneath a spotlit canopy that floated in a vast, bare void; the isolation of the lovers at their first rapt meeting, the world forgot – in spite of all this, the performance began to lag. It wanted the 'impetuous march of music'. Further, a Shakespeare-trained audience murmured when it found that Brook had cut out the expository passage where Friar Laurence explains to Juliet the working of the potion. At the end he cut the reconciliation of the warring houses. Odd, said the scholars, for previously he had made room for such extraneous figures as Simon Rebeck, James Soundpost, and Hugh Catling: the musicians who argue while Juliet lies cold above, and who offer here their counterpoint to the Capulet mourning.

Finally, while the audience cheered, one realized that the newspapers would frown. A drizzling Sunday had to elapse before the daily paper notices arrived; and at least one important Sunday critic held his review for a week. Brook kept calm; but it was too like a procession of protracted death. Cookman, in *The Times* on Monday, regretted the 'recklessly spectacular version which sacrifices poetry, acting, and even the story itself to pictorial splendour'; Gordon Phillips, in the then *Manchester Guardian,* after noting a 'slightly Levantine Verona', said that Shakespeare appeared sometimes to be 'fighting a losing battle against his determined producer'. Lionel Hale described 'a contest of ballet versus the Bard, with the Bard an easy loser' (London *Daily Mail*). As the week ebbed, Philip Hope-Wallace, in *Time and Tide,* applauded the look of the thing, Rolf Gérard's impression of space, 'with little bits of isolated realism bathed in translucent light as it might be in a picture by Carpaccio'. He disliked a certain freakishness – the tomb, for example, might have been 'a fragment of bomb damage' – but he did enjoy what was often 'a wonderful whirling ballet of Verona'. Conceding that the performance lacked sudden lyrical incandescences, he said firmly: 'If this kind of production were to be given in Prague or Moscow, we should never hear the last of it.'

Few had much praise for the acting, yet the revival, for all its caprice, lives now when many others are clean out of mind. Fourteen years later – by the time the Memorial Theatre had become the Royal Shakespeare – its merits would have out-balanced its curiosities. But in 1947 Brook was already before his hour. The performances gave what he asked for. Daphne Slater kept the distraught, child-like quality he needed, that of 'a girl swept off her feet by a series of wonderful and terrible events'; Laurence Payne drove at Romeo as Romeo himself at Tybalt; and Paul Scofield acted Mercutio in the spirit of the Renaissance, flag in air. He uttered the Queen Mab aria while stretched upon the stage in the torchlight, his caped cloak flung round him, his arm raised, and his eyes intent as he let the speech flower into the silence of the grotesquely-visaged masquers. Mercutio had Hamlet's gifts: the courtier's, soldier's, scholar's eye, tongue, sword. Eric Keown, in *Punch,* precisely hit off Beatrix Lehmann's Nurse as a dry, rheumatic creature, 'something between the Red Queen and a Piccadilly flower-woman'.

John Harrison, who was Benvolio as well as Chorus, has remembered for me Brook's early Stratford productions:*

* From 1962 to 1966 John Harrison was Artistic Director of Birmingham Repertory Theatre.

That *Love's Labour's Lost* was a joy to be in, though killing on the feet. The whole stage was ablaze with style and light and comic crankiness. I never expect to see a better. It saved the artistic features of Barry Jackson's first festival after that disastrous *Tempest* and old-fashioned *Cymbeline*. The mad blood was stirring all right. But I always felt it stirred to less effect the following year in *Romeo and Juliet*.

Success was making Peter more dictatorial in his methods. He was obsessed with his central pair and let many of the rest of us go hang. I remember Paul and I, desperate for rehearsal, eventually taking ourselves off to the circle foyer and working out something for the Mercutio conjuring scene after the ball; then literally grabbing Peter by the scruff of the neck and forcing him to watch it. He chuckled a lot and pronounced himself perfectly satisfied. So that's how we played it. He was very high-handed with us all in the ball and fight scenes, master-minding through a megaphone, and only Nancy Burman [then Production Manager*], pouring oil on troubled waters, prevented downright mutiny. He also left a great deal to chance inspiration at the dress rehearsal. It was not until then, for example, if memory serves me right, that he decided to cut the reconciliation of the houses (the only point to the play, apart from the poetry which he'd strewn on the floor) and awarded the Prince of Verona's final speech to me as Chorus.

Chorus, also, was improvisatory. He had originally intended a recorded disembodied voice, and even had a go at recording it himself. I still have the result (though he doesn't know it). Anyway, dissatisfied and a little amazed by the sound of his own voice, he then had a bunch of us record it. My version was selected. Then he decided to let me do it traversing the stage in a black cloak and this worked rather well. He even put back, at my request, the second chorus which had been cut. He still trusted the tyros from Birmingham implicitly. I remember he asked me to cut Benvolio's long speech about the fight myself – merely saying that it had to come down in length.

That reminds me of a similar instance in the previous year. He knew that though I was playing Longaville, I had a great affection for Dumain's poem, 'On a day, alack the day'. So he switched the poems.

To him I was very much the poetic young actor, the ideal Ricki-Ticki-Tavy in *Man and Superman*, which was the first part I played for him. He couldn't understand why I wanted to direct. 'Why?' he asked. 'You're a good actor.' Almost as if, at that time, if *he* had been a good actor, he wouldn't have bothered to direct. I remember him saying once, 'Of course, the only part I would be right for is Hamlet. I long to see it.'

I was tremendously fond of him. When he came up to Birmingham a few years ago to collect an honorary degree, he didn't seem to have changed. He's never needed to put on airs. Same small, smiling, squeaky

* Later, for many years, Administrator at Birmingham Repertory.

presence. Very much the cuddly toy. I think that is how we thought of him in those far-off days — as our mascot. The kind of mascot, like Alec Rose's, that gives all the orders.

IV

One valuable supporter of *Romeo and Juliet* was Peter Ustinov, also of Russian parentage, in *New Theatre* (June 1947): 'This production had quite a few faults by any standard, but it translated into dramatic terms what the mind reads in the written page. Its huge, blue, empty cyclorama was a glorious background, not only for the passionate riot of colour but also for the rushing imagination. . . . It may well be that Peter Brook has been wrong entirely all the way down the line. If that is so, all I ask for is the privilege of being wrong with him.' Brook threw aside the sackcloth. 'A production,' he said during 1948 in John Lehmann's miscellany, *Orpheus,* 'is only right at a given moment, and anything that it asserts dogmatically today will be wrong fifty years from now. . . . Any attempt to fix productions by tradition is doomed to lead to the lifeless cul-de-sac of National Theatres.'

Probably because of the argument, *Romeo and Juliet* was the season's favourite play. The furious rapier-swishing of the duels became a cliché of Shakespeare production, though Peter Fleming, in *The Spectator* that autumn, murmured that the rapiers treated so gaily were in fact 'lethal and expensive tools with very sharp points'. From Stratford, after noting that the revived *Love's Labour's Lost,* his Watteau fête-champêtre, was greeted as thankfully as if it had mellowed to a classic – which indeed it was – Brook returned to London, to another wildly diverse production, to his ballet notices, and to his continued observation of the international stage. 'In Paris,' he said to Ivor Brown, 'you can almost guarantee success by jazzing-up a bit of Greek mythology. But here it's fatal – unless you've got the Lunts on your side.' One day he would have them.

He was not jazzing-up Greek mythology in his next task, a return to violence but to modern violence, a double bill at Hammersmith (in July) of plays by Jean-Paul Sartre: *The Respectable Prostitute* and *Men Without Shadows*. Each was labelled 'Peter Brook's Production'; at twenty-two he was more than ever a name. Neither piece mattered a lot, even if people fainted every night (once there were six) over-wrought by the torturing of men and women of the Resistance, prisoners of the Vichy militia. Rolf Gérard – with Brook names have recurred throughout his career – designed the suitably squalid décor; the *New Statesman* praised 'formidable ingenuity'. After the brief run Brook still appeared on a Hammersmith programme, now as producer of a Japanese Noh play – again with Gerard's décor – that was transiently in the first half of an intimate revue. It had vanished when the revue opened in Shaftesbury Avenue during October, the month that *Romeo* came up to His Majesty's in a few weeks of Stratford Shakespeare. The Memorial Theatre had been crowded; but scholars ('is the play about hot weather?') had not forgiven him, and memory tricked Dr Dover Wilson in 1964 when he talked portmanteau-fashion of '*Romeo and Juliet à la* Watteau'. Even the loyal Barry Jackson had to admit that there could be other readings of the tragedy. Brook's name was not on the Stratford list during 1948. He might have reflected that Komisarjevsky at his most excessive had never been attacked for his Stratford productions in anything like the terms used for *Romeo*. But 'Komis', as Stratford called him knowingly, was fifty when he directed at the Memorial Theatre, and Brook was twenty-two.

Continuing to review ballet, he summarized it as 'an artificial paradise that never comes very close to reality'. It was the hour to move to another artificial paradise. In March 1948, twenty-one days before his twenty-third birthday, and to the consternation of older music critics, he was appointed first Director of Productions, a title he invented, at the Royal Opera House, Covent Garden: good news for Simon Rebeck, James Soundpost and Hugh Catling. Reporting this, the *Evening Standard* said that he resembled a well-fed cherub – the analogy was common form – and talked like an impish don. His voice, according to another newspaper, was a mezzo-soprano mumble. Whatever the volume of his speech, he was a linguist at home in half-a-dozen languages, and he would have no trouble in this cosmopolitan world of opera. For variety's sake, about now, he was editing for the gramophone a potted musical version of *The Wind in the Willows*, which could have been a collective phrase for the Stratford reviews of his *Romeo*. 'That young man knows what he wants,' Mabel France had said on a summer day in Birmingham. At the moment he wanted change; but, like Keats on leaping headlong in the sea, he would soon be acquainted with the soundings, the quicksands, and the rocks.

III

The Garden: 1948-1950

I

A NEW British resident company had been assembled at the Royal Opera House towards the end of 1946. Little more than a year later, Peter Brook arrived at the age of twenty-two. In one sense this had been his ideal theatre, but he had known it from the other side of the curtain. Reaching it now as a director, he saw it in a stranger, colder light, coming though he did with the warm recommendation of Barry Jackson who loved and understood opera as much as the classical stage. Karl Rankl was musical director and David Webster the Garden's General Administrator; but no one had been responsible for artistic unity, for supervising the producers and keeping work from drifting to the slovenliness of routine. Peter Brook was an iconoclast. In his opinion the operatic stage was roughly where the Shakespeare stage had been fifty years before, overlaid, unimaginative. He held that an artistic director, after distinguishing the qualities of a score, had to translate the composer's need and intention into theatrical effect. Musicians might be unsympathetic, singers traditionally temperamental; no matter. He was resolved to find the appropriate style. Always, too, he had detested a merely haphazard association of composer and archaic décor ('mauve and orange *Tannhäusers*'). It sounded reasonable, yet his experience at Covent Garden would be disheartening. Twenty years on he said simply: 'Grand opera is the Deadly Theatre carried to absurdity. Opera is a nightmare of vast feuds over tiny details; of surrealist anecdotes that all turn round the same assertion: nothing needs to change. Everything in opera must change; but in opera change is blocked.'* In another place he had written that, whatever his nominal position, a producer of opera was still compelled to be second to the conductor: thus there was no one person to blend the impressions of the ear and the eye.

* *The Empty Space* by Peter Brook, 1968.

38

Covent Garden, in the quiet spring of 1948, waited aloofly. What would Brook do? Bow Street was no place to encourage an Infant Phenomenon. True to his Russian descent, the Phenomenon opened with Mussorgsky's massive *Boris Godunov,* the first opera he had ever directed: Rankl as musical director; sets by the Russian designer, Georges Wakhevitch, whose work in ballet had impressed him. Jonathan Griffin, poet and dramatist, and later author of *The Hidden King,* was at the British Embassy when Brook, in quest of a designer, crossed to Paris and asked for his help. At once they went round to Christian Bérard. He would love to set Boris, he told them, but it was a task for a Russian and Georges Wakhevitch was the man. So it proved when the opera went into production. Brook, having chosen the expanded 1874 version without the Rimsky-Korsakov sugaring, resolved to present the great tragedy of guilt and loneliness in an 'epic' style dictated by the sombre music; it would contrast entirely with the usual operatic Technicolor carnival. Designs and groupings were contrived about a central axis running downstage; he hoped to handle the chorus in such a way that it would behave more like a contemporary crowd. The nursery scene he set on a gallery in the Kremlin, with cupolas and domes visible behind Boris, alone in the realization of his tragic failure. Wakhevitch stayed up all night painting ikons on the wall. The belfry, in the Coronation scene, was so big that it had to be stored in an East End warehouse and brought by lorry to the theatre where twenty men waited to hoist it into position. The opera, with Paolo Silveri as Boris, duly opened on 12 May 1948, after the company had had acting drill rare in an opera house. According to Beverley Baxter, Brook ordered the singers about until they nearly collapsed from fatigue: 'As a tenor said to a large soprano; "It's like being kicked by a canary." But he should have added that the canary had a kick like a mule.'

So had some of the music critics. They had not previously known a Brook, and he might have said with Pinero's schoolmistress, 'It is an embarassing thing to break a bust in the house of comparative strangers.' True, *The Times* perceived an imaginative sweep, and Philip Hope-Wallace, also a drama critic, found the night 'wonderfully vivid and stirring'. But Martin Cooper (*Spectator*) condemned a production by a novice, 'the pantomime opulence of the coronation scene', and the automatic doors and theatrical use of the ikon motif in the death scene; and Ernest Newman, doyen of the corps, opened in the *Sunday Times* his sustained fire on a director who thought more of the direction than the music. Brook, indeed, split music criticism down the middle. On 16 May the *Observer*'s notice by 'Charles Stuart' (Charles Reid) was headed 'A Touch of Genius'. Reid made various criticisms; he was averse from numbers and sumptuousness for their own sake; but at the last he could write movingly of the final scene in the Kremlin council chamber:

Harried by self-torment, Boris comes panting and reeling to his death down an endless corridor, with doors sliding silently behind him, sealing off light, air, and sanity. The ultimate door, when its wings meet, forms a great image of the Christ, dark-bearded and Byzantine, with piercing eyes. Those luminous eyes are the last thing we see as the curtain falls on a darkened stage: the imperial corse is folded in blackness and forgotten.

For Reid over-lavishness was the main fault. 'But the production does offer a solid half-hour of genius.' This could be set beside a *New Statesman* article (August 1948) in which Desmond Shawe-Taylor asked the Opera House management to reconsider the relative importance of 'fancy production and sound singing. . . . Good singing is the very heart of opera.' At the middle of the conflict, Peter Brook lay ill for a fortnight in the Great Northern Hospital, where he managed to write a film script, a television play, two short stories, and three articles on the theatre.

His next works, *La Bohème*, a revision of the then current production, and *Le Nozze di Figaro* (Geraint Evans and Elisabeth Schwarzkopf), with Rolf Gérard's sets, came through fairly well in spite of the tangle of accents in *Bohème*. Brook told Charles Reid much later that he never forgot his first *Bohème* rehearsal with Ljuba Welitsch, the Bulgarian singer, and Schwarzkopf. He asked one of them to do something she did not wish to do. Her companion took her aside for a moment and whispered (as a listener reported to Brook afterwards) 'It is our first day. Today be good. Then *können wir diktatirien.*' In *Bohème* he enjoyed working from the glass-plate photographs of Paris that Puccini himself had taken; faded tints used in the sets and costumes matched the wistful romanticism.

So far, hopeful; but Brook must sometimes have felt the ground shaking beneath him. No one in living memory had dared to challenge the theories of operatic performance. He rejected any idea of animated dolls in a cardboard world: such an exhibition as worried Sir Isaac Newton who was never at more than one opera: 'The first act he heard with pleasure, the second stretched his patience, at the third he ran away.' Throughout his Covent Garden life Brook kept up a running fight with the musicians. The art of production was in an endless state of evolution and flux, yet musicians could never grasp why a composer's stage directions were not valid for all eternity.

II

With relief, as well as a truant's guilt, he slipped back into the theatre in the spring of 1949. Here, at the Lyric, Hammersmith, not a prima donna in sight, he had a play of a dozen scenes that followed each other unbroken. With them went the challenge of a tiny stage and no machinery whatever. Howard Richardson and William Berney had written this indulgent fantasy, *Dark of the Moon,* a title that attracted Brook when he saw pictures in an American magazine and observed with rapture that there were witches in the cast. Securing a script, not very easily, he opened it one night in the Underground, noticed that the action began in swirling mist on a mountain ridge, wondered about the dialect which was as thick as the mist, and grew so absorbed that he overshot his journey by six stations. Soon he was hunting solutions to the problem of the Lyric stage where Tennent Productions (the Company of Four) had agreed to do it. A folk-tale from the Smoky Mountains – in America 'a legend with music' – the play was based upon the ballad of Barbara Allen:

> A witch-boy from the mountain came,
> A-pinin' to be human,
> For he had seen the fairest gal . . .
> A gal named Barbara Allen.
>
> O Conjur Man, O Conjur Man,
> Please do this thing I'm wantin',
> Please change me to a human man,
> For Barbara I'd be courtin' . . .

Apart from the matter-of-fact people of Buck Creek, the text demanded the witch-boy (acted by William Sylvester), a 'Conjur Man' and 'Conjur Woman' of a superior order in Smoky Mountains society, and two siren-witches who haunted the peaks: no secret, black, and midnight hags, but a couple of blithe alley-cats ready to nestle in a tree or to hang head downward.

Dark Witch and Fair Witch were hardly in the murky-eldritch manner Shaw was thinking of at an amateur performance of *Macbeth:* he suggested that 'the impersonation of witches as a profession is almost as precarious as the provision of smoked glasses for looking at eclipses through'. Brook, in his romantic mood, cherished this freak of the imagination, its interrupted barn dance, the general-store wedding, and a flare of revivalistic emotion when the congregation of Buck Creek strives to win Barbara Allen's soul from her witch-boy husband. He had kept his decision not to plan too closely too soon. For that matter – and he had Covent Garden in mind – nothing should be staged according to some impersonal algebraic formula supposed to fit any production anywhere. When he directed the Buck Creek revival meeting, every player was told at rehearsal to try to steal the scene, and they were ripely and helpfully egotistical. So were many of the critics – though one held that *Oklahoma!* had merged with *The Immortal Hour,* which may or may not have pleased Brook – and during April the piece came into the Ambassadors and a run of more than a hundred performances. Irreverence that shocked some people would have seemed hackneyed in 1970. It would not have appealed to my Cornish Nonconformist ancestors; at the 1949 première I found pleasure mixed with guilt.

This production foreshadowed a quite different style of work to which Brook would not revert for years, indeed until the *Marat/Sade:* that is to say, the animating of a group of young players of not much professional experience, whose intensity grew with every rehearsal. They were encouraged to work with as much noise and gusto as possible: an animation Brook was able presently to order as he wished. In its way *Dark of the Moon* was very close to the kind of performance that became current in the theatre only during the last half of the Sixties. If one could bring that production from the past, take it out of a box, as it were, its idiom and style would appear contemporary. In 1949 it generated a quite unexpected theatrical energy at a time when one felt that this word was the prerogative of *Oklahoma!* and the Americans. Early in rehearsals Brook knew, by a director's sixth sense, that things were running well for him: he had a rare feeling of pure pleasure. Victor Cookman, writing in the *Tatler* (23 March 1949) as Anthony Cookman, put it plainly: 'The producer sets the company a pace which rivals that of *Oklahoma!* The two productions have also this in common, that all the variations of pace are managed with the utmost smoothness and that the

greater number of the small parts have each a telling individuality.
. . . There are more good little performances than there is space in
which to praise them.'

Brook accepted praise and blame calmly. 'I'm not sure,' he said,
'whether it's a good thing to be original in the theatre. The critics
slated my *Romeo and Juliet* for being too original, but they applaud
the quality in *Dark of the Moon*.' Just after this and its surge of
scene and character, he became for one night a television dramatist.
Box for One, which would be often revived, needed only a single
actor and a square yard of stage: there, shut into a kiosk, a fugitive
from a Soho gang endured a progressive frenzy of telephoning
before the gang got him.

Too quickly Peter Brook was again at battle stations before and
behind the scarlet and gold curtain of Covent Garden. He disguised nothing. 'In opera,' he said to a *John Bull* interviewer, 'there
are so many people who fight with complete selfishness for their own
point of view. Getting what you want is simply a matter of making
the biggest fuss for the longest time . . . at an early age I learned to
scream a little longer.' His new production was *The Olympians,* a
work with an Arthur Bliss score to which J. B. Priestley had written
the libretto: a midsummer night's enchantment in a small French
town. There for a few hours, a scratch company of strolling players,
pomping folk who are the ancient gods in whom mankind has
ceased to believe, return to their true selves; during one night they
exercise their power in a pagan masque. The opera had been written
during the four years since Bliss and Priestley, old friends, had met
in Cheltenham at the first British contemporary music festival.
Before the Covent Garden production, Brook spent some time with
Priestley at his Isle of Wight house, adapting the text from a director's
point of view. I do not now remember much except a constant
beauty of grouping against the profound blue and silver of the
midsummer night. Generally, score and singing were approved;
but Ernest Newman, at the head of the anti-Brook faction, let
himself go in the *Sunday Times* (9 October 1949) about the visual
side of a production that cost £10,000:

I found it difficult to imagine a worse handling of the second act. This
was . . . something near musical comedy. Regardless of expense, the
stage was packed with people going through those fidgety exhibitions
that have contributed so much to our exasperation or amusement at
Covent Garden during the last few years. . . . The first thing a theatrical
producer has to do in an opera house is to learn his true place there.

III

The fuss over *The Olympians* was a nursery squabble beside the typhoon that blew up on 11 November 1949. That night Covent Garden revived Strauss's *Salome,* directed by Brook and conducted by Rankl, with 'scenery, costumes, and special effects' by Salvador Dali. Salome was Ljuba Welitsch; Herod, Franz Lechleitner. The opera had been chosen eight months previously. Brook began at once to study Wilde's original French, Lord Alfred Douglas's clotted English version, and the German text commissioned by Strauss. In his St John's Wood home, score on knee, he got a pianist to play to him until every bar was in his head. That Easter in Rome, having observed a show of Dali's *As You Like It* designs* in the foyer of the Eliseo Theatre, he decided that this was the very artist, the man of macabre theatrical imagination, to express the heat and eroticism of Strauss's music. It was honest but rash; he must have been prescient enough to know what would happen. But it was a gesture of independence, and if in making it he pulled down Covent Garden about his ears, he would not much mind. Dali was in America; they met in Paris during May at the home of the Vicomtesse de Noailles; a young woman *répetitrice* from the Paris Opera played and sang her way through the score. It delighted Dali; he was prepared, so it seemed, to abjure arbitrary surrealism, to the relief of Brook who had warned him that any designs with headless dogs and three lemons suspended above a derelict taxi would be refused. Peaceably the two men worked together in Paris and at Cadaques, Dali's Catalan seaside home: he finished the designs in ten days. Brook would find it was only when people called that Dali – preserving tradition – duly wore for the occasion a ceremonial flower in the nostril.

Towards the end of August Brook returned from a visit to Cadaques, two hundred miles from Barcelona. All had been smooth except that he dismissed Dali's notion of turning the stage into a huge bed. He did not want a flying hippopotamus, and certainly he had no wish to equip Salome's brassiere with fireworks that would spark off at the end of her dance. Otherwise, no complaints: merely an incident on the journey home. After leaving Cadaques he and four other passengers were driving to Barcelona along a desolate

---

* Four years later (1953) Brook introduced the Folio Society's *As You Like It,* with the Dali designs: 'The producer who, taking his cue from the title, reconciles the vivid excitement of Dali with the sober responsibilities of the Folio, is, I am sure, on the right track.'

road when two armed brigands – each carrying a Sten gun, a
rifle and a hand grenade – stopped them in a Spanish forest.
Shouting 'Get out, in the name of the Spanish republic!' the
brigands demanded the car and anything useful its passengers
carried. Brook, with some forethought, asked them to take his silk
pyjamas but to leave the original Dali designs which he was carrying
in a suitcase. He was lucky. After the prisoners had been tied back to
back in the middle of the wood, the bandits returned in a few
minutes and threw the designs – on stiff board, three feet square – at
Brook's feet. Hours passed before the five managed to untie their
knots; then they had to walk for a long time through the darkness
to a village where the police also greeted them hospitably with Sten
guns before driving them into Barcelona.

That was a curious prologue to the great event. Describing his
production, two months before it finally went on, Brook did not
hesitate. He never did. *Salome,* he said, thinking of the music
critics, would be 'the most extraordinary spectacle since the six-
teenth century. We have made a hallucinatory fantasy that does not
depart one iota from Strauss and Wilde.' Again (here the future
foreshadowed): 'To me the theatre should be a miracle with a certain
amount of ritual.' One of Dali's designs, on Brook's Covent Garden
desk, had a heading strongly underscored, '*Must* be used'.
In spite of the imperative, nobody could decipher the writing:
not that it mattered, for the designs already chosen were quite
enough.

Talking to Charles Reid, Brook said the decision to go ahead was
taken only two months earlier when they could be sure of Ljuba
Welitsch. 'For you, Peter *mein Kind*, I sing it back to front,' she had
exclaimed accommodatingly, and this without seeing the designs.
Brook had resolved that these must reflect Wilde's imagery and
avoid any pompous Germanic manner, Fritz Lang-cum-Reinhardt,
with real well and real moon. He described to Reid the essentials of
the production: an extraordinary, gleaming moon, the main
image; an equivalent for 'in the air something like the beating of
wings' to reinforce the music at Herod's entry; a banquet that should
express, in one *coup de théâtre*, the height of oriental luxury and
decadence; the appearance of the head; Salome's crushing by the
shields – 'really lethal shields'. Finally: 'We think it is wrong that
the curtain should fall where Strauss indicates it. He was neither
actor, producer, nor electrician. He miscalculated his curtain, which
is indicated to come down when the crushing is only getting under

way, though the whole work leads to this inexorable climax. I am
not taking the curtain down – a quick one, of course – until one bar
after the last note.'

Rehearsals were sultry. Rankl would not speak to Brook, and
they had to communicate through a third person. On the night
Rankl, in protest, did not take his call, whereas Brook took his and
was mildly booed. There were fourteen curtains. Next day, all that
weekend, and for weeks ahead, the producer faced a Lear's Heath
storm. Harold Rosenthal, historian of Covent Garden, has said that
this *Salome* seemed to be bent deliberately on disregarding the
composer's professed intentions: 'Perhaps if [it] were seen again in
the mid-1960s, it would be more readily accepted by audiences and
critics who have in the meantime become accustomed to the excesses
of Wieland Wagner and his imitators.'*

The Times had been amiable: 'Apart from some head-dresses
that threatened decapitation to their wearers, the general effect was
properly macabre, and the special effects, pomegranates, peacocks,
and a pavilion, served to mark the progress of the drama without
calling too much attention to themselves.' But most critics failed
to exercise Coleridge's 'willing suspension of belief for the moment,
which constitutes poetic faith'. Thus Richard Capell, in the *Daily
Telegraph*, wrote bluntly: 'The new production is the abyss. The
nature and intentions of Strauss's work were disregarded *in toto*.'
Ernest Newman said in the *Sunday Times* that both vocally and
orchestrally it was 'the most miserable *Salome*' he had ever heard; as
for the production, one absurdity followed another and the de-
capitated head looked like a large steamed pudding. The *New
Statesman* attacked 'idiotic, exasperating, and hideous costumes' and
the 'four miniature umbrella frames' that rose and fell over Herod's
pavilion. There were more tolerant views. Philip Hope-Wallace
(*Time and Tide*) said: 'Regarded as something other than a successful
staging of Strauss, it is an impressive bit of "theatre". If the costumes
touched a high-water mark of absurdity, the set itself was a pic-
turesque piece of surrealist decadence.' Robert Muller (*Theatre
News Letter*), not yet the power he would be as a drama critic, was
glad to have lost studied mechanical gestures, over-weight prima
donnas in faded costumes, tenors affronted when asked to act,
'and other incidental food for parody retained under the motto
of "Music First".' Caryl Brahms, years later, recalled Salome
running swiftly across the inner stage, her scarlet nylon cloak

* *Opera at Covent Garden: A Short History*, Gollancz, 1967.

floating behind her almost the stage's length, a river of blood.*

Peter Brook decided to reply after Eric Blom, who admired the performance musically, had written on 27 November in the *Observer* of which he was now music critic: 'Nobody can produce an opera, or for that matter, design settings for it who has not studied and thoroughly come to understand the score.' Also: 'The lighting is mishandled in the most irritating way.' Next Sunday Brook retorted that music critics had missed all the points. Music and libretto determined the style of a production. Because in *Salome* these were strange, poetic, unrealistic, should the visual counterpart – sets, props, costumes – be straight? To put the fantastic myth of Strauss-Wilde into a document of Judaean décor would be as absurd as to play *King Lear* in a drawing-room for *Quiet Week-End*. Dali was the only artist in the world whose natural style had what one might call both the erotic degeneracy of Strauss and the imagery of Wilde; after studying the score together, they had set out to make a true music-drama in the style of the great religious painters. That was bold enough. And he added:

Why should we be afraid of fantasy and imagination, even in an opera house? When the curtain rises, strange vulture-like wings beat slowly under the moon; a great peacock's tail, opening with the opening of the dance, suggests the decadent luxury of Herod's kingdom. A handful of such visual touches over the ninety-six minutes of the opera are designed to lift the audience into a strange Wilde-Strauss world, and to point the essential stages of the tragedy.

Further, he could safely say that where his *Salome* departed from traditional production, the aim was musical. Acoustically, the singers were all better off; by stylizing the scene with the Jews in a formal group downstage on one side, the Nazarenes in the other, and Herod raised in the centre, there could be a musical effect far stronger than usual. He had tried, he said, to create a style of opera that was dramatic, exciting visually, and yet did not pretend that the artists involved were actors, dancers, or, in fact, anything but singers.

Eric Blom, on 11 December, was unpersuaded. Brook had not refuted the accusation that he took an opera to be mere raw material for a producer's fanciful extravagances. That same day Peter Brook was writing in the *Sunday Times,* agreeing that stage business and scenic effects must not distract one from the music. 'But what

* *Guardian,* 19 September, 1970.

exactly is a distraction? Here we part company. Isn't ugliness distracting? Isn't clumsiness distracting? I find the scenery of most traditional opera productions so tedious that I cannot listen. To me all the traditional paraphernalia of opera, the meaningless positions, the exaggerated agony, the stock-in-trade gestures, the out-of-date scenery, are so removed from the style of any great composer that they destroy all pretensions to drama.' Again: 'He [the producer], must do exactly what the score dictates to him, and what he believes to be right.'

Presently, Charles Reid, in *Theatre News Letter*, joined Muller in admiring 'the plumed, fantastic pavilion upstage, the mammoth peacock tail which spread itself for the Dance of the Seven Veils, the scarred, sinister moon, the tunnel with iron grille which sloped to Jokanaan's dungeon: these things were not only good to look at in terms of colour and pattern, but also completely congruous with Richard Strauss's music and Oscar Wilde's adapted text. The score is something between a hothouse and a jeweller's shop; Wilde's imagery chill, perverse, and exotic. Both score and imagery found their counterpart in Dali's designs.'

IV

There it remained. Higher musical circles might have thought that *Salome* would be forgotten as an ephemeral caprice: in the words of Rabelais, so much enjoyed by Mr Fox in *Melincourt*: '*Sa mémoire expira avec le son des cloches qui carillonèrent à son enterrement.*' Higher musical circles were wrong, for the night would slip into legend. It was Brook's last production at Covent Garden, though he turned from it in the late autumn to revive *Boris Godunov:* in this the Bulgarian bass, Boris Cristoff, appeared without orchestral or full-stage rehearsal. He had a brush with his producer. Appalled to find that he had to play a scene against the interior workings of an immense clock that dominated the centre of the stage, he insisted that instead he should have upon the wall a small ornamental clock of the type familiar to him. Otherwise he could not sing. Brook would not remove the complicated mechanism. There was deadlock until David Webster, the Covent Garden administrator, suggested a compromise. Why not two clocks – the big one and a smaller one upon the wall which would be Cristoff's? Mischievously, Brook responded by supplying the most miniature travelling clock the theatre could provide. At rehearsal Cristoff exclaimed: 'You have betrayed me. I have not got my clock, and tomorrow night I will not perform without it.' Brook said mildly, 'There is your clock, Mr Cristoff.' In a fury the singer left the stage, shut himself in his dressing-room, and refused to return. Promptly Brook looked round and observed on the stage a Polish bass who could do the part in Russian. Would he? Certainly! The man began to sing; Brook had the dressing-room amplifiers switched on, and Cristoff, hearing suddenly the voice of another Boris, rushed back, swept aside the singer, proceeded with the rehearsal, and appeared on the following night.

Sheer disenchantment had impelled Brook's action: the end of the Covent Garden story was approaching fast. By 1950 he had met a shield-wall of distaste. People had talked in the words of Lord Harewood (*Opera*, February 1950) of 'a series of more or less un-musical productions'. Towards the end of June, by mutual agreement, Brook's contract was not renewed. He said merely: 'After two years' slogging I came to the conclusion that opera as an artistic form was dead. It could be brought to life only if existing music critics were put on the retired list, and all singers and composers could undergo a complete change of heart.' He was tired of a world where opera singers had no regard for their fellow-artists, and, having been dominated by musicians, had no room for new-fangled ideas in stage production.

Brook was bitter with the bitterness of a man before his time. Though he had taken cheerfully the response to his Stratford *Romeo*, at Covent Garden he had found an opposition impermeable to argument. One fine day he would produce opera elsewhere; and in fact he was asked within five years to return to Covent Garden for *Otello*. If his engagements had allowed him, he would have done so. Today there is a chasm of twenty years between the Covent Garden Brook knew and the freer air of the nineteen-seventies. Two decades ago the young man, only twenty-five, went back resiliently to the dramatic stage. At the Opera House his post, which someone had described cynically as a Bow Street Runner's, ceased to exist.*

---

* In 1971 Peter Hall took over – it proved transiently – a similar post in an entirely new Covent Garden climate. Brook, during his period there, might have taken heart from the words of Jean Cocteau: '*Lorsqu'une oeuvre semble en avance sur son époque, c'est simplement que son époque est en retard sur elle.*'

IV

Moon And Stars: 1950-1952

I

AT twenty-five Peter Brook longed to be his age. For years he had
been the subject of articles either entitled 'Wonder Boy' and calling
him an *enfant terrible* or an *enfant prodigue,* or else simmering with
some venerable musician's rage. Everyone had begun conventionally by saluting genius; now they asked, just as conventionally,
what the devil he meant by it. Brook, seldom puzzled, was baffled
here. He did not recall productions that old hands compared with
his. When he was told that Whatsisname never did this thing or the
other, and therefore it must be wrong, he listened with courteous
disbelief, never having heard of Whatsisname. But in the spring of
1950 he had little opportunity to reflect. While still officially at the
Garden he was involved already in Shakespeare at Stratford and in
his first major production on Shaftesbury Avenue. This was *Ring
Round the Moon* at the Globe Theatre; original text by Jean Anouilh,
translation and adaptation by Christopher Fry. It fitted into the
theatre of the period that he would come to remember as one of
'colour and movement, of fine fabrics, of shadows, of eccentric,
cascading words, of leaps of thought and of cunning machines . . .':
the theatre of Jouvet and Bérard and Jean-Louis Barrault, Clavé at
the ballet, *Don Juan, Amphitryon, La Folle de Chaillot, Carmen,*
Gielgud's revival of *The Importance of Being Earnest,* the Old Vic
company's *Peer Gynt,* and Olivier's Oedipus and Richard III, *The
Lady's Not For Burning* and *Venus Observed,* Massine at Covent Garden
under the birdcage in *The Three-Cornered Hat.*

At this hour, the beginning of a new decade, he said in a Third
Programme talk much of what he felt about the theatre. Why was
there such vitality? Why – it lay heavily on his mind – had Covent
Garden 'a struggling and kicking opera company whose new
productions provoked louder screams than any other birth
announced in the daily press?' Why was Stratford's 'dismal mauso-

leum where for years the grey effigies of Shakespeare's plays used to
be watched in respectful gloom no longer a graveyard?' Why, in
the commercial comedy-stricken West End, was the uncommercial
making money? There was a ready answer:

Before the war the audiences were comfortable, complacent people. For
the most part their lives had the things they thought they wanted – easy
money, easy travel: life didn't seem too colourless. Then, sharply, with
the war and the black-out, the restrictions and austerity, colour went out
and has never been seen again. The war-time tours of the Ballet and the
orchestras only fed an increasing famine, and as time goes by the newspaper picture gets more and more black. The theatre is one of the few
compensations left. People with theories call this escapism, and so it is. It
is escapism in the very best sense: a ballet, a comedy in verse, an artificial
play with movement and colour, are both escapes and reminders of all
those things that Europe has fought for, for five hundred years.

It was a young man speaking, as young men have always spoken.
Invariably older generations have seemed to be comfortable and
complacent. Stratford-upon-Avon has usually been emerging from
the depths, though nobody – and not Brook himself, had he known
– could have accused Bridges-Adams and Komisarjevsky of presenting Shakespeare in grey effigy. But Peter Brook liked the broad
sweep of argument, the tingle of immediacy, the exciting present,
the beckoning years ahead. Soon in his talk we had the Brook of the
future: 'In the theatre there is no stopping place, no sudden final
solution* in which the atom is exploded. The moment anything
stands still it dies, and every answer begs a new question.' Further:
'Any theory that restricts the theatre is a wrong theory. It may be
an interesting idea to perform all plays in arenas, or in theatres
without a curtain, or in costumes without rostrums, or on rostrums
without costumes. Each one of these contains a notion that can be
used . . .'

II

When he gave the talk he had already, that year, two productions
behind him with nothing whatever in common except his sense of
theatre, his intuitive sense of fitness. He had begun in January with
Ring Round the Moon, a 'charade with music' translated by Christopher

* 'The whole thing . . . is all in a state of finding; of not expecting final solutions,
  but keeping open. . . . We want to be in a world of experiment' (Peter Hall
  at Stratford, 1963).

Fry from the French of Jean Anouilh. It had a Firbankian quality:
to describe it now is to grasp a handful of moonshine. Fry, in his
own plays, had been restoring a sense of language to a tone-deaf
theatre. Choosing, weighing, and blending his words like an
alchemist, he asked audiences to lend him their ears, and he never
repaid them with what an earlier poet called the loose-lipped lingo
of the street, something that in all senses would become one day the
common form of the stage. Fry taught dramatic poetry to dance
again: no pomp, no massively slow progress in which the verse
must move like a captive in chains during a Roman triumph. He
would be in key with the prose of Anouilh, a man, prolific and
diverse, who was the French dramatist of the hour. *L'Invitation au
Château*, its original title, was the play of his, a *pièce brillante,* suited
particularly to Fry's method: a silver charade that, on the stage of
the Globe Theatre, was penned within a soaring Messel winter-
garden in spring. Brook, too, though he might still consider the eye
more than the ear, had a natural affinity with Fry. In the December
of 1949 they were together at an old, magnificently-sited hotel at
The Lizard, in the farthest south of Cornwall, discussing their
fantasy while the waves foamed into the curve of Housel Bay
beneath Lions' Den, and the great beam of the Lizard light swung
steadily across the cliffs. During the early spring, only a week before
Ring Round the Moon, Olivier had appeared at the St James's in
Fry's *Venus Observed,* more balm to ears afflicted by the gravel-
tramping of colloquial dialogue. At the Globe young Paul Scofield,
by now in almost telepathic sympathy with Brook, chased himself
in and out of the winter-garden and the château ball as a pair of
identical twins, one a heartless schemer, one voluble and shy. Many
still remember Margaret Rutherford, cigar-smoking in her wheel-
chair, Marjorie Stewart and Richard Wattis as they danced an
absurd tango while discussing their affairs, and Cecil Trouncer
shredding banknotes all over the stage. The night, said Siriol
Hugh-Jones, was 'as elegant as a staircase epigram.' When a heavier
hand, again for Tennents, directed *Ring Round the Moon* at the Haymarket twenty years later, the lights were dead, the music fled, the
banquet-hall deserted. Fry's translation glittered yet, but it needed
Brook to animate the party on the stage, the crumbling butler, faded
companion, melancholy millionaire (this was Trouncer, with his
carved-out Grinling Gibbons voice), lepidopterist, ballet-dancer,
aunt.

In 1950 nothing was wrong. It was the theatre of grace Brook

admired, one that seemed apt for the West End stage of its time.
When the comedy had begun a run of two years, he took a formerly
familiar path to Stratford-upon-Avon. The play was the dark
comedy of *Measure for Measure* in which what he would define later
as the Holy and the Rough elements of the theatre are found
together. Sir Barry Jackson, acutely hurt, had left Stratford at the
end of the 1948 season. To the surprise of all, the Governors had
failed to renew his contract, insensitive treatment after the three
years during which he had restored the Memorial beyond imagination. The theatre, Peter Brook's 'mausoleum', under the heat of
unaccustomed publicity, was committed to fresh methods, a star
policy that would have alarmed some earlier Boards and to which
Sir Archibald Flower, for so long dominant, would never have been
a party. Still, though John Gielgud was to appear as Angelo, his
debut at Stratford and in this character, there was an almost
untried Isabella, a young actress, Barbara Jefford. The play opened
on a windy March night: no cherry-blossom frosting the gardens or
swans skimming an Avon of willowed glass. Brook had planned his
sets and costumes* as a reaction from his own pictorial Shakespeare:
a sharp change, for nobody had decorated the plays more than he
had done. Since then, Stratford – and particularly *A Midsummer
Night's Dream* in 1949 – had been scenically overwhelmed. Not so
Measure for Measure. The costumes, designed by Brook himself,
were largely in the style of Breughel and Hieronymus Bosch. The
curtain rose (for it was an age when curtains did rise) upon a perma-
nent frame of grey stone pillars, a double range of lofty arches like a
triangle with its apex downstage. This, in several variations, with
flats or grilles added, could suggest, in colonnade and cubicle,
every Viennese milieu: convent, prison, street. Brook brought the
action steadily downstage. Gielgud, as the fanatic with a twist in
the brain and frost in the voice, came down a long vista of flaring
cressets to receive his appointment from the Duke. Lighting varied
between extreme brilliance and dense gloom. We had the sense of
Vienna's sultry days and its sultrier nights before the unfolding star
called up the shepherd.

Brook sought to present Shakespeare in a more heroic manner,
asking his actors to summon their courage and to act even at the
risk of being, in the knowing hack phrase, 'ham'. He believed that

---

* Peter Fleming wrote in the *Spectator*: 'Brook's use of detail is unobtrusively
felicitous – the tarboosh on a gaolbird's head to remind us that the frontiers of
Asia are not so far away; the domesticated pheasants in the moated grange
bequeathed not so long ago by the Romans who used them as poultry.'

after his experience at Covent Garden his sense of rhythm had been heightened, and that it gave a new tempo to the play. Incidental music he banned – for the moment he had had too much music – though he wrote a plaintive little tune for 'Take, oh take those lips away', sung without accompaniment. The dramatic scenes had a strong austere force. The prose comedy in what he called later a 'Dostoevskyan setting', was rough and inventive. One day he would probably have expanded his inventions; as it was, the house enjoyed George Rose's Pompey, spiv from any Soho corner, as he dispensed the cards that advertised Mistress Overdone's amenities. An extraordinary array of prisoners was seen at full in the progress of the crippled and deformed: Master Rash, Master Caper, young Dizzy, Master Deep-vow, Master Copper-spur, Master Starve-lackey, young Drop-heir, Master Forthright, Master Shooty, and the near, cataleptic spasmodist, the veteran 'wild Half-can' that stabbed Pots.

At the end Brook used another of his charged and daring pauses, this time before Isabella, at 'Look, if it please you, on this man condemn'd', knelt to plead for the life of Angelo. He asked Barbara Jefford to pause each night until she felt that the audience could stand it no longer. The silence lasted at first for about thirty-five seconds. On some nights it would extend to two minutes. 'The device,' Brook said, 'became a voodoo-pole – a silence in which all the inevitable elements of the evening came together, a silence in which the abstract notion of mercy became concrete for that moment to those present'.

He would have claimed then that his work in the theatre could be summarized in a simple phrase: that, in the direction of any play, he sought to create another place, another world, using means either semi-realistic or totally unrealistic. In *Love's Labour's Lost* he evoked what he needed by using the Watteau chiaroscuro; in *Dark of the Moon* the bare stage of the Lyric, Hammersmith, was rapidly transformed as if one were watching a cinema screen; for *Ring Round the Moon* (which returned, in a sense, to *Love's Labour's Lost*) he created a romantic, wistful world opposed to everyday reality, one with a special mood, a tune, a colour. *Measure For Measure* lived in its own Dostoevskyan milieu. The play rose towards the key moment for Isabella: a good deed that could shine only in a naughty world. Brook had been shocked by a recent Stratford revival that had sought to turn everything to favour and to prettiness: Shakespeare's Vienna had to be a place that could combine the saintly and the sordid. The Brook set, much praised, was not intended to be merely functional; he hoped that at every rapid change the audience would imagine that it was seeing a naturalistic film set built for just that moment, another part of this strange, baffling city of Vienna. *Le Balcon* (Paris, 1960, a decade forward) would be his last 'illusionist' work; his change of direction would come with *King Lear*.

Measure For Measure in 1950 was the heart of the Stratford season.* Free at length of Covent Garden, Brook turned to a French light comedy, *The Little Hut*. (Always the cry from adolescence: 'I want to change and develop and dread the thought of standing still.') Previously he had been defending the picture-frame proscenium. 'A theatre,' he said in a broadcast, 'is like a violin. Its tone comes from its period and age, and tone is its most important quality. What actually is the aim of production if not to strike a living bond between the house and the stage? And how much easier this is in the warmth of an eighteenth-century theatre than in the frigidity of many new theatres, however wonderfully equipped?'

Certainly *The Little Hut,* originally *Island Fling,* was a proscenium-theatre play, a puff-ball by André Roussin which Nancy Mitford had adapted. 'Sir,' as Dr Johnson said in another context, 'a man might write such stuff for ever if he would *abandon* his mind to it.' Brook had a name now for directing French plays; fashion followed success, though it would be hard to type-cast him for long together. He had a gift for concentrating on the work in hand – Johnson's abandonment of mind – and then, as journalists do, moving at once from a completed task to something fresh and strange. *The Little Hut,* for Tennents, ought to have been relaxation, but Brook's painstaking work on it, largely a matter of the technical timing of jokes, never excited him. His leading man, that grand individualist Robert Morley, believed wrongly that he enjoyed rehearsals too much and tried to spin them out whether or not they were achieving anything. Morley did not get on well with him, but added candidly: 'Sometimes it's a good thing for the play not to have a mutual admiration society backstage.'

In Brook's view, the director of a French comedy in England should intensify any essentially foreign element for the benefit of

---

* Sir John Gielgud, during 1967, in a televised interview with Derek Hart (printed later in *Great Acting,* edited for the British Broadcasting Corporation by Hal Burton), said of Brook: 'He's immensely imaginative and immensely patient. He is in his element making plays like *Titus Andronicus* or *Measure For Measure* or *Venice Preserv'd* (which are not the greatest plays in the world), into thrilling plays in which everyone has the right balance and the right orchestration.'

English playgoers. *The Little Hut* was a boulevard fantasy about a husband and wife and the wife's lover, all marooned on a desert island and trying to live together. In Paris one saw the matter through the husband's eyes, rather as if he were telling a group of friends about his wife's infidelities; it was all worldly and amusing. In London they thought it wiser to tell the story from the wife's point of view, that of a girl who saw everything simply. So the desert island was much larger than life, its flowers vast and its fruit gigantic, and all the people simpler than life, everyone acting from the best motives. In order to make the wife elegant and desirable, but remote, she was turned to a New Yorker.

On the opening night at the Lyric I thought instinctively of *Enoch Arden:*

> No sail from day to day, but every day
> The sunrise broke into scarlet shafts
> Among the ferns and palms and precipices;
> The blaze upon the waters to the east;
> The blaze upon the island overhead;
> The blaze upon the waters to the west . . .

The setting was tropical Technicolor. The husband's inventive faculty provided as many designs for living as the whole of the *Swiss Family Robinson*. Oliver Messel, working with Brook for the second time that year, provided massive breadfruit and coconuts, exotic plants, and extravagant butterflies; and the cast, led by Robert Morley, David Tomlinson and Joan Tetzel, gave suitably extravagant and exotic performances. Critics were benevolent and the public more so. With various cast changes, the piece would run for more than three years. Whether it deserved to is another matter. Still, *The Little Hut* did not pretend to be more than a two hours' scamper from reality, and the theatre cannot always be what Shaw once described thunderously as a factory of thought, a prompter of conscience, an elucidator of social conduct, and a temple of the ascent of Man. Shaw had a fifth category, 'an armoury against despair and dullness', and there at the time it was written, *The Little Hut* could fit in snugly enough.

III

The following year, 1951, brought the Festival of Britain, a brave if inevitably self-conscious exercise in communal gaiety. It was also a festival year for Brook. He began by leaving London during four spring weekends, the entire time allotted to him for a production of *La Mort d'un Commis Voyageur* (Arthur Miller's domestic drama, *Death of a Salesman*) at the Belgian National Theatre. For the rest of the week the company was rehearsing something else. The play cost just £200 to stage in Brussels; its ultimate rehearsal which Brook did enjoy (without trying to spin it out) went on for thirty-six hours. Shortage of material was embarrassing; in Belgium then one could not get even coloured gelatine for the lights. But Brook, *le remarquable technicien anglais,* survived, and so – though it hardly blazed across Brussels – did the production. By the time it had opened, his year's first London play had failed, astonishingly, at the Haymarket where it had seemed to fit perfectly into the gold frame.

A Penny for a Song was the second work by a thirty-three-year-old actor-dramatist, John Whiting: his earlier, the revolutionary *Saint's Day,* had yet to win the Arts Theatre prize against a fury of criticism. Styled farcical comedy, *A Penny for a Song* was a mooncast caprice from the Dorset summer of 1804 when Napoleon's invasion fleet was likely to arrive at any hour. Possibly the dramatist had read the fifth scene of the second act of *The Dynasts,* in which an old man with a pike, acting as one of the beacon-keepers on Rainbarrows' Beacon, Egdon Heath, is called John Whiting. Previously in Hardy's chronicle, a stage-coach passenger on a Wessex ridge says to another, 'People who live hereabout feel the nearness of France more than they do inland'. In Whiting's play we find a gardener up a tree* – it is his task to watch for Napoleon's sail – a crazily ingenious Squire with a gush of dog-French, his single-minded brother in charge of a fire-engine, an urbanely observant philosophic dilettante, and a genial personage – splitting his time between cricket and the local Fencibles – who once stumped Nyren, captain of Hambledon. Established in a garden flower-sprayed and arbour-guarded, and designed by Rowland Emett of *Punch*, it was the gentlest of fantasies. On the night its graver passages seemed less plausible (as indeed they did in an altered version staged in 1962 by another director). Brook's production and his company easily created the appropriate atmosphere of wars and wassailings. Emett made a graceful set of a lawn before a small Georgian house, with the line of the Channel beyond; Brook

* This was George Rose, who had been Pompey in the Stratford *Measure For Measure*.

gloried in the observation balloon that floated decoratively into mid-stage, the stertorous fire-engine (a gift to and from such an artist as Emett), and the couple of cannon-balls that trickled through a garden gate someone asked peevishly to be closed. Fire-engine and balloon may have derived from John Whiting's grandfather who was patron and honorary member of an Edwardian fire brigade in Salisbury and who had his own special enthusiasms and inventions. These included:*

an airborne engine designed to attack fires at the very centre – that is, from directly above. It consisted of a plain wooden platform with one dozen buckets – the whole suspended from a balloon. This contraption proved its excellence at the first trial. While hovering directly above the fire, the balloon became ignited and precipitated the platform, the buckets, and two men into the fire which was immediately extinguished.

A Penny for a Song showed, too, how a director who had come a very long way from the rudimentary switchboard of the Chanticleer, could light a stage both in the full glow of morning against the sky's blue arch, and at night when the lawn was shadowed and the moon was rising after the fury and the heat. A small piece, but with relish in its nonsense, style in its ordering. Brook was told that he had over-directed – at the time criticism's password, a phrase grabbed from the pigeonhole. Whiting, who ought to have known, praised an 'extraordinary sympathy and understanding'.

Though most people tried now and again, Peter Brook still resisted any rapid and facile summary. He was, first of all, a young man, a crime he shared with Pitt; for years he appeared to get no older. In the West End he was a romantic, something else that defied glib definition. In Shakespeare he was moving from his earliest rash blaze of riot towards a stripped austerity; always he was seeking to probe the dramatist's many-layered thought. Critics, fumbling for a label, found that Brook eluded the gum-brush. Admirers were emphatic; older men, in the way of older men, were suspicious and dismissive; actors either trusted him entirely as Scofield – with his own telepathic awareness – had done, or were as unsure about him as Robert Morley was at the rehearsals of *The Little Hut*. Very simply, as in the rehearsal room of the Birmingham Repertory Theatre on that late summer morning years before, he

* 'The Honour of the Fire Brigade', in John Whiting's *The Art of the Dramatist*, edited by Ronald Hayman, London Magazine Editions, 1970.

knew exactly what he needed, and how to get it: a talent observable in a passage from Denys Blakelock's autobiography. Blakelock, at his most endearingly precise as the personage named Lamprett Bellboys in *A Penny for a Song*, found Brook explicitly a genius, friendly, serene and imperturbable. But (he went on): 'He neither slumbers nor sleeps, he would not know a clock if he saw one, and he believes that the Sabbath was made for producers. A few days before the opening night there was an expensive luncheon: [Peter] was a charming host, but from the hors d'oeuvres to the Camembert, in his gentlest tones he destroyed everything I had done up to date. . . . I was on the wrong track, I had to reorganise, to re-orientate, to think again.'* Still, this actor's first or second thoughts had always been a pleasure; nobody complained about his final decision.

IV

Doggedly, critics went on imagining that Brook must continue in the mood of his last play. Once more he baffled them with his production, in late June, of *The Winter's Tale* at the Phoenix Theatre, a stage he would get to know intimately. The play, with probably the most generally misread title in Shakespeare (there has been a conspiracy to call it *A Winter's Tale*†) had not been acted for a run in the West End since the near-definitive Granville-Barker revival at the Savoy in 1912. Now Sir John Gielgud was Leontes; Diana Wynyard, Hermione; Flora Robson, Paulina; Sir Lewis Casson, Antigonus. Down towards the bottom of the list was the author of *A Penny for a Song*, John Whiting, as the Gaoler (twelve lines). George Rose (Autolycus), his third consecutive part with Brook, and Virginia McKenna (Perdita) had come on from the Haymarket. Music, remarkably, was by Christopher Fry. For years there had not been in London a less ostentatious production of Shakespeare. Siriol Hugh-Jones, who would always supply the phrase for Brook, found it again in her *Vogue* notice: 'Having delighted, ravished and infuriated us in former productions with fabulous crowd skirmishings, shock effects, thistledown elegancies of style, and occasional bloody-minded naughtiness, he now straightens his box of bricks into neat piles to build a scaffolding for the play, and nothing but the play.' She remarked on some of the

* *Round the Next Corner*, Gollancz, 1967. Blakelock, who left the theatre in 1953, died in December 1970.
† It goes with such spellings as Thorndyke and Schofield.

incidental felicities: the immense crown suspended above Sicilia; Time advancing through a dazzling whirl of snow – it was indeed as though one of those endearing glass toys had been shaken; the rustic garland of straw above Bohemia; and the whole Bohemian episode lit by the muted, golden sunlight of a Claude sky. She did not mention the bear which – as Philip Hope-Wallace said – splendidly ate the Antigonus, Sir Lewis Casson. I remember how Brook and his designer, Sophie Fedorovitch, turned the stage to a desolate end-of-the-world coast, as eerie a scene as we had known. Customarily we must avert our eyes when an actor, heavily furred, shambles on to hustle Antigonus towards the wings; at the Phoenix I had no desire to laugh while the old courtier, crying 'This is the chase; I am gone for ever,' fled terrified along the angry shore: the first time in at least one experience that 'Exit, pursued by a bear' had been properly realized. At more important moments Brook let the actors govern the night. Gielgud, who had originally suggested the revival to Tennents, contrived to humanize the megalomaniac Leontes, with his jealousy born of fantastic imagining: a critic wrote of 'a naphtha-flare of rage'. As nobody else had done in immediate recollection, he made of the first acts a wild hurtling music, and in the last, as the king repentant, used all his emotional grandeur in the remembrance of his queen:

> Stars, stars
> And all eyes else dead coals!

Brook had studied *The Winter's Tale* and its construction carefully, discovering in it a cohesive pattern some directors had overlooked, and observing that the way to understand the statue scene, so frequently criticized as false, was simply to play it. He would have had Granville-Barker with him here, though where Brook held, after close examination, that the scene was 'the truth of the play', Granville-Barker gave his praise to a craftsman's treatment of a stage effect 'so good that hasty naked handling might have spoiled it'. Earlier, Brook and his actors at the Phoenix – John Moffatt especially – recreated the narrative passage for various Gentlemen and Paulina's Steward, 'Then have you lost a sight which was to be seen, cannot be spoken of'. It is often held that in employing a form of Messenger speech for the King's recognition of his daughter, Shakespeare avoided a challenge. But he was not a dramatist to avoid anything, and how sure his instinct was, Peter Brook proved in the lively conversation-piece frequently scamped.

Sir John Gielgud, in a television interview eighteen years later, remembered that before *The Winter's Tale* the only talk Brook gave was about journeys: Shakespeare's feeling for going out on adventurous journeys and coming home, and for ultimate recon- ciliation. 'This feeling of leaving and returning is a very marvellous and important thing, and that was very helpful to us all.'*

v

On 12 September, while *The Winter's Tale* was running in Edinburgh where it had gone for Festival performances, a brief break in its London run, Peter Brook and Tyrone Guthrie signed a letter to *The Times*. This, from Brook's address at 35 Loudoun Road, St John's Wood, was about John Whiting's *Saint's Day*. Christopher Fry, Alec Clunes and Peter Ustinov had awarded to it the Arts Theatre prize of £700, and they had done so defiantly after the critics, more or less in unison, had dismissed the piece as claptrap. There had seldom been such scorching first-night notices: practi- cally any critic could have echoed Fanny Squeers, 'I am screaming out loud all the time I write which takes off my attention rather and I hope will excuse mistakes'. Yet here, and unrecognized – after all, why should it have been? – was the premonitory trembling of what would one day be the new wave, the stir, the lift, the swell, far out. Whiting explained long afterwards that his theme was self-destruc- tion; nobody perceived this. Arriving from Edinburgh in time for the fourth performance, a matinee, and in an Arts Theatre all but empty – it grew emptier as the play went on – I found the first act and a half absorbing. Then the dramatist shifted to a private world at 'the point of deviation':

Careful! We are approaching the point of deviation. At one moment there is laughter and conversation and a progression: people move and speak smoothly and casually, their breathing is controlled, and they know what they do. Then there occurs a call from another room, the realisation that a member of the assembly is missing, the sudden shout into the dream, and the waking to find the body with the failing heart lying in the corridor – with the twisted limbs at the foot of the stairs – the man hanging from the beam, or the child floating drowned in the garden pool. Careful! Be careful! We are approaching that point. The moment of the call from the other room.

The passage can stand as an analogy to the drama of the anarchic

* *Listener*, 2 October 1969.

C

nineteen-fifties: the laughter, the smooth controlled progression, the call from another room, the end of peace and comfort, the facing of tragedy, the desperate question. Whiting's narrative was relentless. Fry would say a decade later: 'It came before the public was prepared for it.' Brook and Guthrie wrote in their *Times* reproach to the critics:

Saint's Day may well be strange and obscure, and entertaining is certainly a word that cannot be applied to it; but its passion and unbroken tension are the products of a new and extraordinary theatrical mind. The dramatist is writing in his own idiom and describing his own world. For the moment this must seem as strange to us as the private worlds of Kafka and Virginia Woolf must have appeared before familiarity added signposts to the scene. We offer no explanation of John Whiting's work; we only wish to record our own deep faith in his talent, integrity, and promise, and beg everyone truly interested in the theatre to go to see for themselves.

Very few did respond, but a time came when Whiting would be a cult-figure, his work edited in detail, and *Saint's Day* – established at last as a landmark-play* – taken periodically from the shelf. It reached the Arts Theatre too soon, and the stage revolution, still nearly five years ahead, would be governed by rowdier dramatists. Today, when new playgoers regard the years before 1956 as primeval, the sequence of events is forgotten; war-time toleration when practically anything had a ready audience, in London or out of it; approximately five years of slow readjustment and recovery, and another five with playgoers getting more and more selective, the rebels in wait, and production increasingly adventurous and illuminating.

Brook's Festival of Britain year had yet more in it. During October it was announced that he was planning a film of *The Beggar's Opera*. Tyrone Guthrie, eight years earlier, had suggested this to Laurence Olivier as a film subject; it appeared now that Olivier, as well as being co-producer with Herbert Wilcox, would play Macheath for which he had had his singing voice, a light baritone, intensively trained. Rumour said that, when dining with Wilcox and asked what he wanted to do, Brook had said immediately, '*The Beggar's Opera*', and they had begun to cast it on the back of a cigarette packet. It would be eighteen months before the public would see anything. Meanwhile Brook was in constant activity. Not long after the film was announced he had talked on quite other

* It was published first in *Plays of the Year: 6*, Elek, 1952.

matters to the Gallery First Nighters Club in that crowded room – forsaken now – above a public-house behind Shaftesbury Avenue. He perceived, he said, three revolutions in the current theatre: great changes in scenic style, violent changes in the style of acting, and slow changes in the type of play. 'We now feel that scenery should help to throw the attention on to the actors, leaving the audience to imagine the details.' Soon he was saying in an interview: 'I am completely against all movements to revive the Elizabethan open stage. The proscenium stage is a weapon of focus and concentration where everyone can see and hear together.'

He would have one further production that autumn, though none of those he had been thinking about during the spring when he had contemplated both a *Volpone* and films of *Ring Round the Moon* and (with gypsies) *Romeo and Juliet*. Transiently he ceased to theorize, and for a very good reason. Early in November he and the twenty-one-year-old actress Natasha Parry were married. Half Russian, a quarter Greek and a quarter English, she was a slim, pale-skinned and dark-haired beauty, with (it had been well said) the tranquillity of a princess in a Persian miniature. Bred to the stage, she had been the youngest of Cochran's Young Ladies in the A. P. Herbert–Vivian Ellis musical play *Big Ben*, when she was only fifteen. She had acted in repertory at Southampton; but by the autumn of 1951 she was in a French comedy, *Figure of Fun,* by Roussin, at the Aldwych Theatre, London. Peter Brook – whom she had met first at a Covent Garden ballet when she was seventeen – had helped, unofficially, to mould the play during its last week on tour.

They were married at Caxton Hall on 3 November 1951, before their relatives only; no best man. Peter had telephoned the news to his father on the previous day: 'Are you free tomorrow at ten o'clock? I'm getting married.' At nine-thirty his parents arrived at the register office; then his brother Alexis and his wife, and Natasha's mother, her stepfather, and a seven-year-old stepsister. The registrar arrived at ten precisely: no trace of the principals, but they appeared at length, singly and almost simultaneously, ten minutes late. Peter had never been a good time-keeper. When he handed over the marriage certificate for safe keeping, his father realized why nobody else was present, for the entry read curtly: 'Peter Stephen Paul Brook. Occupation: Clerk. Address: Hove.' The couple had no time for more than a quick breakfast; Peter had to leave at once for Brighton where he was directing at the Theatre Royal a Tennent production of Anouilh's *pièce brillante, Colombe,* and Natasha for the

BBC studios where she was recording a sketch. Next week he had moved to Bournemouth. As Natasha was in *Figure of Fun*, she and her husband had to spend their first weeks of marriage away from each other.

Denis Cannan had adapted *Colombe,* a backstage play of a famous actress and her two sons. An experienced cast contained Yvonne Arnaud, Joyce Redman and Esmé Percy, none of whom Brook had directed before; Gurschner and Stanley Moore, who had done the *Dark of the Moon* sets, returned for this; and Tennents put on the production at the New Theatre on 13 December 1951. It was only moderate Anouilh. His tale of a faltering marriage, love's evanescence, a young wife caught up in the Parisian theatre at the turn of the century, for a while seemed to be barren. One could appreciate Brook's way of disguising the fact, and several of the performances were persuasive, even if Yvonne Arnaud, with the *roucoulement* of a ringdove, was miscast as a dominating terror of an ageing actress. Gradually the play strengthened; as a narrative of lost love, and the reason for love, it began to fix the mind; and at length an epilogue whisked us back two years to show the idyllic birth of an affection we had seen dragged in the mud This was stage trickery that succeeded, though some of the earlier passages were sacking next the skin. A section of critical opinion said that Brook had emasculated *Colombe.* I would suggest now that he depended more than usual upon isolated effect, his device, for example, of showing the stage from the back, with another audience supposedly away by the cyclorama. Stage hands and effects men were about their business in the foreground. Beyond them the actors, backs to the house, played out the end of a Venetian romantic drama, run-of-the-piazza stuff put together by a dramatist who could have been a shadow-Rostand. The curtain rushed down at the back; within a few moments the stage was bare.

It may not be reasonable to dwell on this. Brook himself was an admirer of *Colombe* and of Cannan's version which, though it sometimes strayed far from Anouilh's details, never strayed from his intentions: 'Word for word [Brook wrote in an introduction] the French and English *Colombe*s vary; idea for idea they are just about the same. Anouilh's aim is to speak through comedy: to woo his audience into swallowing his bitter pill: Cannan's aim equally has been to divert, so that even those most on their guard against the wickedness of cynical and pessimistic Frenchmen can be seduced into forgetting their suspicions in laughter and tears.'

Early in the New Year, less than two months after her marriage, Natasha was taken ill* and ordered a long rest. During 1952 Peter did nothing in the theatre; his version of *The Beggar's Opera,* unseen in public until the summer of 1953, kept him for most of the year in the film studios. He had a good deal of trouble with it, but various other and more rewarding things would happen before its première. He would direct at Hammersmith in 1953 Thomas Otway's *Venice Preserv'd,* almost forgotten in the theatre. Moreover, the Metropolitan Opera Company of New York, heedless of the London music critics, invited him to stage a production of Gounod's *Faust* for the opening of the 'Met' season in November. When he went across to confer with the Metropolitan controller, Rudolf Bing, during the autumn of 1952, Natasha was with him; and the New York Press flowered in the usual surmises. He was going to direct Arthur Miller's *The Crucible* in London; there was talk of a mysterious piece called *Venice Preserv'd.* What mattered most to him just then was his return to opera. How was Covent Garden feeling about its black sheep?

---

* On Christmas Eve she left *Figure of Fun,* and in mid-January she was in her room at the top of their Kensington house where Peter spent every possible moment with her. By the autumn she was well enough to travel to America with him.

V

Otway And Opera: 1953-1954

THE Lyric Theatre at Hammersmith in West London had its final efflorescence during the cold winter of 1952 and the spring of Coronation year, 1953. When I recall it now, I move back to a moment seventeen years earlier, during a Komisarjevsky production at Stratford-upon-Avon: the raising of those gold, convolvulus-shaped trumpets in a flourish round Lear's throne. Here in Hammersmith was the last great flourish of the Lyric, the old melodrama house (*Secrets of the Harem*), thrust away behind a street market, that Nigel Playfair had made into a temple of style as he interpreted the word. In his Restoration and eighteenth-century revivals he was a supreme interpreter. Since his day the temple had been simply a theatre-of-all-work that renewed itself just after the war as a testing-ground for plays possibly transferable. Though much would happen still, 1952–3 was the Lyric's ultimate splendour. Peter Brook knew the stage inch by inch; he had made three productions there, though none of them was as star-spangled as Otway's *Venice Preserv'd; or, A Plot Discover'd*, third of a Gielgud-Tennent sequence that had begun with *Richard II* (Paul Scofield) and *The Way of the World*.

Thomas ('Gentle') Otway had written during the Restoration the last major English tragedy until *The Cenci,* an actor's play rather than a poet's. Nobody had seen his name on a London programme since the bawdy romp of *The Soldier's Fortune*, with its massive voyeur, Sir Jolly Jumble, had turned up in the West End during the nineteen-thirties. Once they had called him 'next to Shakespeare', not for the quality of his language which runs forcibly without flooding into an Elizabethan cataract, but as a tribute to the pathos of *The Orphan* and, more reasonably, to the dagger-thrust of invention in *Venice Preserv'd* (it is a play of daggers) and to the humanizing of the principals, Jaffier and Pierre. The first of these is impulsive, honourable, but too, easily over-wrought, a fallen Brutus; Pierre, nobly undeviating in the fight for liberty, is ready at the end to encounter darkness like a bride. The plot describes an uprising against tyranny: 'A factious, giddy, and divided Senate is all the strength of Venice; let's destroy it.' But the plan is ruined by a woman's misguided influence on Jaffier; it is as though Brutus had declared to Portia the conspiracy of the Ides of March and answered her appeal.

A change from the Restoration's lacquered comedy, it might have perplexed our ancestors to hear that the play could ever be in the discard. Byron betrayed himself when he wrote of the city of Venice:

> And Otway, Radcliffe, Schiller, Shakespeare's art,
> Had stamped her image in me. . . .

(Radcliffe, in surprising company here, was a reference to Ann Radcliffe and the Gothick murk of *The Mysteries of Udolpho*). Byron was on safer ground with

> Ours is a trophy which will not decay
> With the Rialto; Shylock and the Moor,
> And Pierre, cannot be swept or worn away,
> The keystones of the arch. . . .

At Hammersmith Scofield was Pierre ('Cursed be your Senate! Cursed your constitution!'). Gielgud who, as a young man, had once played a declamatory part in *The Orphan*, was Jaffier, making passionately genuine the love-and-friendship conflict. Brook neither forced the tragedy nor pampered it as a fragile antique. His treatment of the fourth-act dagger scene for Jaffier and Belvidera (Eileen Herlie) reminded us, as it ought, of Garrick and Mrs Cibber in the Zoffany picture. The language is typical Otway, as in Jaffier's final speech when Belvidera has 'leapt on his neck and kissed him':

> I am, I am a coward; witness, heav'n,
> Witness it, earth, and every being, witness
> 'Tis but one blow! yet, by immortal love,
> I cannot longer bear a thought to harm thee.
>   (*He throws away the dagger, and embraces her*)
> The seal of providence is sure upon thee:
> And thou wert born for yet unheard-of wonders.
> Oh! thou wert either born to save or damn me!
> By all the power that's giv'n thee o'er my soul,
> By thy resistless tears and conquering smiles,
> By the victorious love, that still waits on thee,

Fly to thy cruel father, save my friend,
Or all our future quiet's lost for ever.
Fall at his feet, cling round his reverend knees,
Speak to him with thy eyes, and with thy tears,
Melt his hard heart, and wake dead nature in him,
Crush him in th'arms, torture him with thy softness;
Nor, till thy prayers are granted, set him free,
But conquer him, as thou hast conquer'd me.

Coming from a film studio's hyper-realism – he had been directing *The Beggar's Opera* – Brook showed now that he could make the wisest use of flat-painted settings. One can recreate scene upon scene from the production as if they hung upon the walls of the Accademia; the chiaroscuro of the cellar, heavily-arched, where the conspirators assembled; the Venetian Senate in its pomp against the darkly glowing depths, the far distances of Leslie Hurry's design, noble in perspective; a flurry of action by the lagoon's sombre calm; the execution scene suggested without dolorous parade. As performed here the tragedy was romantically durable. Brook cut little, even of the scabrous Nicky-Nacky passages in which Pamela Brown, as the courtesan Aquilina, and Richard Wordsworth as the lecherous Antonio, Otway's caricature of the Earl of Shaftesbury, had full range. One ingenuity went almost unremarked at the time. Brook needed a special sound to blend with Hurry's setting, and his solution was portentous. He and the musical director, Leslie Bridgewater, merely recorded some simple guitar music and played it back in the theatre, grossly over-amplified. The result could have come from a grotesque, exaggerated, but just plausible musical instrument such as Hurry might have invented. It was the beginning of the musical legerdemain that Brook would practice so profitably in the years ahead.

For collectors of his work, it had to be a slide from Otway at Hammersmith to a previous glory of Playfair's Lyric, *The Beggar's Opera*. After long gestation the expensive colour-film had arrived in London with all the to-do of a world première – a phrase first minted in Hollywood – at the Rialto Cinema on 31 May 1953; the audience of 450 was composed glitteringly and exclusively of the Queen's Coronation visitors. An informed public, seeing it a little later, might have observed certain old friends among the credits. Denis Cannan had written the screenplay; Christopher Fry had provided additional dialogue and song-lyrics; Georges Wakhevitch was the designer. Brook's working budget had risen between

films, for this was his first since *A Sentimental Journey,* from £250 at
Oxford to £250,000 at the Shepperton studios.

Though Brook, far from the intimate elegance of Playfair and
Claud Lovat Fraser, would have liked his *Beggar's Opera* in Hogarthian black-and-white austerity, colour was demanded. He would,
too, have liked Richard Burton for Macheath, a pleasure denied
him. Brook and Olivier disagreed basically on the treatment of the
part, and Olivier's highwayman could have been one of Farquhar's
polished young adventurers exercising their beaux' stratagem in
Lichfield. Eric Bentley, in America, would be glum: 'Olivier's failure
in the realm of musical comedy would have mattered no more than
his failure in the realm of musicianship had it not been redoubled by
a failure in the realm of reality. His highwayman is not only no
singer, he is not only no musical comedian, he is no highwayman.'*
Brook's Hogarthian narrative was unsparing: brawls in frenzy,
fights in a hayloft, and a procession to Tyburn Tree, complete – as a
critic said in *The Times* – with 'men on stilts, a child in her nightdress,
a blackened, paralysed dotard, all detaching themselves from the
mob that swarms round and above Macheath's fatal cart'.

Here, as in the *Romeo* mob at Stratford or the prisoners' procession
in *Measure for Measure,* Brook was seeking to animate a crowd of
characters, not to fuse everyone into a characterless crowd; any
doxy on the screen could have related the story of her life. Yet, for
all this and for all the speed of the hurly-burly – Brook, refusing to be
stage-bound, never kept his camera still – the film did leave an
impression curiously faint, probably because one was too conscious
of acting and direction to consider the narrative. Olivier, galloping
off over Bagshot Heath, was an athletic, scarlet-coated light
baritone, and Stanley Holloway a resounding bass Lockit. Some of
the actresses received the dubbed voices of opera singers; thus
Dorothy Tutin was paired with Adele Leigh, and Daphne Anderson
with Jennifer Vyvyan. One music critic raised a wistful memory
when he responded to Brook as most music critics had done in the
fading past: 'The famous songs the producer has no notion of
tackling.' Notices generally were tepid; financially, the film was
disastrous. 'And, you know,' said Brook nine years later, 'when you
flop to the tune of a quarter of a million pounds, you have to do
penance until the people concerned forget you or die off.'†

---

* In *The New Republic;* reprinted in *What is Theatre?*, London, 1969.
† In an interview with Richard de la Mare and Maurice Hatton, *Guardian,* 29
  November 1962.

Even so, a few writers were helpful. C. A. Lejeune said in the *Observer:* 'Peter Brook's production at times approaches his Covent Garden scale, with crowd scenes that craftily suggest Cast of Thousands.' Campbell Dixon, in the *Daily Telegraph,* liked the film very much: 'We may say, as Trader Horn of his account of the elephant hunt, that it makes a pretty splash of activity.' Brook had one small and entirely personal pleasure; nobody else had any idea what it meant. Though he never saw the Playfair version, he did act in the piece at school (Gresham's) where they thought so little of him as an actor that they gave him the poorest part – the Player in the first dialogue with the Beggar. In revenge, it was the one part he cut right out of his film.

II

When, having put Otway and Gay behind him, Peter travelled to America with Natasha in October 1953, he had *The Little Hut,* already more than two years old in London, to direct upon a New York stage. (The cast had whisked through a provincial tour in England.) Already the *Beggar's Opera* film had preceded him; and, presumably for exercise, he was about to direct Orson Welles in a compressed *King Lear* for a Sunday-night television show sponsored by the Ford Foundation, as well as preparing for a complete *Faust* on the opening night of the Metropolitan Opera. It was a protean performance, even in the record of a grand old *enfant terrible,* as Caryl Brahms had called him tactfully in London, or (as a New York newspaper preferred, less tactfully) 'this fantastic tot of twenty-eight'.

The tot had to wait until *Faust* for any stentorian enthusiasm, though amiable notices of *The Beggar's Opera* spread wide: 'A rollicking return to the past' (New York); 'a trampoline for the ups and downs of its highwayman hero' (San Francisco); 'no mere respectful re-hashing' (Boston); 'preserves the ironic artlessness of the original raillery' (Baltimore). Theatre criticism was another matter. One day Brook would describe New York critics as 'the most powerful and toughest in the world', and it was probably a compliment that *The Little Hut* could survive their mauling for as many as twenty-nine performances. In London the girl Susan had been an American. At the Coronet, New York, Brook, who wanted to preserve the out-of-the-world quality of the fable, translated her to a French girl (Anne Vernon) with a quite uncomplicated attitude to life; Henry

(Roland Culver) was an ultra-moral Englishman. The reception was glacial; Brook may have worried too much about adaptation to a presumed American taste. 'None of the cast has much comic electricity,' said Brooks Atkinson. Years later Peter would be saying: 'Fun continually needs a new electric charge; fun for fun's sake is not impossible, but seldom enough. Frivolity can be its charge; high spirits can make a good current, but all the time the batteries have to be replenished: new faces, new ideas, have to be found. A new joke flashes and is gone; then it is the old joke that returns.'

Eric Bentley blamed over-production: 'Not every six-tier wedding-cake tastes better than a bun.' Whatever the reason, *The Little Hut* had all but faded by the time Brook had added to his star-cluster by directing Orson Welles on television. This was a seventy-three-minute version of *King Lear*, a play he would come to know better. Briskly, he abolished the sub-plot, combined remarkably the characters of Edmund and Oswald, and allowed Edgar only a single brief sequence as a really mad 'poor Tom'. Natasha Parry was Cordelia, the first part in which Peter had directed her. Welles emerged, said the *Philadelphia Bulletin*, simply as 'a fierce, ranting thunderous-voiced old ruffian getting his just deserts'. The actor had only a few temperamental indulgences as when, in the scene with Gloucester, he insisted on real seaweed to drape over his wig. But it was unexciting Shakespeare, even if the *Cincinnati Enquirer* said, rather charmingly, that the lines were 'reasonably well mouthed'. Brook arranged for Lear and the Fool to take shelter in an abandoned, creaking windmill, and he provided a drenching rainstorm in which the actors worked under a sprinkler system and a device was used to create rain electronically on the screen.

Mitford-Roussin, and what my first editor would have called pemiccanized Shakespeare, were preludes to the full-scale adventure of Gounod's *Faust,* most operatic of operas, at the Metropolitan; its setting for once would match the mid-nineteenth-century idiom of the music. When Brook reached the crimson and gold opera house, with the 'diamond horseshoe' of its first-tier boxes and the prospect of its diamond-and-ermine première, he was remembering Covent Garden and resolving to let nothing deflect him. To the newspapers – they translated it in their own way – he said that he 'didn't give a damn': if the critics rejected his *Faust,* they did, and that was that. It was smoother than he expected. Certainly he need not have worried about his company; arriving more than commonly aggressive, he found what he called 'a cast of angels'. As his television *Lear* had done, the *Faust* production cost 90,000 dollars – with the difference that one lasted roughly an hour and a quarter, and the other, like the production it replaced, might be expected to last perhaps thirty years. For the television he received 5,000 dollars; for *Faust,* 1,500: in any event it was more profitable than his first look at the Faust story, in the company of Marlowe at the Torch eleven years before.

New York opera-goers, who knew about events at Covent Garden, waited with some anxiety for the imaginings of a 'stocky, sturdy, rather rumpled personage, who looks more like a detective inspector from Scotland Yard than a chap who cracks operatic traditions like nutshells'. The rumpled inspector, unrepentantly intransigent, now told musical New York what he had told London: that grand opera as a form had remained stiff and constricted, with the picture on the stage quite divorced from what the music was saying. That summer, when he and his designer – Rolf Gérard again – talked over the production in London, they had agreed that *Faust* was absolutely French in tone, with the kind of romantic atmosphere that made people believe in Paganini's league with the devil. In the theatre it must be brought from the Middle Ages to the nineteenth century. Mephistopheles would be a kind of Cagliostro with superhuman attributes; not an archetypal Satan with horns, but someone able to command magic and trickery. The production, therefore, would be a sequence of vignettes seen through the French illustrations of the eighteen-fifties: nineteenth-century romanticism in the clothes, neo-Gothicism in the sets, the soldiers jaunty heroic Frenchmen with pomaded moustachios, the young Faust as a sort of Byron and the old one as the Schopenhauer type.

In order to diminish the size of the immense Metropolitan proscenium, Brook had the action framed within a front curtain shaped like an irregular circle. Everything would be entirely different from such a massive production as *Die Meistersinger,* put usually in the same period as *Faust:* one was heavy, Germanic, virile, and the other light, elegant, graceful, sophisticated. Brook insisted again that what the ear received must not be at odds with what the eye saw. Was it not absurd to think of medieval, clod-hopping German rustics in *Faust's* 1830 French waltz?

'Angelic' though the cast might be – Brook was comparing the Met with Covent Garden – one or two troubles recurred. Tradition ruled. If a tall man with a certain figure and walk had created a part a century before, then the part must always be played like that, even if a short, fat man happened to be singing it in our own day. Both principals and chorus were tradition-bound. At first the chorus resisted movements, arranged by the balletmaster, that Brook had commissioned for the waltz scene: the routine, he gathered, was effeminate. Obligingly, he modified it at the next rehearsal; the chorus remained unhappy. Then, instead of continued argument, Brook said nothing, and he got what he wanted.

Criticism would be varied, but the first-night effect, with Jussi Bjoerling as Faust, Victoria de los Angeles as Marguerite, and Nicola Rossi-Lemeni as Mephistopheles, delighted what *Variety* called incorrigibly the 'historic tonsil-emporium'. Faust wore a grey frock-coat and white cravat, and the malevolently suave Mephistopheles, losing red tights and long-feathered skull-cap, was a mid-nineteenth-century gentleman in tails and white tie and a black, red-lined opera-cloak. Some critical opinions must have had a familiar sound. Olim Downes, in the *New York Times,* though he applauded the liveliness and fluidity of the new *Faust* and its conspicuous absence of stiffness and convention, had this to say in a surging paragraph: 'One gets the impression from the procedures of most of the stage directors Mr Bing has engaged to renovate chosen works of music-drama, that they regard opera as a kind of adulterated theatre, a form to which they must apply the methods of the spoken theatre to redeem it from its ways, or else throw up their hands and consider it as an impossible species of musical extravaganza, and treat it as such, regardless of any plausibility or cohesion of dramatic effect. . . .' Irving Kolodin, of the *Saturday Review*, did not like the sets but believed that much of Brook's work could be admired highly: 'His general plan of action struck me as sensitive, respectful of the music and responsive to it; without impulse to call attention to himself.' At their gloomiest, the critics lacked the note of high outrage general in London, and Brook got on very well with his septuagenarian conductor, Pierre Monteux.

III

Faust established in its appropriate century, he returned at once to London to prepare for a verse play established in much the same period, Christopher Fry's *The Dark Is Light Enough.* The same period, no doubt, but a thousand leagues from Gounod and his tame librettists, Barbier and Carré. Here was the third part of Fry's seasonal progress. *The Lady's Not For Burning,* 'approximately medieval', had spoken for spring, and *Venus Observed,* with its theme of loneliness, for autumn: now Fry had turned to winter – three plays within six years, though it would be another sixteen before he completed the quartet in 1970 with *A Yard of Sun* (summer in Siena). While Peter was planning *The Dark Is Light Enough*, Natasha, back at last to the theatre, went into Gielgud's production of *Charley's Aunt:* there she coped fearlessly with those desperate lines about Oxford's dreaming spires and sculptured nooks, 'like silent music – a scholar's fairyland'.

Verse drama, slackening a little, had continued its post-war renaissance; each in his fashion, Eliot and Christopher Fry, inseparable names to the drama critic, governed one province of the theatre jointly. Fry's publishers spoke of his 'long-needed reinstatement of the comic spirit in English poetic drama': he had done much more than this, defying two contemporary sins that he called the fear of language and the fear that no audience could be adult. In *The Dark Is Light Enough* his language, as fitted a winter play, was less luxuriant than it had been; it held the spare beauty of branch and twig in the anatomized traceries of December. Three lines from it can stand as Fry's personal epigraph:

> Music would unground us best,
> As a tide in the dark comes to boats at anchor,
> And they begin to dance.

More than any other writer of his time, he has caused the anchored boat of verse drama to dance. The title of the 'winter comedy' derived from Fabre on the flight of the butterflies in stormy weather and profound darkness: 'It was across this maze of leafage, and in absolute darkness, that the butterflies had to find their way in order to attain the end of their pilgrimage. Under such conditions the screech-owl would not dare to forsake its olive-tree. The butterfly ... goes forward without hesitation. ... So well it directs its tortuous flight that, in spite of all the obstacles to be evaded, it arrives in a state of perfect freshness, its great wings intact. ... The darkness is light enough.' In the play we see the Countess Rosmarin Ostenburg as she moves, unfaltering towards the end of her pilgrimage through winter and rough weather. It is 1848, the hour of the abortive Hungarian revolution against the Austro-Hungarian Empire. The Countess's country house is in the direct path of the rebel troops – roads 'sour with men marching'. The rising must affect her life, those of her daughter, son-in-law, all concerned with her. But she has only a week to live. When she dies on a stormy evening we realize how she has held her course through a world she has loved, upon 'an earth which has entertained me'. She has been wayward, her sense of direction eccentric; but she reaches the end with faith untarnished.

Brook, at the Aldwych Theatre, kept faith with Fry. Still looking, somebody said, like a wistful undergraduate and ruling like Ivan the Terrible, he had brought his company* through the agonies of a prefatory tour and the exaction of many rehearsals. The cast was tired; but at the première (30 April 1954) the play, its wings intact, completed the course on a night of many beauties. Dame Edith Evans's Rosmarin, a woman of infinite pity for mankind, moved in her own radiance through the gloom and confusion of a life whose people were an everlasting excitement to her. She was fortunate to have Oliver Messel as the designer of her country house; and in word and atmosphere Fry and Brook could powerfully evoke the state of winter. The first night had one remembered alarm. Between the second and third acts, when there was a quick change of set, someone had failed to stabilize off-stage, upon its slender stand, a heavy arc-lamp that gave back-lighting to a narrow entrance. The hoop of Margaret Johnston's crinoline caught the stand and brought the whole thing crashing down, missing the actress's head by inches. A great gasp, and the play went on.

IV

It did so for six months; and it was still running when, just before midsummer, Brook had the easier task – on paper at least – of directing a light comedy at the Apollo. Entitled *Both Ends Meet,* it was Arthur Macrae's treatise on tax-dodging and official dentistry: the pretence that any tax inspector must be a Front-de-Boeuf: 'Tell down thy ransom, and rejoice that at such rates thou canst redeem thee from a dungeon, the secrets of which few have returned to tell.' In fact, a Front-de-Boeuf, iron man, can be most embarrassed. Hence the decision of the relevant character – acted by

---

* In it was that charmingly substantial actor, Peter Bull, who would write in *I Know the Face But* . . . : '[My part] was that of Dame Edith Evans's medical adviser, and it meant that she had to address me as "Little Doctor" throughout. ("Largeish Doctor" did not quite fit in with Mr Fry's verse.) I was therefore battling against heavy odds.'

Macrae – to call himself an accountant (permissible) instead of a tax official (deadly): a sharp move that obliges him, unwillingly, to hear the ways of tax evasion favoured by his potential fiancée's guardian and a knowing solicitor. Such comedies as this have long curled from our stage like vanishing smoke-rings. *Both Ends Meet* was likeable in evanescence, though, except for the spluttering, dry-syphon expostulations of that grand comedian, Miles Malleson, chinless and apoplectic, I remember little from it: maybe an unfair sense, while walking up Shaftesbury Avenue, that after the problems of *The Dark Is Light Enough*, Brook could have had nothing simpler: the equivalent of falling off a log. Directors by now are used to these innocent misapprehensions.

That September Brook escaped for a while from every kind of fiscal comedy by going with Graham Greene on a fortnight's holiday in Haiti: a prelude to directing on Broadway a musical play, *House of Flowers* by Truman Capote (music by Harold Arlen), with a cast of American and West Indian Negroes. It was a narrative of two rival brothels on a French island in the West Indies: the House of Flowers, run for the comfort of visiting sailors, had to compete with a Madame Tango's establishment. There was also a story of the love of one of the Madame Fleuri girls for a bellboy. With a voodoo ballet added, it seemed on the whole to be a reasonable entertainment for Brook's decoration. Reasonable, perhaps, but hardly entertaining for Brook, though one would have thought it all right on the first day of rehearsal when Harold Arlen, a blue cornflower in his buttonhole, turned up with champagne and presents for everybody. Truman Capote whispered to Brook: 'It's love today; the lawyers will be in tomorrow.' Within a few weeks they were; Pearl Bailey, the lead, who objected to a second re-writing of the second act, served a 50,000 dollar writ on Brook while the play was still touring. Later, in New York, he had to do most of the direction at long distance, from his hotel room by way of the choreographer. In spite of fairly favourable notices, especially for the first act and the Oliver Messel sets – Messel in these days was as busy as Brook – Louis Kronenberger spoke for the majority when he wrote: '*House of Flowers* was genuinely individual, with tropical colour and fragrance and profusion. . . . Unfortunately, what made it fresh and flower-like also made it droop and fade; what conferred a unified tone also created a monotonous effect. In the nose-in-the-air gentility of its bordello girls it had a satiric theme its book somehow failed to exploit; and it gradually sank into the languor of a tropical afternoon.'*

Two days after the opening Brook hurried to Jamaica to stay with John Gielgud, pondered on the second act, and on returning to New York had his third or fourth thoughts put into production. There had been problems during rehearsal, he said; but these had been solved, settled and reconciled. By now Pearl Bailey had torn up her writ. Altogether it was a lively period, especially back-stage where Marlene Dietrich seemed to be round for much of the time as an honorary wardrobe mistress, and two melancholy-eyed little Jamaican boys, ten years old, were constantly escaping from rehearsal to the pin-table arcades. They were known, charmingly, as Do and Don't.

* In *Theatre 1954–55*, edited by Ivor Brown, London, 1955.

VI

The Year Of Titus: 1955

I

By the spring of 1955 Peter Brook, a man of the professional theatre for eleven years, seemed to have been settled in it since before Noah was a sailor. (*Twelfth Night* he has not yet directed.) On the edge of thirty, he was twice his own years in theatrical wisdom. Already, apart from Tyrone Guthrie who could never remain in one place, he was the director most honoured on both sides of the Atlantic. Furiously imaginative but less boyish, less anxious for the extraneous effect, and, as somebody put it, less rumpled than he was, he remained open to idea and experiment: he wanted, as he told an interviewer rather dizzily, to live in 'ever-widening spirals'. For a time he had to content himself with ever-widening ripples while, from the centre of the theatre's calm lagoon, he aimed round the compass-card, inventing a new theory for any fresh throw. In some other countries he would have had his own stage: in England he had to work when and where he could, though as a rule – for he was permanently in demand – he could choose among the plays offered to him. Certainly this was so in 1955; he was at work that spring on both Anouilh's *L'Alouette,* under its English title of *The Lark,* and, astonishingly, the long-despised tragedy of *Titus Andronicus* for a festival production at Stratford-upon-Avon.

Two years earlier, when he saw Suzanne Flon in Paris, he had decided that Dorothy Tutin, among British actresses, would have the special simplicity for Anouilh's Jeanne d'Arc. 'She is singing like a bird in the sky,' says the Earl of Warwick, 'over the heads of your French armies on the march, where all take aim to shoot her down.' Brook nursed his casting until an hour came to use it. Then in May 1955 he did the play for Tennents at what had so far been a lucky theatre for him, the Lyric, Hammersmith (once, his only chance of a personal London stage, he had been offered, and refused, its directorship): now he had the gift of Dorothy Tutin's sensibility; he had an English translation, expert in rhythm, by Christopher Fry; and the scenery and costumes – scenery that appeared to be a set of wooden gates or hurdles variously assembled by the actress herself – was by Jean-Denis Malclès. *L'Alouette* had run for eighteen months in Paris; in England it would have to face Shaw's definitive portrait of the Maid as a pillar of faith and fire. Anouilh's work was less nobly imagined, infinitely less straightforward, now and then an exasperation. In the ordered mosaic of its first part, confusing sometimes, Joan on trial was also Joan at Domrémy, Vaucouleurs, Chinon; and it was dangerously late when Anouilh reached the core of his task, the Maid faced by a pitiless Inquisitor, not at all like Shaw's, who could stand as a manifestation of intolerance. Behind Shaw's chronicle was the tragedy of a world not yet ready to receive its saints; Anouilh's was the human tragedy of a peasant child ('You can't explain Joan, any more than you can explain the tiniest flower growing by the wayside'). It ended not with the caged lark, the agony at Rouen, but with a sudden flash of theatrical bravura, stake and faggots torn down, and Cauchon exclaiming: 'It isn't the painful and miserable end of the cornered animal caught at Rouen: but the lark singing in the open sky. Joan at Rheims in all her glory. The true end of the story is a kind of joy. Joan of Arc: a story which ends happily.' There, upon the Lyric stage, Joan stood leaning on the staff of her banner, smiling upward, while among the pealing bells the Dauphin was crowned at Rheims.

'The curtain,' says Anouilh, 'falls slowly on this beautiful illustration from a school prize.' For some watchers the scene had the exhilarating lift of lines from an English poet:

> Equal the horn of Roland high on the Pyrenees;
> Equal the lance of Joan in the gate of Orleans.

For others, Ivor Brown among them, it was surprising folly at the end of a play that had promised so much. But most writers, Brown included, respected Dorothy Tutin's quality and noted Brook's art in his control of the stage, in his disposition of the low hurdles that formed the setting, and in the subtle gradations of his lighting plot. This, in particular, reminded his friends how much he had learned since a Birmingham Repertory play long before. Then he had rectified the evils of his hit-or-miss lighting at the dress rehearsal by taking an intensive crash course from the theatre electrician; the result was a première excitingly-lit.

II

So to the miracle of *Titus Andronicus*, least respected of Shakespeare's plays and never acted at Stratford-upon-Avon where the Governors were frightened of it. They did agree to it unwillingly for the jubilee year of the Shakespeare Memorial in 1929 – its stage would have been that of the temporary theatre, the cinema in Greenhill Street – and at the time there was sound enough reason for the choice. With *Titus* the Memorial would complete its record: the production of every play in the Folio and one (*Pericles*) outside it. Further, the Festival cast included the Titus (Wilfrid Walter) and the Aaron (George Hayes) of the Old Vic revival in 1923. The tragedy was announced; then the Governors recanted: instead, they decided to put on *Much Ado About Nothing,* in memory of the Birthday night of 1879 when Barry Sullivan and Helen Faucit had acted Benedick and Beatrice. No doubt it was a proper decision. The theatre wanted all the money it could get; *Much Ado*, its mascot, was sure to draw while *Titus* might have waned after half-a-dozen performances. As a cynic said during one of Irving's Lyceum years: 'There are few Shakespearians, but there are many lovers of *The Merchant of Venice.*'

Titus Andronicus needed a Peter Brook, and he had long contemplated it. Once he had thought of directing it with a Negro cast. On another occasion he had imagined sets by Epstein. Its neo-Senecan horrors absorbed him as work for a theatre theatrical: murders and massacres, acts of black night, complots of mischief, treason, villainies: a casualty-list in blank verse. For collectors it was the last play of the thirty-seven, an ultimate shore: desolate beach and ensanguined tide. Most people shivered, though Robert Atkins, who feared nothing, did resurrect *Titus* for a few performances at the Old Vic in the year of the First Folio centenary, 1923. 'They told us that two or three people had been carried out fainting, and I could well believe it,' wrote Doris Westwood* who walked on as, unpredictably a Senator and a Goth. In the end the play entered a Stratford programme 360 years after it was written: on the night of 16 August 1955, the bloodstained thumb at last left its print upon the page.

Peter Brook had been scheming his *Titus* for a year, and actively preparing it for eight months: designing costumes and sets and working out the music as well. For this he received an average, over

* *These Players: A Diary of the 'Old Vic'*, London, 1926.

the entire period, of ten pounds a week. The piece, a shocker to outmatch *The Spanish Tragedy,* triumphed in its own period. Its violence, thirteen deaths of one kind and another, and more to come, transcended Kyd's: Hieronimo biting out his own tongue was no real competitor to the involuntary cannibalism of Tamora, the final Thyestean feast. T. S. Eliot followed modern fashion when he thrust *Titus* roughly into the bin as 'one of the stupidest and most uninspiring plays ever written, a play in which it is incredible that Shakespeare had any hand at all, a play in which the last passages would be too highly honoured by the signature of Peele.' (I do not know if Eliot saw the production at Stratford.) Elizabethans would not have worried in the least. They wanted a few direct hours of murder and rapine: it was nothing odd to them to watch a bear-baiting while lute-music drifted across the river; and they saw nothing strange when Marcus Andronicus, instead of bringing a surgeon to his niece, the ravished and lopped Lavinia, addressed her in a stream of classical conceits. Marcus has here some splendid lines that Logan Pearsall Smith, after being contemptuously dismissive of the tragedy as a whole, confessed that he had passed over.

As usual, revisers went to work, taking the remorseless affair and turning it into something far worse; thus a third-rate Restoration playwright, Edward Ravenscroft, provided his own collocation of horrors. But after about 1725, *Titus* in any form proved to be the rarest of Shakespearian curiosities: one of the vaults, far beneath the main building, among rats and ring-bolts, where no light penetrated. During the eighteen-fifties a Negro actor, Ira Aldridge, the 'African Roscius', entered the vault and played Aaron at a tumultuous old melodrama house, the Britannia in Hoxton. It was a version wildly altered and expurgated: Aaron, it seemed, became the hero, 'a noble and lofty character', and a scene from a piece called *Zaraffa, the Slave King* was added for good measure. Aldridge had not penetrated far into the vault. Disheartened, *Titus Andronicus* – the real play this time – did not turn up again until the Old Vic night seventy years later. Another gap then until 1953; in that spring I made a version for the Third Programme of the BBC*; and almost simultaneously the amateur cast of the Marlowe Society appeared in *Titus* at the Arts, Cambridge: half of a night's double bill that included *Friar Bacon and Friar Bungay.* A link between the two had been established by the actor of Demetrius, who is made into a

* Wilfrid Walter as Titus; George Hayes as Aaron.

pasty for the Bloody Banquet at the end of *Titus*, and who appears, eating the same pasty, at the opening of *Friar Bacon*. One might have said: 'The funeral baked meats/ Did coldly furnish forth the marriage tables.'

Both the radio and the Cambridge performances swept from the dark like an angry gale; but we had to wait two years for the fullest theatrical *frisson*, for Peter Brook's achievement at Stratford, with Laurence Olivier as Titus, Anthony Quayle as Aaron the Moor, and a programme bound ominously in black. Curtain-fall that August evening brought the longest, loudest cheer in Stratford memory. One heard people, normally decorous, shouting at the pitch of their voices, hardly knowing that they did so, and denying it afterwards; a critic said it could have been the scene at a Cup Final. In *Titus* the actors had something to act. It had never occurred to them or to Brook that the play was the worthless affair academic writers claimed, and we could feel at once the response to strong, uncomplicated emotions: violence, hatred, cruelty, fear, presented (said Brook) in 'a form that became unrealistic, transcended the anecdote, and for each audience was quite abstract and thus totally real'. He said later that the play began to yield its secrets the moment one ceased to regard it as a series of gratuitous strokes of melodrama, and looked instead for its completeness. Everything in it was tributary to a dark, flowing current out of which surged the horrors, rhythmically and logically related. 'If one searches in this way one can find the expression of a powerful and eventually barbaric ritual.' He had manipulated the uneven text so that his actors could let fly without dread of mocking laughter; whenever he spied a possible laugh, he either cut the offending phrase or unmasked his protective atmospherics. The immoderate atrocities he kept slightly out of focus; the rest was in sharp definition. Grimness remained; at the same time Brook imposed an austerity, a formalized dignity. We were not sickened as at the blinding of Gloucester in a far greater play. When Laurence Olivier was on stage we found ourselves for once in the empyrean of classical acting.

It was odd at the première to see how embarrassed, uneasily jocular, the audience was before curtain-rise; far more than either players or director, who had no thought of jocularity. Laughter faded from the moment Brook revealed the tomb of the Andronici: his basic design, given to Michael Northen to model, looked like a grove of organ pipes, ribbed and fluted; it would contain a tomb and a throne-room and open later to the 'bare, detested vale' and the tangle of the forest thicket. But Rome first, though Rome only in name, a shadowed, brooding city of the fitfully torch-lit imagination: before a word was uttered in it we knew that we should reach the heart of grief. Music of Brook's own devising wailed and thudded; slowly, processions coiled, and priests, green-habited,* moved in hieratic solemnity. When Titus entered from victory over the Goths, 'Hail, Rome, victorious in thy mourning weeds', he came as a man doomed. Certain of the early lines are mere bathos:

> Romans, of five-and-twenty valiant sons,
> Half of the number that King Priam had,
> Behold the poor remains alive and dead. . . .

When Olivier spoke them we were not derisive. This Titus was a white-haired warrior, desperately tired. The lines of his body drooped; his eyes, among the seamed crowsfeet, were weary; though he greeted Rome because it was a thing of custom, his voice had neither spring nor light. The business must be endured; later on, no doubt, there might be surcease from these eternal wars, heroic rants, useless lengths of rhetoric. Immediately Titus was real to us, and having established him as a man, fixed him in our thoughts as he first appeared, Olivier was able to move into a wider air, to expand the part to something beyond life-size, to fill stage and theatre with a swell of heroic acting. Similarly when Brook had established his remote haunted Rome, we were ready for anything that might follow.

Later we realized that the Titus we had seen at Olivier's entrance would have an affinity with Lear: the ancient on the edge of the gulf. In quietness the actor terrified; his voice cut each word in flint. But it was the quietness at the core of a hurricane, and in rage we felt the storm-wind of the equinox. Lear became identified with the storm in his mind, Titus with the sea. The sea had been his constant image. 'What fool,' he cried, 'hath added water to the sea?' And again: 'For now I stand as one upon a rock, Environ'd with a wilderness of sea.' With his right hand sacrificed, he fell to

---

* Praising the aspect of the stage when *Titus* was in Warsaw two years later, Professor Jan Kott spoke of Romans as seen and painted by the Renaissance, and noted (*Shakespeare Our Contemporary*: London, 1964) that Brook had freely taken from Titian a full range of yellows, dressed the priests in the irritating greens of Veronese, and derived from Rubens the black-blue-and-gold costume of the Moor. It did not matter, he added, whether the colours had really been derived from the Venetians, or whether the dramatic visual composition of characters was indebted more to El Greco or to Rubens. 'What matters is that it is painting as seen through film experience.'

entreating heaven; he bowed this 'feeble ruin' to the earth. Then, as Marcus urged him, 'But let not reason govern thy lament,' Titus cried suddenly:

> If there were reason for these miseries,
> Then into limits could I bind these woes:
> When heaven doth weep, doth not the earth o'erflow?
> If the winds rage, doth not the sea wax mad,
> Threatening the welkin with his big-swoln face?
> And wilt thou have a reason for this coil?
> I am the sea: hark, how her sighs do flow!
> She is the weeping welkin, I the earth:
> Then must my sea be movèd with her sighs;
> Then must my earth with her continual tears
> Become a deluge, overflow'd and drowned.

As Olivier cried 'I am the sea', its surge beat on the world's far shore. The waters receded; Titus met the mockery of Saturninus, his sons' heads, 'thy hand – in scorn to thee sent back'. He leant forward, silent in grief; Marcus Andronicus turned on him with 'Now is a time to storm; why art thou still?'; and the slow, answering laugh was like the menace of a tide upon the turn.

Earlier, there had been the ghastly pause, the almost unbridged gulf, at the sight of Lavinia. When the girl, gripping a staff between her arms, mercifully not guiding it by her mouth as in the text, had traced on the ground the names of her ravishers, Titus's voice changed from the metallic 'I will go get a leaf of brass/And with a gad of steel will write these words/ And lay it by,' to the hissing fury of 'The angry northern wind/Will blow these sands, like Sibyl's leaves, abroad.' After the crazed opening of the archery scene – Brook, master toxophilite, enjoyed riddling the palace with arrows*– Olivier had another pause on the simple, 'Ah, Rome. . . . Well, well; I make thee miserable.' Lastly, before judgment and revenge, the old man, bounded by his red study walls, kept a stark calm in the colloquy with Tamora and her sons, disguised so foolishly, so fondly secure. The actor had thought himself into the hell of Titus; we forgot the inadequacy of the words in the splendour of their projection. Anthony Quayle's volcanic Aaron made no effort to rationalize a fiend Ira Aldridge would hardly have known; and Vivien Leigh was a piteous Lavinia, though I still think a few more hairs might credibly have been misplaced after her morning in the wood.

---

* 'Wear double-breasted dinner-jackets,' Noël Coward is reputed to have said; 'I hear Peter's shooting arrows at the audience.'

Constantly Brook's invention fortified the piece: the design of that disastrous pit into which Bassianus falls (we did not have his ring that 'lightens all the hole'); the folding set that within seconds could transform the stage to a place fit for rape and murder; the crimson framing of the banquet, a feast that kept laughter dumb even if its feasters collapsed in their due order like a range of broken skittles. To vary the pattern, Michael Denison's Lucius killed Saturninus from above with a dagger-cast strongly aimed. Once at least, in the Clown's part, Brook collaborated with Shakespeare, offering no excuses as he had done a decade before in *King John*. The stage direction is: 'Enter a clown, with a basket and two pigeons in it.' Titus calls: 'News, news, from heaven!' Brook now had Edward Atienza lowered in a basket, with the line, 'My uncle the gibbet-maker and I have been up on the walls.' We lost some beauties, such as the lines (for Marcus) Logan Pearsall Smith had admired,

> O, had the monster seen those lily hands
> Tremble, like aspen leaves, upon a lute,

because Brook had lopped the scene, believing wrongly that it got in the way of the action. Elsewhere such a dangerous phrase survived as my favourite synonym for holding the baby:

> Say, wall-eyed slave, whither wouldst convey
> This growing image of thy fiend-like face?

When it was spoken with straightforward force, nobody laughed.

Brook suggested Lavinia's mutilation, never insisted on it; at the end she did not hold that dreadful bowl between her stumps. Tamora's involuntary cannibalism roused barely a murmur in the house ('baked in that pie' was cut): again we shuddered where we had prepared to laugh. Throughout, music – Brook's own *musique concrète* without being *concrète renforcée* in Henry Reed's phrase – strengthened the atmosphere. *Titus Andronicus* was a collector's rare primitive. Its night was lanced with fire. Ivor Brown spoke for critics and public when he wrote, in a survey of three Stratford Festivals:*

Peter Brook's production had been a masterpiece of salvage and a display of extreme cunning in the art of covering up. Shakespeare had been rescued from his 'prentice self and appeared almost as a matured master ... despite the fact that the producer had culpably cut some of the few lines in the play that carry the obvious signature of the Shakespeare that was to

* *Shakespeare Memorial Theatre 1954–56,* Reinhardt, 1956.

be. . . . Brook's method was to drain off the rivers of gore, never to parade the knife-work, and, instead, to symbolise a wound with a scarlet ribbon. . . .

There had to be positive development of the play's merits as well as a cloaking and evasion of its faults. To this end Sir Laurence contributed nobly. . . . The audience were coaxed into believing that this was indeed a worthy play about a man both sinned against and sinning; if young and foolish in much of its writing for the melodrama market, it now became, under the persuasion of our strongest actor, a sounding-board of terrible, yet authentic passions and of agonies monstrous but not beyond bearing by mankind.

III

In *Titus Andronicus* Brook developed as a musician for the theatre: his work would probably have horrified his old antagonists, the critics' corps. In *Measure for Measure* his plaintive tune for 'Take, O take those lips away' was sung without accompaniment; he contributed a frisky recorder tune to *A Penny for a Song,* and another to *The Lark*. But *Titus* was totally different. The choice of music for it derived from a small seed, the success of an experiment in *Venice Preserv'd*. There he had wanted something that, musically, should be eighteenth-century, yet decadent, corrupt. After much searching he and Leslie Bridgewater found fragments of sixteenth-century Spanish lute music and other things which Bridgewater sewed together. But the texture was the thing. Brook had been studying *musique concrète*, absorbed in its possibilities for the theatre. He now had the music scored for harpsichord, guitar and bells, then over-recorded and played slowly so that it sounded as if strings were being plucked on a fantastic instrument as high as the proscenium.

Brook could not contemplate getting from any composer he knew music that would be primitive enough for *Titus:* undoubtedly he could not think of anyone who could write it down. What he needed was music addressed to a quarter of an ear, whereas most composers, writing for the theatre, did so on the assumption that everybody had three ears. He insisted that the *Titus* score had to be Roman in a way primitive and barbaric. He brought in a young composer, William Blezard, who was his répétiteur for *The Beggar's Opera* film, and they had any number of sound-and-music experiments at Brook's house in Gordon Place, Kensington, where he had a baby grand piano and a tape recorder on the top floor. Realizing that, for their purpose, only texture, rhythm and timbre were important, they worked with such things as ashtrays and pots and pans, pencils on Venetian glass phials, and wire baskets used as harps. For the opening 'Enter Titus to a funeral march, bearing three sons in coffins', no ordinary march would do; Brook wanted something gigantic, and he got it by putting one microphone inside the piano and one underneath, stamping on the pedal in such a way as to make all the strings shudder, and then recording it slowly. He added an off-beat cymbal; on top of that a recorder tune, simple, pentatonic, over-recorded, and slowed down, so that it seemed to come from an instrument twenty feet long. There were overtones of melancholy and tremendous blast-furnace breathiness. Yet the tune was almost 'Three Blind Mice'.

For the hunting scene after which Lavinia is raped and mutilated,

> . . . the babbling echo mocks the hounds
> Replying shrilly to the well-tuned horns,
> As if a double hunt were heard at once. . . .

Peter mocked-up brass rhythms on an ivory and blue plastic trumpet that Natasha had bought for him in the toy department of Harrods. He and Blezard discovered a simple little tune for trumpet and trombone and split it between the instruments, playing it very slowly with lots of slurs and slides before speeding it up in recording. Passed through an echo device, the whole thing became inhumanly brilliant, light, echoing, babbling, and just right for the stage hunt that was suggested against a green background. To get a fresh open-air effect, Brook could have plunged from the darkness of his first setting by the tomb of the Andronici to a blue cyclorama. Instead he used this green colour, bright and unearthly. On Lavinia's entrance, 'her hands cut off and her tongue cut out, and ravisht', a small stylized tune was played on harp harmonics followed by piano: one microphone rested on the harp pedals, one on top of the harp. It had to be an eloquent, not a horrific, moment when the girl appeared through completely unrealistic trees, holding up her stumps from which long ribbons of brilliant red velvet fell and wavered. Later, for the scene in which Aaron cut off Titus's hand, Brook used a throbbing effect; he played two alternating chords quite slowly on the piano within which was a microphone, over-recorded the result, and slowed it down to make it deeper. Played back loudly, it resembled an alarming mixture of an immense organ and a gigantic double-bass in a primitive blood-lust rhythm.

Brook was able to solve the problem of the archery scenes where

Titus's henchmen shoot insulting letters into the palace of the Emperor. At first we saw the arrows shot into the wings ('Here, boy, to Pallas; here, to Mercury'); next we saw them quivering in the palace walls ('Sweet scrolls to fly about the streets of Rome!'). Hidden in the scenery, they sprang out as needed, and whenever one arrived we heard a weird sound that Brook had made by striking single notes on the piano and immediately switching on his recording machine. Though the note's impact might be unvaried, there was an extraordinary contortion of pitch: a tape, when switched on, starts slowly and needs a couple of seconds to get on true pitch as it whines up from below. The entire sequence of 'pings' formed a mad little tune.

Towards the end, during the second scene of the fifth act, the crazed Titus was revealed in his study, attended by Tamora, the queen, as Revenge, and her sons Chiron and Demetrius as Rapine and Murder. Slowly the top half of the set opened to show the old man sitting at a red desk in a blood-red room. Here Brook wanted to get the effect of time dragging – as it were, a chime slowed down – and for the purpose he hunted through his house for wine-glasses; the search produced a set, including some Georgian champagne glasses, that would give the appropriate ringing note when hit with pencils. Half a dozen were enough; and the combination of a little tune and one chord played on them, while Brook's assistant plucked a piano string rhythmically, provided the most haunting of knells.

IV

Even for *Love's Labour's Lost*, Brook had never had such a Press as for this. By now, with *Titus* and its regularly fainting playgoers behind him – every night had its casualty list – he had directed more than twenty plays, half a dozen operas, a musical comedy, and a film. He had also written for television, and he had spoken, if without much enthusiasm, on five Brains Trusts, rousing passion most easily when he was attacking schoolmasters. For him this was quite natural; formal education he had regarded as a luckless mistake. Thus, of four preparatory schools, he had said (though tactfully, he did not say it on television): 'My anxious father withdrew me from one because the Head went mad, from another because the Head went bankrupt, from a third because the Head retired very suddenly, and from a fourth because the Head's wife left him. I disclaim responsibility, but I highly approved on each successive calamity.' He probably disliked school memories all the more because people continued to suggest that he was in last term's Sixth Form, or that he had left the day before yesterday. Nobody made sterner efforts to escape from the British habit of labelling a man and using – as Hilton Brown said in another context – quite imperishable gum.

Brooding slightly, he rounded off the year with a *Hamlet* that had already possessed him while *Titus* was still packing the Memorial Theatre. He had met the greatest play of them all very early. When he was seven his father had made from three-ply, and given to him, a toy theatre that worked: curtains, lights, trap door, and all. On Christmas afternoon, having discovered Shakespeare precociously and thought well of him, he presented a four-hour *Hamlet*. 'This,' he said, 'is my day, and I can do what I want.' What he wanted was to act every part himself, with his elder brother Alexis to help back-stage. Scenery was changed continually, and the characters seemed to be more acrobatic than the text indicated. Up to a point – no interval is recorded – Peter's parents did everything an audience should; they rebelled only when he decided to work through the play again to try a clutch of new ideas (an early notebook is in-scribed '*Hamlet*; by P. Brook and W. Shakespeare'). Frustrated, the director went moodily to bed.

Now a more ambitious, if more austere, *Hamlet* would set the hornets buzzing. Few writers knew what they had wanted from *Titus Andronicus*, but they were prepared to concede that Brook had given it to them. Every writer knew precisely what he wanted from *Hamlet* and all were, as usual, exigent. If Shakespeare could observe the cairn of literature about the play, he might quote beneath his breath, 'Now pile your dust upon the quick and dead,/ Till of this flat a mountain you have made.' Editors tie themselves in intricate coils; simplifiers believe it is the story of a man who could not make up his mind. That is another way of putting Matthew Arnold's phrase about Man viewed as being *ondoyant* and *divers*, balancing and indeterminate, swayed by a thousand subtle influences, physiological and pathological. Everyone has a personal idea of the Prince with what Granville-Barker called 'a rash and lonely mind', his native faith in life stunned as he lapses into impotent despair, crippled faith, enfranchised reason at odds in him.

It was Brook's sixth major Shakespeare production. Apart from *Romeo and Juliet* eight years before, it was so far his least successful

in England, though admirers, and there was a small band of the
faithful, have not ceased to acclaim it. Paul Scofield returned now to
Hamlet, seven years after he had acted it in Victorian costume at
Stratford for another director. Then he had been a romantic,
haunted figure 'most dreadfully attended' by the thronging phan-
toms of his brain; a spirit in torment no less than his father; as
A. V. Cookman said, a spiritual fugitive who sought not so much
the fulfilment of his earthly mission as 'some steadfast refuge for the
hard-driven imagination'. Equally touching in the Brook revival, he
had lost something of the vulnerable youthfulness Barry Jackson
said was the quality he needed in any Hamlet.* Even so, Scofield
would be potent; again he used his rifted voice, tones (I speak for
myself) that could bring an image of light diffused and fretted across
a broken classic column. The voice was always of the blood-royal,
for Hamlet, in spite of later modish exercises, cannot rise from a
street corner, and it spoke movingly for the troubled soul of
Denmark living summoned by the soul of Denmark dead. At the
time I wrote of 'a desperate music'; in memory the phrase is valid.
Speaking for objectors, Anthony Hartley (*Spectator*) felt that 'the
daemonic brutal character of the Renaissance prince was much
underplayed, and we are left with a Renaissance melancholy, the
muted note of a sonnet by Du Bellay or a lyric by Nashe'.

Before it reached London, *Hamlet* undertook a surprising tour –
Brighton, Oxford, Birmingham, and Moscow, where this was the
first British company to appear in Brook's ancestral land since the
revolution of 1917. He directed the play in a chameleon-set by his
old Covent Garden associate, Georges Wakhevitch: an arched hall
with its crannies, galleries, and windows put to as much inventive
use as in a later set (by another hand) for a long-running production
in Budapest with Miklós Gábor. A writer in *The Architect* summarized the design as 'a heavily arched and ribbed apse'. To this
basic set were added cannon, crimson hangings, and the piles of a
pier. Brook himself was not sanguine about his production;
looking back, he considered he had treated it too traditionally, in a
convention too academic, an austerity that detached it from the
theatre. Admirers did not think so; the slings and arrows in London
came unkindly after a Moscow visit where 15,000 Russians received
this *Hamlet* with the sharpest enthusiasm. On arrival at Moscow
airport the players (Scofield, Mary Ure, Diana Wynyard, Alec
Clunes, Ernest Thesiger, and the rest) found snow falling in thick

* As in the young Ian Richardson's at the Birmingham Repertory in 1959.

flakes and the Customs shed like a Turgenev drawing-room with winter landscapes framed heavily in gold. Presently, in the distance, they saw the blood-red stars upon the dark towers of the Kremlin.

Externally, the famous Moscow Art Theatre resembled an English county library in red brick; inside, seating 1400, it looked like a lecture hall, a pair of earphones at every seat for the simultaneous translation. An anxious company was disheartened; dress rehearsals could not begin because the costumes, eighteen baskets of them, with properties and gramophone records, had been left in Berlin under the care of the Russian Minister. Fortunately, Diana Wynyard remembered his name; Brook telephoned during the small hours; an aircraft with a door large enough to take the property baskets, was flown to Berlin at once; and halfway through rehearsal the costumes arrived at the Art Theatre from the airfield, guarded by special escort. The company had even brought its own powder to charge the cannon that fired a salute at the end of the play ('the soldiers' music and the rite of war speak loudly for him'); indeed, the travelling schedule included 'twenty-two arrows, a cannon and cartridges, and one collapsible coffin.'

All twelve performances at the Art Theatre – the seagull upon its curtain – had been sold out. On the snowy night of the première listeners seemed to find a text of three-and-a-half hours too short; they followed it with solemn appreciation, and the only laugh came when Polonius, the seventy-six-year-old Ernest Thesiger, stopped the First Player at 'This is too long'. The Gravediggers were greeted with polite silence. The sole trouble, noticed by few, occurred in the front of the house where Brook had to pitch a photographer's camera into the corridor; earlier he had protested to the theatre manager about these interruptions, and he exploded during the second act when, just before a vital soliloquy, a man set up a tripod to take yet more pictures. Everything by the end had been forgiven; the company took twenty calls; Brook, to a roar of cheering, thanked the audience in Russian. Soon *Pravda,* in the customary delayed notice – Russian drama critics have more time than writers elsewhere – praised Scofield's' 'truthful, honest, lively, and noble youth'.

Russians were astonished that *Hamlet* had been rehearsed for only a month; they would have taken a year and more and regarded it as perfectly reasonable. While he was over there Brook took a chance to see one of the long-rehearsed *Hamlets* as directed by Okhlopkhov at Baku on the Caspian: here the director had identified nobility with opulence, a conception vastly different from what Britain would know as 'the Moscow *Hamlet*'. The Art Theatre seagull was a symbol of the visit. 'We never touched ground,' said Brook. From the whirl of official receptions, Scofield still remembers one when, tired after his performance, he noticed upon a side-table a large china jug, like a piece of old-fashioned washstand-ware, and filled with a colourless liquid, obviously water. He poured out a glassful and drank with satisfaction. It proved to be excellent vodka, and his conversation that night had rarely been more spirited. Vodka was not among the parting gifts; but the Soviet Ministry of Culture presented everyone in the cast with a lacquer box, Russian cigarettes, and a book on Moscow; the stars received medals, and Hugh Beaumont of Tennents a framed picture which he hung in the foyer of the Phoenix Theatre.

v

Gratified by their reception but very weary – most of them, worn out, fell asleep at once on the return flight – the players opened in London on 8 December. The stage was the Phoenix where Brook and Scofield would be doing three plays with Tennents: *Hamlet*, a version of a Graham Greene novel, and Eliot's *The Family Reunion*. After the first première Alec Clunes had the strongest critical applause for his redoubtable Claudius, almost too impressive to have been a satyr to the dead King's Hyperion. There was division about Mary Ure, an Ophelia sex-ridden and terrifying in madness, for at that time, as Robert Speaight would say in reviewing another production fourteen years later, no part in Shakespeare had suffered more from the sentimental evasion of sexuality. Scofield had to endure comparison with his own past, though for his devotees the new Hamlet was a natural growth. Brook, with whom he has had so close a fellowship, has pictured him definitively.* From youth, though verse hampered him, he would make unforgettable verse from lines of prose:

It was as though the act of speaking a word sent through him vibrations that echoed back meanings far more complex than his rational thinking could find; he would pronounce a word like 'night', and then he would be compelled to pause: listening with all his being to the amazing impulses stirring in some mysterious inner chamber, he would experience the wonder of discovery at the moment when it happened. Those breaks,

* *The Empty Space.*

those sallies in depth, give his acting its absolutely personal structure of rhythms, its own instinctive meanings: to rehearse a part he lets his whole nature – a milliard of super-sensitive scanners – pass to and fro across the words. In performance the same process makes everything that he has apparently fixed come back again each night the same and absolutely different.

Siriol Hugh-Jones continued to speak most surely for Brook's supporters when she described the production as 'shining, taut, as urgent as a plucked string, with *rallentandos* like Schnabel's that never sag'. Memory is the most searching and most selective critic. Looking back now across fifteen years, I remember a good deal of Scofield and Clunes with pin-sharp certainty, but the production has dimmed; often I cannot say, without seeking a crib, what effect Brook was making in this passage or the other. While *Titus* and even *Love's Labour* are in full light, *Hamlet* can be in tantalizing shadow. Brook himself was dubious; he had always been so. For one thing, he regretted that he had made the Ghost into a human figure, played naturalistically, as a father to his son: reasonable in theory, it was yet against the entire conception of the supernatural, so the scene, through no fault of the actor, appeared to be drab and underplayed. Criticism generally suggested that if Brook were given the impossible, as in *Titus Andronicus,* he would solve it: he would fail simply when a play was proof against failure. One actor said sadly of his *Hamlet:* 'I'm afraid he's just trying to show it's as good as *Titus.*'

He had some poor luck with this production. Towards the end of its stage run he directed it on commercial television – only to see the last half-minute faded out and Fortinbras swept aside by a singing advertisement for orange juice. Murder most foul, as in the best it is; but this most foul, strange, and unnatural.

D

VII

Grand Tour: 1956-1957

IN spite of the critics, who are often forgotten after the first month, *Hamlet* went on to the play's third longest unbroken run in stage history: 124 performances. Immediately after it ended, in April 1956, Peter Brook directed a version of Graham Greene's novel, *The Power and the Glory,* about a persecuted priest in a Mexican police state, viciously anti-clerical. The novel analysed the changes in a fugitive's soul; but the play, by Denis Cannan and Pierre Bost, had to be about a priest in flight round a land where Catholicism was forbidden. It could have had many epigraphs, one possibly from *Hamlet:*

> Oft it chances in particular men,
> That for some vicious mole of nature in them,
> As in their birth, wherein they are not guilty. . . .
> Or by some habit, that too much o'erleavens
> The form of plausive manners – that these men,
> Carrying, I say, the stamp of one defect,
> Being nature's livery, or fortune's star,
> His virtues else be they as pure as grace,
> As infinite as men may undergo,
> Shall in the general censure take corruption
> From that particular fault.

Here was all the atmosphere of stifling heat and moral decay formerly familiar in melodrama much less subtle; Brook turned to his *musique concrète* for a 'range of exotic percussive clops' appropriate to the background of sets by Wakhevitch that either burned with livid colour or expressed a deadly gloom. All, as so often, rested on Scofield; practically unrecognizable now, he was a shrivelled, shabby little man, a 'whisky priest', his voice parched, his gait a shamble. Though the man's life had been anything but immaculate, he believed unflinchingly in his calling. Whatever else, he knew that he had the power of saving sinners; it was this that aided him in his last colloquy with the Lieutenant of Police, fanatically bent upon driving religion from the state. Once faith perishes, a world where only evil reigns must perish with it.

The priest, wizened, pitiable, and desperate, paradoxically a gallant craven, took the Phoenix stage in a performance of heart and craft. Similarly, Brook could create the scorch, the squalor, and the loneliness of a forsaken land. Robert Marsden, from Chanticleer days, was in the cast: he saw how his director's method had varied in the twelve years since *The Infernal Machine:* how he would let the company express itself instead of pinning it at once within a pre-conceived pattern.

The play had a reasonable reception, hardly overwhelming. It was the kind of night when a veteran critic, ready to adapt Shakespeare to his purpose, would push back the grey lock from his forehead, fidget a little and murmur: 'Let it have needful, not lavish means.' Between this production and Brook's next, the English stage would tremble from a seismic shock; the epicentre was in Sloane Square, at the Royal Court Theatre where a fierce little play had appeared without any hint of trouble. This was John Osborne's *Look Back In Anger,* as unexpected an event as the Bishop of Bradford's speech which, unwittingly, twenty years before, had sparked off the Abdication. I am sure the English Stage Company had not realized what might derive from the production of an indifferent play – well-made in the old manner, with five characters and a box-set – that depended upon the white heat of its invective. It succeeded at the première, in spite of some third-act bursts of ironical laughter from above, because Osborne was saying what many young people wanted to hear; moreover, he said it with a command of current idiom. A few critics seized upon his impetuous expression of dis-content, and the play became the centre of a cult and a key period piece. It was lucky because it had found fortuitously, the exact moment: John Whiting's *Saint's Day,* five years earlier, had been premature. Now, from May 1956, a new drama would take charge; rumble after thunderous rumble in Sloane Square, and George Devine, of the English Stage Company, announcing that one of his intentions was to give dramatists the right to fail. The observation could remind us of Wilde on Irving's Lear: 'Surely a gentleman has the right to fail if he chooses.'

These excitements were only just beginning when Peter Brook directed, as his third play at the Phoenix, a revival of an older showpiece. T. S. Eliot's *The Family Reunion:* a Solemn Musick that was an acquired taste in the theatre: one had to be aware of a self-conscious author testing and observing rhythms, of his typical insistence on the definite article, and of such daunting phrases as 'Let your necrophily feed upon that carcase' and 'The aphyllous branch ophidian'. A Greek myth chilling the English scene, the play developed in stylized naturalism: a tale of sin and expiation, with choral voices of conscience and prophecy; a flight from the Erinyes who become the Eumenides; and various Aeschylean properties in a modern setting. It had hardly seemed to be work for Brook, but here it was, and acted by an extraordinary cast. Paul Scofield was the hunted man, Lord Monchesney, of whom A. V. Cookman said in *The Times:* 'Whether as the sleepless-eyed youth flying with pale, haunted face from the Furies, or as the sudden spiritually-composed fugitive turning pursuer and flying towards the purgatorial flame, Scofield spoke as a man who felt every word.'

Dame Sybil Thorndike was in the company, with Sir Lewis Casson, Gwen Ffrangcon-Davies, Nora Nicholson. Even those who had been gloomiest about Eliot seventeen years before, acknowledged an experience as sharp as the 'present moment of pointed light . . . when you stretch out your hand to the flames'. Brook had his own idiosyncratic moment when the Shapes were seen first beyond the tall, country-house windows of Wishwood. Lights faded; fire-glow, pulsing round the room and its copper-hued ceiling, filled it with undulating, wave-like shadow. Embrasure curtains slipped back; outside the windows were the pursuing Shapes, vaguely like Henry Moore figures but only dimly visible; there for us to picture in any form we would. Later, and before Henry knew that he must 'follow the bright angels', light glimmered where all had been grey, as if a moon were shining serenely above Wishwood and touching those dim outlines with silver. Brook allowed our imaginations to take charge; Cookman noted, too, how easily he had contrived the abrupt movements from consciously played 'conversation' to the degree of formality needed for a choral effect.

II

That summer, while the theatre was wondering how far a new rebellion might go – it was the time of the Berliner Ensemble's visit with its Brecht plays – Peter Brook went out to see an older rebel, the legendary Gordon Craig, living then at his last home in the little mountain town of Vence in the South of France.* For a long time Peter and Natasha had been exchanging letters with Craig and had seen him often. Once, at the request of Granada Television, a talk between Craig and Peter was recorded, and issued later in Britain. Craig, a man who had crossed the frontier from the stage of his time, was young still at eighty-four, a buoyantly mischievous figure to whom much was 'cracky', who remembered the theatre of illusion he had spent his life in battering, and who could dream yet of new productions that would never be. Brook's own production, when he returned to London, was the American Arthur Miller's taut wire rope of a drama, *A View from the Bridge*. Because of a homosexual kiss, it had to be performed, theoretically at least, in private: this would seem comic a dozen years later, but it was then an act of defiance, much publicized, to throw it open to thousands of club members, recruited at a nominal sum, for club showing at the Comedy Theatre. Brook himself was resolutely against the Lord Chamberlain and all his works. 'Censorship prevents the author from following the implications of a relationship.' And again: 'Serious playgoers have a right to see plays which present provocative themes seriously and with perspective.'

Most of stage London, as well as the author and his wife Marilyn Monroe (in cherry-red) appeared to be in the house at the opening. The theme was an eternal passion, jealousy. Eddie, an inarticulate Brooklyn longshoreman (Anthony Quayle), with no one to prompt him, was as jealous as Othello; it was this that caused him to destroy himself, even if something else, a simple protective instinct, went with the raging possessiveness. Miller said that he saw the play 'sparely, as one sees a naked mast on the sea, or a bare cliff'. Brook's production never dulled device by coldness and delay; he designed an ingeniously composite folding set in which two walls swung together to make a street corner and opened to disclose an interior; it was 'a whole neighbourhood built vertically', wrote Sheila Huftel. Brook knew how to treat the last scuffle in and about the stairs in the murk of a Brooklyn evening; and he provided his own sound-score of dockyard noises, hoots and clangs.

One trouble was that the text expanded an earlier play, and Sheila

---

* Edward Gordon Craig, in *Gordon Craig* (London, 1968) writes that his father 'admired Peter and thought Natasha adorable. They brought him presents and did their best to make his life happier.'

Huftel, who has written the definitive book on Miller, regretted this.* She felt she was watching a street accident with the dramatist as casualty, and she could wonder only why Miller had ruined his own work. She was writing, of course, as a specialist; strangers to the play were unaware of the points she made in a close analysis of the texts. She did say:

Mr Brook tried to draw out all the warmth in the play, increasing its naturalism by creating an entire Brooklyn neighbourhood. The immigrants come not to the New York of bright lights, and dollars lining the gutters they had imagined, but to a steel trap, an iron cage. They come to a nineteenth-century red-brick tenement not economically worth rebuilding. The bright lights are there, even in view, but just across the water, and a world away. Then the steel cage opens and you find the warmth of the family, warmth that Latin groups create and hold to all over the world. For this reason it had to be a worker's home, warm and comfortable, not bleak – a home where Eddie would spend his evenings, and that Beatrice would cling to and protect. This centre is all they have, which makes its destruction the more poignant. In this way Peter Brook brings out the sense of family that is always strong in Miller.

'I am inclined to notice the ruins in things,' says the lawyer-chorus of *A View from the Bridge*. This might well have been an epigraph for the next play Brook directed, his first in Paris, Tennessee Williams's *Cat on a Hot Tin Roof*. It was a period when, in speaking of the American drama, everybody would automatically couple Miller and Williams much as Eliot and Fry (a very different pair) would be bracketed in Britain, or, long before this, Pinero and Jones. The names followed each other on the same breath; Williams had a more flamboyant sense of the dramatic, even if he could over-write in prose that an addict described rapturously as 'fuelled with human speech, taking off and soaring with a warm, jet-driven roar'. *Cat* was one of his more nerve-straining pieces ('What is the victory of a cat on a hot tin roof? Just staying on it, I guess, as long as she can'). It had not previously arrived in Paris where a critic looked forward to *La Chatte sur un toit brûlant* as '*la pièce la plus érotique de l'année*'. Brook, having dealt with Miller in London, now crossed to Paris in December and had a high time at the Théâtre Antoine with the atmospherics of a great house on an oppressive sun-baked Mississippi plantation. He supplied the climate as he had done in *The Power and the Glory*, and he made relishing use of storm effects and of the dazzle of off-stage fireworks. Superficially, the

* *Arthur Miller: The Burning Glass*, New York 1965; London, 1966

'*drame de la sexualité, de la famille, de l'alcoöl*' contained everything as Max Beerbohm would once have recognized:

> Death and disease, disaster,
> And downfall were our joy.
> The fun flew fast and faster. . . .

but André Obey's version was curiously tame; Brook and Jeanne Moreau (in pink chiffon) as Maggie the Cat, had to do what they could for an all-in play that considered human extremities of emotion and for a time made of Tennessee Williams a target like the side of a house.

Back in London in January 1957, Brook, in search of other roofs, was saying with some feeling: 'Each year I try to add something new, to stretch out in a different direction. A couple of years ago it was designing scenery and more recently experimenting with music. I want to be different at thirty-five from twenty-five, and different still at fifty and seventy. I have a horror of people who never grow old.' Having said this, he travelled with Natasha to New York and Hollywood for six weeks. After her appearance in *Charley's Aunt* and a long stay with Peter in New York and the West Indies, Natasha had resumed her career with a sequence of exacting television parts. Suddenly, in the hot summer of 1955, she was taken ill, both lungs were affected, and she was not cured completely until the spring of 1957. Now, on this American visit, they left Hollywood without regret: Peter found it rather like London Airport and Hampstead Garden Suburb merged somewhere on the upper reaches of the Thames. Their return to London coincided with the showing on television of a film entitled *Heaven and Earth,* the scenario of which Peter had written in 1951, with Denis Cannan, and directed himself, Paul Scofield as the star. It had been shot in ten days at Elstree, for ATV, on Brook's story and Cannan's shooting script; but complications and contracts prevented it from being shown in the cinema. The plan was a modern version of the Jonah myth. An aircraft, bound across the Atlantic for the Riviera, is endangered when all four engines are in trouble; realizing that disaster is near, and believing him to be the cause, the passengers jettison a young evangelist, a Billy Graham-like character, handsome, haggard, and, owing to exceptional circumstances, full of whisky and remorse. A court of inquiry is held; just as the truth is emerging, he arrives on crutches, miraculously saved.

John Osborne, guest critic for the *Evening Standard* (it was ten months after *Look Back in Anger*), enjoyed a film that its director had enjoyed making. Brook had had to devise the right sounds to underscore his long aircraft sequence. Feeling that the convention of an omniscient symphony orchestra was dubious in the strato-sphere or in mid-desert, he tried to exploit the impression one gets sometimes, in an aircraft, a motor-car, or a train, of hearing melodies in the engines' change of pitch. Thus he fabricated electronic hums, re-recording them at different speeds in a curious quarter-tone scale. These he interwove with realistic engine noises so that the listener to this peculiarly Petrine music from the spheres never knew when one sound ended and another took over.

III

For once, instead of stretching in a different direction, he redis-covered *Titus* from two years earlier, with the *musique concrète* once summarized charmingly (by Penelope Gilliatt) as 'a barbaric col-lage . . . sounding rather as if it were scored for Malayan nose-flute, deep-sea tuba, and the Gorgon's eyeball'. In May 1957, acted by the Stratford company, still with Olivier as Titus, Quayle as Aaron, and Vivien Leigh as Lavinia, the play went to the Théâtre des Nations in Paris. There Olivier was applauded for the greatest tragic performance since Mounet-Sully. If perplexed by the choice of play, nobody quarrelled with its acting, *un spectacle stupéfiant*, that made Francoise Rosay swear she would become a vegetarian. Thence to the beautiful Venetian Fenice Theatre, off the Grand Canal, and to Belgrade where Pitera Bruk directed *Tit Andronik,* with Ser Lorens Olivije, Antoni Kvejl, Alan Veb, Ralf Majkel, Maksin Odli, and Vivijan Li. It was a raging success – Marshal Tito came backstage to say so – and the players duly went on to Zagreb, Vienna, and Warsaw (*Tytus Andronikus*). Brook decided, as he would assert later, that the play touched audiences directly because it had tapped a ritual of bloodshed recognized as true. One of the profound admirers was Professor Jan Kott, of the University of Warsaw. Believing as he did that the films had discovered the Renaissance Shakespeare, he held that the most amazing quality of the Brook *Titus* was its return to true Shakespeare in the theatre through the experience of the film. He noted how the production was composed not of scenes but of shots and sequences; a production with tension evenly distributed and no 'empty places', the text cut but the action developed. Intervals of time were marked by blackouts; scenes faded, one into the other, film-like; dramatic encounters and soliloquies stood apart from crowd scenes like big close-ups. Attention would be concentrated on a given character which seemed to grow and move nearer to the audience; as if a film camera were tracking from Titus to Lavinia, from Tamora to Aaron. 'I found this performance,' Kott said, 'among the five greatest theatrical experiences of my life.'*

At length the tragedy entered the hollow London cavern of the Stoll in Kingsway: the final production in a vast, cold building that, either as an opera house or an all-purposes theatre, had never been much loved. That night, after addressing us as ladies and gentlemen in seven languages, Olivier said in his speech of thanks that *Titus*, once so obscure, was now so popular that it might be filmed, set to music, or skated. Critics agreed. There had not been in our time a more compelling feat of legerdemain than this reclamation of something untouchable, a poison-bottle of sinister dark glass from a forgotten shelf.

From it Brook went far across Shakespeare to *The Tempest,* the ultimate fantasy that dwells, like Claribel of Tunis, ten leagues beyond man's life. None of the plays he had found so baffling and elusive. He directed it at Stratford in August with his own music and designs, and with John Gielgud as a sombre Prospero of grizzled middle age, lonely and truth-seeking; Doreen Aris as a particularly good Miranda, who deserved more notice than she had; and Alec Clunes never quite sure what to do with Caliban. Hardly the 'thing of darkness', he could be acutely comic in the Stephano-Trinculo scenes, and we could trust him to respond to 'the isle is full of noises' (so it was: Brook's own *musique concrète:* 'no mortal business, nor no sound that the earth owes'). At the Stratford opening the ingenuities could be excessive, but the shipwreck, silhouetted against an indeterminate, violet-green sky, was fiercely plausible, a matter of flailing ropes and lanterns swaying in a dizzy arc; it reminded me of a Ben Greet revival in the early twenties when a lantern on a tall mast swung fiercely to and fro, dipping to the waves and back. At Stratford Brook supplied burning fire-balls and clambering sailors; then, a moment few directors had vouchsafed, a spell-stopped, ominous quiet before the final split. As soon as we had reached the island, meeting-ground of elemental forces, caves opened and closed, grew and shrank; actors, poised in close harmony, shot from trap-doors or disappeared into them as if they had

* See *Shakespeare Our Contemporary.*

been hardened to the business since boyhood; diaphanous spirits floated downstage, gauzes dissolved, outsize tropical fruits hung from branches as thick as drain-pipes (a hint here, maybe, from Messel in *The Little Hut*). The *musique concrète* was at its busiest, either a thousand twangling instruments that hummed about our ears, or others that tolled like bells from *la cathédrale engloutie*. The music reached us from what Brook called a 'mescalin-world of sound'. Again the actual nature of the first sound was unimportant; through a process of re-recording, with a mosaic-maker's patience, he could create complex and extended patterns of tone and rhythm.

The epithalamic masque, with its all-white goddesses, had a sign of the Brook to come, a reiterated fertility-rite chanting of key phrases about barns, garners, vines and plants. (For collectors, Eileen Atkins was a Nymph.) John Gielgud's Prospero employed all the majesty of the English tongue; I had never heard a nobler ground-swell at 'Behold, sir King, the wrongèd Duke of Milan, Prospero'. The Ariel had little voice. Patrick Wymark's Stephano, looking (for me) like George Robey, might have cried 'Desist!' at any moment. Other writers said that he and his Trinculo (Clive Revill) were a Shakespearian Oliver Hardy and Stan Laurel. All said, the revival kept a balance between Brook's Decorated and Undecorated periods. If his sets were basically austere, those craggy caverns, South Cornish in feeling, by a 'sea-marge, sterile and rocky-hard', his effects were capriciously inventive: a harpy rising and falling, like the growing and shrinking Alice, upon the telescopic lift of a mushroom; a stumbling progress among twined creepers; figures coming from or melting into the distance. It was by no means complete, for no English production of *The Tempest* has yet been right, but Brook, who would never cease to battle with its problems, got nearer to the play now than he would later. Always he has felt what Eliot calls 'the instinct to return to the point of departure' – to try again the play in which nothing is what it seems:*

When we realise that it takes place on an island and not an island, during a day and not during a day, with a tempest that sets off a series of events that are still within a tempest even when the storm is done, that the charming pastoral naturally encompasses rape, murder, conspiracy and violence; when we begin to unearth the themes that Shakespeare has so carefully buried, we see that it is his complete final statement, and that it deals with the whole condition of man.

* *The Empty Space.*

Brook and Sir Arthur Quiller-Couch might have had a great deal to say to each other. I wonder especially how Brook might have replied to 'Q's' linking of *A Midsummer Night's Dream* and *The Tempest:* 'Of all Shakespeare's plays these two *require* to be acted by (shall I say?) amateurs. The amateur may miss or hit. The professional mummer has never made any hand with either play; nor (I think) ever will'.

IV

Needing continual change, Brook was in New York during the autumn of 1957 – opera had fewer worries for him now – directing Tchaikovsky's *Eugene Onegin*, those so-called 'lyrical scenes in three acts', in new décor by Rolf Gérard. It had not been done at the 'Met' for forty years; George London was now the Eugène, with Dmitri Mitropoulos, who agreed entirely with the new conception, conducting. Once Brook might have spoken firmly of opera production in a phrase from *The Family Reunion:*

> There are certain inflexible laws
> Unalterable, in the nature of music.
> There is nothing to be done about it,
> There is nothing to do about anything. . . .

But he had ceased to feel like that in the congenial atmosphere of the 'Met'. This time, he explained, he and Rolf Gérard agreed that they could do *Eugene Onegin* in only one legitimate way, in accord with Russian tradition. They needed the old-fashioned technique of painted vistas and realistic scenes: Brook recalled how, when he was doing *La Bohème,* scene painters at Covent Garden had spoken of Puccini's method; his way of bringing along photographs, for the *Butterfly* décor, that he had taken in Japan with a plate camera. Similarly now, Brook arrived at the 'Met' with his own photographs, for the scene-painters' benefit, of crumbling palaces in Leningrad. He wanted to present a complete cross-cut of Russian provincial and town life at a particular moment in the last century, and to bridge the four waits during major scene-shifting with interludes arranged and orchestrated from the score of the opera. He wrote in the *New York Times.**

When one thinks of Tchaikovsky and Pushkin, of Russia and the nine-teenth century, the word 'romantic' springs easily to the lips; it is a word

---

* 27 October 1957.

that seems the opposite of all that one means by 'realistic', yet oddly enough the truth is a paradox: it is through their utter realism that the great Russian masterpieces are romantic. Realism is one of the strongest traditions in Russian art.

And then:

When Rolf Gérard and I started work on *Onegin*, we both agreed that we had no choice; the only legitimate manner in which we could stage this opera was precisely in accordance with this particular Russian tradition. It seemed to us that we needed the very elements that in other operas one so often deplores; we felt that it was through the old-fashioned scenes that we could arrive at a climate in which the opera belonged.

The last scene he and Gérard found incomplete and unatmospheric in spite of the formal beauty of so much of the music. Yet the end of Pushkin's poem was satisfying, partly because it balanced Tatyana's letter to Eugene which first precipitated the action, with Eugene's final letter to Tatyana. On the Metropolitan stage Brook attempted to create a similar parallel, contrasting the two secret meetings: falling leaves in the autumnal garden where Eugene rejected Tatyana's love were echoed by the formal ironwork and falling snow of the St Petersburg garden where Tatyana finally rejected Eugene. For this reason, Brook and Gérard moved the action from a boudoir to the more summoning set of a public park at night. Various writers demurred, on the principle that any change must be a bad change. Even so there had been no marked alarm at a première where nearly 4,000 people, some of whom paid the equivalent of £12.50 for their seats, had waited for the rise of the great gold curtain. Generally, critics and public approved of the period piece. Their response was that of a writer in the *New York Times* who said that *Onegin* was 'often as affecting as a sentimental old chromo'. The writer meant well, though Peter Brook would not have put it in those terms.

Within weeks, and with the usual quick change of mood, he was reviving *The Tempest,* brought from Stratford to the so-often-squandered stage of the Theatre Royal, Drury Lane, where long ago he had done the ENSA *Pygmalion*. Over and over, the most tepid nonsense had been cheered there simply because it happened to be at the Lane; generally the management could be as philistine as Alfred Bunn, the sensitive Macready's torturer. It was moving when the house reverted to splendour on the night of 5 December 1957. Outside, all the evening, a dense fog had draped the wintry streets.

Inside, cheering rang hearteningly after Gielgud, a man who had fought long and fiercely with the forces of magic, had paced down-stage in his turquoise robe to speak the epilogue, the ship behind him. The audience knew nothing about events before curtain-rise. Brook was angry that he had to use *The Tempest* to try out the new equipment and lighting set installed for *My Fair Lady*. 'We have been treated as guinea-pigs,' he said. But his anger drifted away in the night's sure progress. He had revised the epithalamic masque, all-white at Stratford; at Drury Lane Iris appeared rightly as the 'many-coloured messenger', and Juno descended on a rosy cloud that seemed to float unsupported. It was even more of a *coup d'oeil* when the three goddesses, posed in classical pomp, moved skyward above the dance of naiads and reapers. Somebody said, with a gallant dab, that it would have commanded the respect of 'Indigo Jones' himself. This was not yet the entire *Tempest*; but Brook knew where he was heading.

He had little time to review any fresh campaign. Already he was off to end the year by directing the Lunts, Alfred Lunt and Lynn Fontanne, in a 'satiric parable' adapted by Maurice Valency from the German of Friedrich Dürrenmatt. This, called *Time and Again*, a feebler title than the original, *The Old Lady's Visit*, was tragi-comedy sharpened to a spire of terror. Brook staged it in the key of nightmare. Very simply, a former prostitute, risen to be a woman of fabulous wealth, returned after a lifetime to the little German town of her birth – a derelict town waiting for its salvation – intent upon one thing only: revenge for the wrong done to her as a girl. 'The highest justice,' she said, 'has no pity'; for the life of a small shop-keeper, the object of her vengeance, she offered one billion marks. A woman of ice in a dress of flame, she descended suddenly upon her birth-place, borne in a palanquin and surrounded by a complex and frightening entourage; what followed had a Kafkaesque inevit-ability, though in retrospect it did not seem to be especially well written: all was sacrificed to situation.

The French version of the dance of death had much impressed Brook at the Marigny in Paris; but after a three months' tour of provincial England, no London theatre was ready for the nervous terror of Lunt as the man in the toils and for Fontanne's 'rattlesnake beauty'. Instead, during May 1958, with ten of the London cast, the strange, glowering simplicity of the Teo Otto settings, and Peter Brook continuing his Transatlantic shuttle service, Dürrenmatt's play would open in New York.

VIII

All Over The Place: 1958-1960

I

BEFORE New York, Paris; there was a chance to get in a production at the Théâtre Antoine. He had done Tennessee Williams there; and Paris, in the natural run, should be ready for a Miller. The obvious choice was *A View from the Bridge* which Marcel Aymé had just translated, as *Vu du Pont,* from the text Miller had provided for London. Aymé had sought an equivalent for the *argot* of the New York waterfront by scattering Miller's dialogue with French slang. The production, in which Brook employed his dramatic and admired skeleton set and had the film star, Raf Vallone – never seen on the legitimate stage outside Italy – as Eddie, Marcel Boffuzi as Marco, and the Russian Lila Kedrova as Beatrice, broadly resembled the Comedy Theatre treatment; but Sheila Huftel, never absent from a Miller première, was at the Antoine to note certain psychological changes essential for a French audience. Miller purist though she was, she observed the entire dedication of the house and a production 'as tense as a well-timed gesture'.* No other would have this general as well as intellectual success. Peter Brook, who said of it, 'It attracted the audiences of *My Fair Lady* as well as those of *Long Day's Journey Into Night*', was not there to hear the first-night reception; already he was on his way to New York for the Dürrenmatt (*Le Retour de la Vieille Dame*). Anxious about the Antoine, he could not resist ringing up from Orly Airport. Vallone had just left the stage after the calls while the house was still applauding, when Simone Berriau, the Antoine director, told him he was wanted on the telephone. He picked up the receiver. '*Allo, Raf. Ca a marché?*' asked Peter; and Vallone, nearly crying with relief and fatigue, told him: 'Your name was called so many times I came out to take the applause.' Through the year *Vu du Pont* was running strongly in Paris.

* *Arthur Miller: The Burning Glass.*

Meantime, on 6 May, the Dürrenmatt opened in New York at a theatre, once the Globe, that had been re-christened the Lynn Fontanne, a luxurious place, expensively-priced, decorated in powder-blue and gold, crystal and silver. New York critics liked the play, now named *The Visit*. Brooks Atkinson, recording that two illustrious drawing-room comedians had their harshest roles in a quarter of a century, said that nothing on the current stage could match Brook's orchestration of moods. For Walter Kerr in the *Herald-Tribune*, the play, 'as hard as nails in the coffin that waits patiently in the wings all night', had an appalling fascination. He admired Peter Brook's manipulation of abandoned figures in constricting space: 'The idle, silky, subtly threatening movement of presumably innocent townsfolk as they halt their man's escape by night, the terror of a line of stubborn backs blocking his every turn, the infinitely slow and quiet encircling that ends in a most discreet murder – all are images of encircling power.'

It was in *The Visit* that Alfred Lunt so endeared himself to Brook by the kind of suggestion only an obsessed actor would make.* During the first act, while sitting on a bench, he would take off his shoe, rub his foot, and shake the shoe to empty it before putting it on again. One evening, as he was making-up after a walk on Boston Common, he told Brook that it worried him, on shaking the shoe, that nothing fell out; he wondered whether he might not put in two small pebbles so that the audience could see and hear them drop. Gravely, Brook agreed; but Lunt was not really satisfied yet. He considered the matter again, looking anxiously at the two pebbles in his palm before he spoke. 'You don't think,' he said, 'that it might be better with just one?'

III

Peter Brook had not directed so far what used to be called a musical comedy: experts in elegant variation would speak of 'the lighter lyric stage'. To do something like this after Shakespeare, Tennessee Williams, and Dürrenmatt, was for him a fairly natural progress; and the musical he chanced upon would be one of the stayers of his period. It was entitled *Irma la Douce*; it had already governed Paris; in England, after a provincial opening, Brook's production reached the Lyric Theatre in Shaftesbury Avenue on 17 July 1958. Before this it had gone off splendidly at Bournemouth in a large,

* *Stagestruck: Alfred Lunt and Lynn Fontanne* by Maurice Zolotow, London, 1965.

ugly theatre where it defied the conditions so easily that the cast
went on without fear to the intimacy of the Royal at Brighton. Just
as inexplicably, Brighton hated it, and in London it took a night or
so to settle.

The mercurial adventure derived from a musical, *Expresso Bongo*,
in which Scofield played a Cockney agent; having seen this, Brook
proposed to its trio of authors, Julian More, Monty Norman, and
David Heneker, that they should try to naturalize the French *Irma*,
an invention by a former Parisian taxi-driver, Alexandre Breffort,
with a score by Marguerite Monnot. It was a highly Parisian affair,
flickering from Pigalle to the Caribbean. Irma herself was a *poule*, a
girl about Montmartre; you might have said that she was ready for
a new version, and in another milieu, of what Browning described
so discreetly as 'the fond tale o' the Frail One of the Flower, by
young Dumas'. A law student, Nestor-le-fripe, to keep her from
returning to the streets, impersonated (in a beard) a staid 'protector'
who would pay her enough to remain at home. But, as student, he
grew jealous of himself as protector, apparently murdered his *alter
ego* – like Gilbert's Chancellor he was there in two capacities and
they clashed – and for the imaginary crime was sentenced to life
imprisonment on Devil's Island. The piece being an uninhibited
fantasy, no one was in the least surprised when Nestor turned up in
Montmartre after a fairly rapid journey on a Kon-Tiki raft. Brook
directed with great relish: Elizabeth Seal, as quick as a willow-
wren, and Keith Michell were Irma and Nestor; and the whole
affair was rightly gay and *faux-naif*. Clive Revill, who had been in
The Tempest, clowned through innumerable parts, and Rolf Gérard,
inevitably, designed the sets with their make-believe readiness.
Some people disliked *Irma,* seeing in it only a type of French
humour that did not travel: they called the production frisky and
Elizabeth Seal suburban. But those that did like it, far more of
them, were glad that Brook had trusted any audience to have at
least a tithe of his imagination. It was designed, said Anthony
(Victor) Cookman in *The Tatler,* to survive both its scenic expansive-
ness and the turning into English of the thieves' slang of Montmartre: a problem in equivalents. When *Irma* had begun, it would
not stop. As late as October 1959, the Shakespearian John Neville,
new from *Hamlet* and the First Folio record at the Vic, replaced
Keith Michell, making so discreet a debut that Shaftesbury Avenue
hardly noticed it. For six months he sang the numbers, by then as
familiar in London as they had been in Paris, 'The Bridge of

Caulaincourt', 'Our language of love', 'She's got the lot', and 'There is only one Paris for me'.

For a while, after *Irma* was in train, Peter had a gap that must have seemed like one of his own stage pauses; Natasha, on the other hand, was occupied now both in the theatre – a revival of *Lysistrata* – and the cinema. Peter, too, had the cinema in mind: here only the beginnings of an idea to be realized far ahead: the earliest stirring of talk about a possible film of William Golding's allegorical novel, *Lord of the Flies,* for a Hollywood producer, Sam Spiegel, with a script by Peter Shaffer. It was a narrative of a group of suburban English schoolboys, wrecked on a tropical island, who revert to barbarity and ritual murder. Obviously a promising subject, there would be time for it later. For the moment Brook was thinking discontentedly about the stage, and as ever being articulate. He wrote in *Encore* (January–February 1959):

The theatre is on a catastrophically low level: weak, watery, repetitive, drab and silly. Why are there no plays that reflect the excitement, the movement, the change, the conflict, the tragedy, the misery, the hope, and the emancipation, of the highly dramatic moment of world's history in which we live? Why are we given the choice between colour and poetry in the classics, or drab prose in contemporary drama? Why has no one followed on Brecht's track? Why are our actors lazy and passionless: why do so few of them do more than two hours a day: why do so few of them think theatre, dream theatre, fight for theatre, above all practice theatre in the spare time at their disposal? Why is the talent in this country – and the goodwill – frittered away in a mixture of ineffectual grumbling and deep complacency? I think that to find the causes one must not look for individual villains or for a race of villains: I think the villain is deeply buried in the system: it lies in laws that operate at almost all levels.

This, and much more, sounded very much like a later Brook. No one, he said, could any longer take a flop: empty seats had always to be the crowning argument. During the last decade in the English theatre most of the experimenting had been at Stratford. He asked what were Europe's really exciting theatres and replied to his own question: the Théâtre National Populaire of Vilar, the Komische Oper of Berlin, Glyndebourne, the Berliner Ensemble, Theatre Workshop. Some of these were classical and formal, some revolutionary and proletarian. One thing they had in common: 'They are totally independent of the box-office, the Press or the audience. The need to make a "reasonable success" does not exist for them.' For him:

National Theatres, many of them, of different shapes and sizes, would be part of the answer. Of course, we can't ever get one – because the Government will never spend the money. And anyway, it would be such a cumbersome organisation, inevitably in the wrong hands, bound to pass through so many ghastly years of teething troubles, that it could not affect the scene as far ahead as we can look. No, I think we should clamour for the big National Theatre, as a thorn in the flesh of successive Governments, but actually hope for something more realistic. I would like to see a start made – and the principle established – with one tiny theatre with a hundred seats, even fifty seats, but *subsidised to the hilt*. By this I mean that the subsidy should cover all that such a theatre could lose even if every seat were empty at every performance. . . . It will be run by a director and a new sort of committee. The committee will applaud the director if he announces that he has lost every penny – he is entitled to do this. It will chase him with furies, however, if he has failed to keep his theatre alive. . . . Its appeal must be that it can *dare completely;* that it can *dare* offer any author with a completely uncommercial idea a stage *immediately*. It would be an actor's studio of writers, it would be our avant-garde.

And finally:

Where is the vanguard of the theatre? Where can one see disastrous experiments from which authors can develop away from the dying forms of the present day? To face new audiences we must first be in a position to face empty seats.

Here was George Devine's doctrine of 'the right to fail' uncompromisingly expressed. All round Brook, as he wrote this, an old theatre was shaking in dismay. It was the period of high rebellion, with the West End trapped between the two fires of the English Stage Company at the Court and Joan Littlewood's Theatre Workshop at Stratford East. Complete conquest would be far less easy than it may have looked then; but in 1959–60, not yet a decade after *Saint's Day*, the rebels seemed to be redoubtably in command.

III

Though Peter Brook would spend much of 1959 in France, making his film *Moderato Cantabile,* he was in New York during November and December to direct at the ANTA Theatre Anouilh's *The Fighting Cock,* called originally *L'Hurluberlu,* or reckless idiot. Rex Harrison, ruling the night in spite of 'a maddening habit of not listening when others are speaking',* was the General, educated by

* *Seasons of Discontent* by Robert Brustein, London, 1966.

various things that did not fit into his programme; Natasha Parry, taking over from Odile Versois, whose accent would have been odd among the other players, all of them English, was beautifully composed as the wife with more honour than love. 'She is a slight woman,' said Brooks Atkinson, 'with classical features and a limpid acting style. She conveys the soft melancholy of a woman who has been wounded by the simple realities of experience, and she never reaches for a stage effect.' The General, an authoritative diehard unused to a world that no longer turned as it did once, had continued in retirement to fight his battles, seeking to remove the 'maggots' from public life and to restore the old notion of honour; France had to recover its roots in the nation and the family. All very well; but the unhappy man had still to learn about what Tennyson called in an inspired phrase (even its derivation was misplaced), 'the ringing grooves of change'. It was a play, sharply ironical and appreciatively noticed, that Brook, with sets once more by Gérard – 'transparent, water-colourish, the work of an unusually bold yet delicate imagination'* – wove closely into the 'pattern of living' Atkinson had praised in the *New York Times.*

A new Peter Brook had begun to make his own pattern of living in theatre and cinema. Back in Paris, he directed during May 1960 *Le Balcon* at the Théâtre de Gymnase. It was the symbolic fetishistic drama by Jean Genet that had been acted only once before, in London at an inferior club production when the author, who had objected to it strongly, was banned from the theatre. Genet, *un poète maudit,* made no secret of his sultry private life and his years in and out of prison. Commanding a world of ritual and fantasy, he was much applauded by connoisseurs of 'superb and scabrous prose', the kind of credential that would at once establish a resolute opposition. This revised piece, about a brothel keeper (Marie Bell) and the visitors to her House of Illusions, a so-called General, Judge, and Bishop who must play their assumed parts in reality when revolution comes, had a curious esoteric appeal in the complicated floridities of its manner and matter. Its production (*'mise en scène et décors de Peter Brook'*) mixed actors of very different backgrounds: some classically trained, some in film or ballet, and some who were simply amateurs. 'Long evenings,' Brook said, 'of very obscene brothel improvisations served only one purpose: they enabled this hybrid group of people to come together and begin to find a way of responding directly to each other.' Use of the impro-

* Brustein.

visatory method had grown on Brook: it had been one of his marks as a director from the day he was first getting his crowd scenes to work.

His sets in *Le Balcon,* his last 'illusionist' production, were particularly important. He reorganized the piece. Seven of its original scenes he cut; for the remaining eight he designed, on a revolving stage, a series of hinged open frames that had to be pivoted between the various locations: mirrors were everywhere. The play, intended for a *'théâtre des intellectuels'*, lasted for fifty performances in a limited run. Its future notoriety in the theatre was assured.

Brook was more excited by what he described as 'an anti-audience film', *Moderato Cantabile,* which had been occupying most of his time and was shown, also in May 1960, at the Cannes Festival: his first film since *The Beggar's Opera.* He liked it more than anything he had done: the camera had been the first love of his life and here he was using it in a type of experiment for which he had longed, with his admired Jeanne Moreau, who had worked for him in *Cat:* 'She is for me the ideal contemporary film actress because she doesn't characterise. She acts in the way Godard films, and with him you are as close as you can be to making a document of an emotion. . . . She works like a medium, through her instincts. Her performance gives you an endless series of tiny surprises.' It took him a year to get Raoul Levy to sponsor the film – with its narrative by Marguerite Duras and Gérard Jarlot – and then he insisted upon a clause in the agreement that Levy should have no say in artistic matters. This was to be wholly Brook; Levy agreed to back the film solely on his faith in director, authors, and actress.

Brook regarded *Moderato Cantabile* as an experiment to see whether it was possible to photograph an almost invisible reality; whether it was possible, in photographing nothing but a surface, to get under the surface. He used no conventional script, merely suggested locations and approximations of the needed shots: a flexible form of planning that greatly troubled Levy who looked for a detailed statement of intention. Briefly, Brook wanted, without any of the usual tricks and without the intervention of a script-writer's 'false arrogance', to capture two people's emotional experience, something that could happen only once. The scene was a small town on the Gironde estuary near Bordeaux in winter. A married woman (Jeanne Moreau), wife of a rich ironfounder, had heard the screams of a murder victim – a lover killing his mistress in a café – and become fascinated by possible motives for the crime. Meeting a man, one of her husband's employees (Jean-Paul Belmondo), with whom she discussed the affair, she fell in love with him and insistently sought him out. When at length he ended the association, she found herself screaming as the murdered woman had done on that winter day.

Duras's title came from the first movement of Anton Diabelli's piano sonatina which the woman's son was heard practising at the start; Brook had no other music. Most of the action was cerebral and internal; the camera, set up at a single point, simply acted as a recorder. Brook said of this in a *Sight and Sound* interview:*

The great criticism of *Moderato Cantabile* was that I didn't move the camera enough, that I set it up and allowed things to happen in front of it, and it was assumed that I did this because I came from the theatre and didn't know any better. In fact, there was a lot of conscious thinking behind it. The narrative we were trying to capture in that particular film was neither an external one nor entirely an inner one – you can't say that the characters behave as they do because they live by a river in a dull town, but you can't ignore the way these things relate to them either. So, having found the landscape and these particular actors, my task seemed to be to set up a camera that didn't comment; to let you watch, as it were, a documentary record of something so intangible that you could feel it was really happening.

Moderato Cantabile had by no means a unanimous greeting at Cannes, though critics observed the director's devotion to the title-phrase, 'moderately paced and singingly', which informed every movement; they praised, too, the long tracking shots and the vistas of reeds and river. Jeanne Moreau shared with the Greek star, Melina Mercouri, the Festival jury's prize for the best actress. When, in October 1960, it arrived at the London Film Festival, it was re-titled *Seven Days . . . Seven Nights*, the period of the love affair's birth and death during which the two, man and woman. met on a ferry, in a deserted park, in a ruined building, in a café, Some critics said bluntly that the film was soporific; others recognized how Brook had explored a single mood and ignored all but essential background details; how he exploited the study in morbid psychology, the woman's increasing obsession and the man's increasing uneasiness; and how in the background he made haunting use of wind and trees and the wintry chill. He spoke himself of 'this completely lost little town where there is no distinctive feature whatsoever. We take out everything that dramatizes the

* By Penelope Houston and Tom Milne: Summer, 1963.

story. We take away the element of narrative. We avoid scenes, big scenes in the dramatic sense, and avoid underlining and pointing anything, avoid anything in the camera work, in the movement of the camera, the lighting, the music and the cutting that might dramatize it; eventually one has done a process of total elimination.' What remained, he said, were character, mood, idea, conflict and emotion. It was genuine film direction: making an actor reach a point where this 'total attitude' was true to the character. It was real cinema, devised so that an audience could understand and perceive for itself something truly expressive about a person without being prompted by a line of dialogue, emphasis on camera, or a burst of music.

Record-breaking in Paris, the film did less well in the French provinces. In England it was a luxury, even if the magazine *Films and Filming* praised it as the best work released in Britain during 1961: 'For its emotional and intellectual integrity in analysing simple but vital human experiences; and for its remarkable development and control of technique to this end.' There were many adverse opinions, and more when after a very long interval it reached the United States in the autumn of 1963. '*Moderato Cantabile*,' *Time* said, 'might better have been titled *Adagio Funereo*; it is much too long, much too lugubriously languid.' *Newsweek* held that the film's special stylishness, 'perhaps tolerable and even interesting' in 1960, had grown outmoded: 'The delay in importing *Moderato Cantabile* has been lethal.' Brook had said himself in 1961, and he would stick to it; 'God knows it's been damned, but it has a very special spot in my heart. If somebody tells me he liked *Moderato Cantabile*, I'm fascinated. He's a friend for life.'

IV

Before *Moderato Cantabile* reached a London screen, *The Visit* at last discovered its London theatre. In June 1960 the Lunts opened, under a dual management,* at an entirely new theatre, the Royalty, built into the side of a Kingsway office block that had replaced the cavernous and strangely pathetic Stoll, a building that, in spite of *Titus Andronicus*, had been for too long a forgotten opera-house dressed up with nowhere in particular to go and little satisfaction in the end. *The Visit* had taken two and a half years to get to London at last. Probably no one was more surprised by its arrival than the

* H. M. Tennent Ltd and Two Arts Ltd.

author, Friedrich Dürrenmatt, the Swiss dramatist with the red-apple cheeks, who had written it as *Der Besuch die Alten Dame* in 1954, who had seen it fail in Zurich and in Paris, who had known a surprising lack of enthusiasm for an English version, and who had been even disappointed in England when the Lunts had taken it at the insistence of Peter Brook. There had been a reasonably hopeful provincial opening, but audiences generally – and the play had appeared at such towns as Brighton and Blackpool, Stratford-upon-Avon and Dublin – had suggested that this was neither a play they wished to see nor one in which they liked meeting the Lunts. Stratford seemed to hint that Brook should get back to *Titus*. Then belatedly, there had been the New York triumph; even so it was still two years before the second assault on London when at least one theatre was hospitable. The opening of any new house is an excitement; there was plenty on the night of *The Visit,* and nobody could foresee that within another twelve months the Royalty would be a cinema and remain so for nine years. Peter Brook, though he considered it perfectly workable, wished there had been a more theatrical mind behind its design: he objected also to the lack of cheap seats, 'a new trend and a bad one': the cheapest seat in the house for *The Visit* was seven-and-sixpence.

The play held its compulsive sense of evil. Dürrenmatt had said: 'Claire is neither Justice nor Apocalypse, nor the Marshall Plan. Money has enabled her to act like the heroine of a Greek tragedy. Just play the foreground, and the background will take care of itself.' Brook and the Lunts had taken care of both. T. C. Worsley said in the *Financial Times* that the director's triumph was to have 'caught the curious, removed unreal tone of voice of the expressionist play, and to have kept it absolutely consistent throughout the evening'. This was a period when the foundations of the West End stage appeared to be cracking; managers would wait up after a première to see what two of the drama critics, Robert Muller and Bernard Levin, would say in the *Daily Mail* and *Daily Express* respectively. On the morning after *The Visit* each of them cheered. 'The Royalty Theatre,' said Levin, making it perfectly clear, 'has opened with triumph, triumph, triumph, triumph,' while Muller said mildly: 'A stupendous evening.'

The Visit was a drama of menace. It was essential that it should frighten us, swoop forward as a nightmare swoops, with those sharp plucking movements. We had to feel ourselves surrounded, as the victim was; one jar, one clumsy manoeuvre, and we should wake from the dream. Nothing at the Royalty was clumsy or false. Brook proved, against the spare two-dimensional sets, to be the legitimate theatre's most expert choreographer of doom. The way in which the scenes melted and grew, the patterns formed, disintegrated, and re-formed, the inevitable, brooding, silent terror of it all, was more than Dürrenmatt could have hoped. At one moment towards the end Alfred Lunt was a lonely figure on a bench in a sunlit forest (the stage was empty, but the forest was there): then, in a single flicker, he was waiting, a man beleaguered, to be condemned at the town's meeting: this was nightmare's true clench. *The Visit* did not entirely repeat its American triumph; but it had 148 performances,* and Dürrenmatt made the conquest he once thought hopeless.

By now, for Brook, the transatlantic journey was almost as familiar as commuting between Baker Street and the Chilterns. He went back to New York again for a reunion with an old friend, the opening of *Irma,* with its three original principals, at the Plymouth Theatre in September 1960. This production got Howard Taubman to say that it was as heady as a fine, dry French wine. Peter Brook always liked *Irma* in spite of talking deprecatingly about a well-designed, efficiently-tuned engine. When in the spring of 1962 he was re-directing his production, yet again, for an English tour, he said: 'It's the only play I've come back to with feelings of pleasure. I've never seemed to be away from it during the last four years, staging it abroad and returning to it whenever a new star has taken over. Moreover, I've watched it a dozen times.' *Irma* would be one of his last theatre holidays: a new and exigent Brook was taking over, and the mood would be at the world's end from the young man of a decade before. He was still, as somebody said, listening like a tape-recorder; he was still asking unanswerable questions of any script, any company, and replying to them at once; he was still agreeing with Emerson that a perfect consistency is the hobgoblin of little minds. 'Speak,' said Emerson – and Brook – 'what you think today in words as hard as cannon-balls, and tomorrow speak what tomorrow thinks, in hard words again, though it contradicts everything you said today.'

---

* Brook's loyalties were firm. Myles Eason, once Tybalt in his *Romeo and Juliet,* acted in *The Visit* and was Assistant to the Director; and George Rose played the Burgomaster.

IX

'As Flies To Wanton Boys': 1960-1964

I

ANYONE who arrived, uninstructed, at this stage of Brook's career would have had the greatest difficulty in judging his man. Anouilh, Genet, *Irma la Douce, Moderato Cantabile:* fair stood the wind for France, but what next? Brook had decided to get back to the cinema and the technical problems he was always happy in solving. First, during October 1960, he and Natasha were travelling through Mexico, which was like re-visiting the Graham Greene world of *The Power and the Glory.* Soon after this he settled to the making of *Lord of the Flies,* a complicated process. Sam Spiegel, of Hollywood, had bought the rights of William Golding's novel from Sir Michael Balcon. When one afternoon, by a swimming pool in Monte Carlo, Spiegel asked casually, 'What are we going to call the film?' Brook, to whom he was speaking, had realized what the coming year might be like. Why change the title for the sake of change? At this he knew instinctively that he and his producer would not agree upon a thing.

When first he had wanted to make the film after reading Golding's allegory of development from primal innocence to self-destruction, he heard that Ealing Studios had bought the rights for £2,000 and had a director hard at work. The film was not made; and one day the rights were for sale again, at £18,000. Brook now went to Spiegel, hoping that he might look paternally upon a small low-budget experiment. All Brook wanted was a small sum of money, children, and a beach: no shooting script. Spiegel insisted upon a detailed screenplay which would guarantee that the film had what he called 'world values'. Nothing happened for a year, though an art director searched hopefully for locations in Spain and Africa; Brook went to the Canary Islands; various children were interviewed, and Peter Shaffer was engaged to write the script. (At the same time, and in secret, Richard Hughes was commissioned to write another.)

Shaffer had said to Brook at once that he could not see how they could agree to change the title, to make boys into girls, English into Americans. Still, in the end, he turned up with a screenplay that would have lasted six hours; it included an immense trek up a mountain and what Brook called an extraordinary sequence that lasted for nearly an hour in a cave where three complex rituals, each of which would have served for a whole season of the Theatre of Cruelty, were playing at once. The outline of the novel and the force of the subject vanished like snow-wreaths in thaw. Eventually wisdom ruled, with a return to the book and to Golding's closely-ordered allegorical structure: it was useless to get away from it. Spiegel, on his scale of operating, decided that the film must cost around half a million dollars, shelved it, and went on to *Lawrence of Arabia* instead. So another year passed. It was about then that a young American, Louis Allan, had begun in New York to work out a method by which private backers who were not excessively anxious whether their money would be returned, might invest a few thousand dollars or so in a film. Allen and his partner Dana Hodgdon had just financed Shirley Clarke's *The Connection*; they were ready to work similarly for *Lord of the Flies*. At length three hundred investors responded; they bought oil-well shares, coupled with an interest in the film, and finally Brook could afford to negotiate for the rights, though by the time the deal was through, he and his partners had spent half their new budget of £80,000. The last script, the ninth, had been the answer. Shaffer and Brook had filled it with elaborately detailed descriptions of scenery they had never seen and illusory but most complicated camera movements. On the strength of this the three hundred backers believed that they were dealing with a respectable plan, and Brook got down to work.

II

In America they searched for English boys of the right reserved, civilized quality, having decided at first that they could not bring them from England. A twenty-three-year-old Harvard man, Michael Macdonald, Brook's assistant, who was son of the critic Dwight Macdonald, went to see English business men in various Manhattan offices, explaining that they were looking for English boys on that side of the Atlantic. Nobody responded; indeed all were coolly and unhelpfully polite until Macdonald mentioned a sovereign name: 'We're looking for a kind of Billy Bunter.' Immediately excitement glowed; help was offered, and hope rose. Macdonald also accosted possible families at the docks as they arrived; wrote to Embassy families; discovered in the New York directory clubs for Old Etonians, Old Harrovians, and the old boys of Mill Hill. He traced, moreover, an entire Scottish village which a distillery had moved intact to the heart of New Jersey. In the end they were able to select from about 3,000 children, all anxious to be in the film while their parents were glad to have a quiet summer. No pay was suggested, merely pocket-money and a share in the hypothetical profits.

Ralph, who would be the leading boy, they discovered in a swimming pool at an Army camp in Jamaica four days before filming began. Advertisements in English newspapers had read: 'Why be head of the school when you can be Lord of the Flies? 12/13-year-old prep.-schoolboys needed during June and July for professional film being made in West Indies. Parents apply to . . .'* From this Piggy, the Billy Bunter character, arrived. He sent a letter on lined paper that began: 'Dear Sir, I am fat and wear spectacles,' and enclosed a crumpled photograph that made Peter cry with delight: Piggy himself in Camberley. Other of the forty boys came from such diverse places as Kuwait, Tripoli, Hamburg and Johannesburg: the oldest was fifteen, the youngest seven.

Next the setting: an island called Vieques, a small piece of land nine miles east of Puerto Rico, between it and the Virgin Isles: a jungle paradise with miles of palm-fringed beaches. Woolworth's lent it in exchange for a screen credit, but the military controlled two-thirds of it; it was a nest of US machines, soldiers and helicopters, from which Washington had chosen, if needed, to mount its invasion of Cuba. The boys encamped in an abandoned pineapple factory where a large room became a dormitory filled with Army cots. The twenty adults lodged at a little hotel on a knoll not far away. Rigorous economies were devised; thus no one could fly except late at night, at cut-price rates, and nobody could telephone to New York, hire a car, or stay at a hotel if other methods could be found. In this way the unit saved thousands of dollars and could waste as much film as it wanted. After all, said Brook, a writer was expected to waste paper. He ruled that no one should question the use of film, and once they had begun to shoot, they went on, up to

---

* Brook received, among other replies, a formal and cordial letter inviting him to a meeting of a witches' coven in South London. But the writer, though signing his name, omitted the address.

four cameras turning at once. At last the unit emerged with over sixty hours of unbroken screening, a Laocoön tangle of 415,000 feet of film, four times the usual amount. Daily shipments of exposed film were made to New York, also miles of tape which had been recorded at all times of the day; from this, during the long editing the dialogue would be pasted upon the film like postage stamps, word by word. Regretfully, Brook had had to leave Shaffer's script. He went back instead to his first intention and improvised from the novel. This, briefly, is the story of a group of English schoolboys who crash in an aircraft, during an atomic war, upon an uninhabited tropical island; no adults survive. Someone must be leader; Ralph is chosen instead of Jack, head of the choir-boys and a feud between the two begins. (Jack and Ralph are names from Ballantyne, but there is nothing of the decorous *Coral Island* in *Lord of the Flies:* even less, come to think of it, of *The Little Hut*.) The boys dread an unknown creature, known as 'The Beast', on the mountain-top; Jack and his hunters – former choir-boys who have been seen wearing cassocks and birettas and singing a Kyrie which merges into a hunting-song – kill a pig and leave the head on a stick as an offering. Presently savagery supervenes; two boys are killed; when rescue arrives, a British naval commander discovers only a horde of screaming painted devils hunting down their leader. Then, at once, they revert to the English schoolboys they are.

Brook had to give the word to set a scene in motion, but the boys, all of whom had read the novel in paperback, responded at once. 'The violent gestures, the looks of greed, and the faces of experience were all there. All children cannot act, but they can do things that an adult is too theory-bound to manage. They are all sensible and logical and want to know what they are doing, and why. They took at once technical directions that would throw an adult.'* Golding declared simply that in children all possibilities were latent. Certainly these boys understood; one of the problems was to encourage them to be uninhibited within the shots but disciplined outside them: savagery by day, prep.-school discipline at night. Though the action of the novel occupied three months, Brook believed that if the 'cork of continued adult presence were removed from the bottle', the complete catastrophe could occur within a long week-end.

For three months the children worked well without grumbling. All rose at six a.m., and before filming began, Brook told the day's

* *Observer,* 26 July 1964.

story at a general assembly. At first he and the cameramen had a problem. Tracking shots were essential; but would the children stay on their exact marks and how much time would be wasted if they deviated and the camera tracks had to be re-laid? To avoid this they worked on a flexible plan, using rails that could be moved easily on the sandy beach, and a camera poised on a tripod that the cameraman himself pushed, walking crabwise as he looked through the viewfinder. After two days of agitation the plan succeeded.

When not at work, the children raced hermit crabs, caught lizards, and did some filming on their own, an 8-mm shocker entitled *Murder for Money: or, Something Queer in the Warehouse*. They also published a semi-weekly newspaper, posted to keep the parents up-to-date. It was a period of fantastic action. Again and again enthusiastic intellectuals would appear on the island, anxious to help but finding very soon that their enthusiasm would wither. In the end three people sailed off to France with cans of film and tape; though by now the £80,000 was exhausted, the Paris laboratory gave them credit and the year's editing began. Grim though it had seemed for most of the time, it would be romantic enough in retrospect.

During that summer, while he was making *Lord of the Flies*, Brook wrote:*

The cinema can tap the flood of imagery of existence more easily than the theatre. After all, any flood of images is a film. In fact, I would define a *good* film as a piecing together of living fragments and a bad film as an assembly of lifeless ones. If each fragment – each shot – is a piece of *living* material, then half the battle is won (*Shadows*) – because in academic film-making the *shot* is often a dead word, even though it is part of a paragraph that makes good sense (*Bridge on the River Kwai*). The good film either assembles its fragments into an order that has equal life-like disorder, or into a formal pattern (*Hiroshima mon Amour*) so that the living word becomes the living paragraph – because in the last resort it is only order that can suggest disorder on the most transcendental plane.

III

Probably it was natural that after the pressures and alarms of its making, the final showing of *Lord of the Flies* should have had a certain sense of anti-climax. So much had been written about the film that critics could have hardly come to it untaught – certainly not those at the Cannes Festival when it was shown there in the

* *Mademoiselle*, November 1961.

early summer of 1963: at a time when Brook had long been over-whelmed with other projects. On the whole it was received with respectful intelligence, though after the long pull across the years its director might have hoped for more enthusiasm and less about the need for the discipline of a script. He could have been pleased with agreement in *The Times* that the film had both the realism and the rhythm he regarded as the two most important things in any picture.

New York that August acclaimed *Lord of the Flies* as startling and chilling, and the individual voice of Jonathan Miller said in the *New Yorker:* 'The whole thing has been cut with sabre-toothed abrupt-ness. The sound track is conspicuous for a fine, harsh sibilance – the crackle of branches and the hot whirring of insects.' Britain took its time to respond. It was a year before the film reached the Cameo-Poly, near Oxford Circus, with an X certificate. Notices were gratifying. Penelope Gilliatt, in the *Observer,* said that the direction had preserved the book's character with a fastidiousness that was remarkable. 'I admire very much the bold and bony structure of the film and the freezing way Raymond Leppard's *Kyrie* is used.' Isabel Quigly said in the *Spectator*: 'Almost uncannily faithful to the book. . . . Stevie Smith called the book "beautiful and desperate". I'd apply both words to the film as well – especially in a deep and heart-felt and even far-fetched way, the "desperate".' *Lord of the Flies* ran firmly before its release during the autumn on the Rank circuit. Even then, though the book was prescribed reading for 'O' level syllabuses, it would find such an eccentric greeting as at Birming-ham where in March 1965 the city's Sunday Films Committee banned it for Sunday showing. Critics responded swiftly as a rule, though in the provinces there was always a risk of such a headline, from the East Midlands, as 'Makes Dracula Positively Cuddly'. With the years *Lord of the Flies* developed into a contemporary classic, ripe for revival. Controversy is as soon forgotten in the cinema as in the theatre; and the film has a place today among major experimental work of its period that justifies the toil of that idealistic island fling, so very, very far from Ballantyne.

IV

Long before the Cannes Festival Brook had moved into another form of experience: his production of *King Lear* in Stratford-upon-Avon, at the tail of the Shakespeare Festival of 1962. There had been a sharp change of method at Stratford, governed for three

seasons by a young Shakespearian, Peter Hall. Here Peter Brook
had become one of a governing triumvirate in which the third
figure was an elder statesman, Michel Saint-Denis, more influential
now in theory than in practice. Hall intended to create at Stratford
an ensemble that, after its growing pains, would gradually have the
cohesion and style of which directors dream, though they wake
often to a rainy morning. Several artists were put under long-term
contract. By 1962 the Royal Shakespeare Company, as it had been
re-christened – to prevent the Memorial Theatre from dropping
into line with the other museums – had a fresh authority both in
Warwickshire and, in London, at the Aldwych. This was taken as a
West End home for a repertory of non-Shakespearian classics and
new plays as well as the major Stratford revivals: a sharp change at
the pleasant all-purposes theatre known for the 'Aldwych farce'
sequence of Ben Travers between the wars.

The Royal Shakespeare's world was to be one of experiment
where 'everything, stage, setting, costumes, speaking, creative
acting' must be 'in a state of finding; of not expecting fresh solutions, but keeping open'. Peter Brook himself looked back, alarmed,
at the methods of post-war Stratford. It was time, he said, to move
away from romance and fantasy and decoration; once they had been
necessary 'in shaking the ugliness and boredom off these well-worn
texts. Now we must look beyond an outer liveliness to an inner
one.' It could have been put less contentiously; and Brook found the
same type of response he remembered from Covent Garden,
especially when he said: 'I am more easily bored with Shakespeare,
and have suffered more ghastly evenings with him, than with any
dramatist I know.' However, there could be no question of the
excitement, as well as of the antagonism, he would generate with
his revival of *King Lear*. Something long contemplated, it was at a
Polar remove from either the nobler-than-life approach of what he
would call the Deadly Theatre, or from his own theories in a long-
forgotten past.

When I came first to the theatre I had believed obediently that
King Lear was unplayable, a bourne from which no actor could
return in triumph; certainly each of the first two actors in my
experience was a man battling against superman, now piping shrilly,
now bellowing into a snowdrift of beard, now coping with a wind
machine, while in the middle distance a respectful company hovered
in Anglo-Saxon attitudes. But many later men had revealed the
splendour: Randle Ayrton at Stratford, a crumbling crag; the young

William Devlin, almost Olympian in presence; Werner Krauss, with his early parade-ground imperiousness; John Gielgud, both broadening and subtilizing his performance through the years, though in a last production the absurd Japanese décor defeated him; Donald Wolfit, more memorable as Kent, but with a massive quality on his best nights; Laurence Olivier, never turning the part to an assemblage of detached effects; Michael Redgrave, Paul Rogers, the curiously intermittent Charles Laughton. Now Paul Scofield, as directed by Brook, would be a Lear entirely new, the old charts tossed aside.

Brook had been powerfully impressed by the Polish essayist and Shakespearian scholar, Jan Kott. They had met in a nightclub in Warsaw one agitated early morning; after a beautiful girl had been arrested in error, he and Kott, whom he had never seen before, set about obtaining her release. Towards daybreak he heard the police addressing his companion as Professor, and discovered that in fact he was Professor of Literature at the University of Warsaw. Telling the story in his preface to Kott's book, *Shakespeare Our Contemporary* when at length it appeared in England (in 1965), Brook observed: 'Here we have a man writing about Shakespeare's attitude to life from direct experience. Kott is undoubtedly the only writer on Elizabethan matters who assumes without question that every one of his readers will at some point or another have been woken by the police in the middle of the night. . . .' Here was somebody far from the 'sheltered figures behind ivy-covered walls' who wrote most of the commentaries on Shakespeare's passions and politics. The preface continued:

Our greatest problem in England where we have the best possibility in the world for presenting our greatest author is just this – the relating of these works to our lives . . . England, in becoming Victorian, lost almost all its Elizabethan characteristics – today it has become a strange mixture of Elizabethan and Victorian worlds: this gives us a new possibility of understanding Shakespeare side by side with an old tendency to blur and romanticise him. It is Poland that in our time has come closest to the tumult, the danger, the intensity, the imaginativeness, and the daily involvement with the social process that made life so horrible, subtle, and ecstatic to an Elizabethan. So it is quite naturally up to a Pole to point us the way.

Jan Kott, as we have seen, intensely admired the revival of *Titus Andronicus*. When he reviewed it after the Royal Shakespeare Company's Warsaw visit in 1957, he congratulated Brook on

Peter Brook in 1946, the year of *Love's Labour's Lost*

Man and Superman (*above*) and *King John* (*below*) were the first two of Peter Brook's three productions for Sir Barry Jackson at the Birmingham Repertory Theatre in the autumn of 1945, and the first time he worked with the young Paul Scofield. *Left to right above:* Paul Scofield (John Tanner), Herbert Vanderfelt (Roebuck Ramsden), John Harrison (Octavius). *Left to right below:* Mabel France (Queen Elinor), David Read (King John), Paul Scofield (the Bastard), Denis Quilley (Robert Faulconbridge)

A scene from *Love's Labour's Lost,*
Peter Brook's first production at
Stratford-upon-Avon in 1946, at
the age of twenty-one. *Left to
right:* Paul Stephenson
(Ferdinand), David King-Wood
(Berowne), Donald Sinden
(Dumain), John Harrison
(Longaville)

The opening scene of Brook's controversial production of *Romeo and Juliet* at Stratford, in 1947. Myles Eason as Tybalt, in black, is in the centre; John Harrison as Benvolio is on the right

'Tomorrow! O, that's sudden! Spare him, spare him! He's not prepared for death.' Barbara Jefford as Isabella pleads with Angelo (John Gielgud) for the life of her brother in Brook's production of *Measure for Measure* at Stratford in 1950

Above: The opening scene of Peter Brook's historic production of *Titus Andronicus* at Stratford in 1955. *Left to right:* John MacGregor (Martius), Leon Eagles (Quintus), Michael Denison (Lucius), Ralph Michael (Bassianus), Alan Webb (Marcus Andronicus), Vivien Leigh (Lavinia), Frank Thring (Saturninus), Alan Haywood (Soldier), Geoffrey Bayldon (Æmilius), Laurence Olivier (Titus Andronicus), Ian Holm (Mutius), James Grout (Roman Captain)

Right: Paul Scofield as Hamlet in the Brook production that went to Moscow in 1955 before it came to the Phoenix Theatre in London. *Left to right:* Richard Johnson (Laertes), Alec Clunes (Claudius), Paul Scofield, Diana Wynyard (Gertrude), Michael David (Horatio)

In 1957 Brook directed *The Tempest* both during the Stratford-upon-Avon
festival and in December at the Theatre Royal, Drury Lane. *Above,* in the
Masque scene: *left,* Richard Johnson (Ferdinand), John Gielgud (Prospero),
Doreen Aris (Miranda); *back,* Joan Miller (Juno), Jane Wenham (Iris),
Stephanie Bidmead (Ceres). *Below,* John Gielgud as Prospero speaks the Epilogue

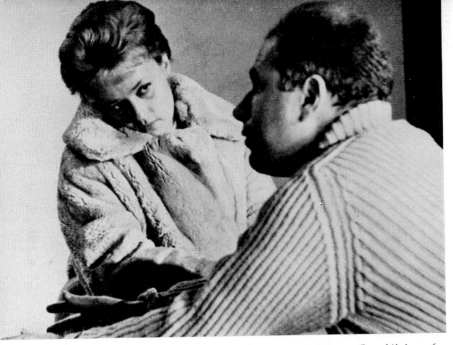

Above: Jeane Moreau directed by Peter Brook in the film *Moderato Cantabile* in 1960

Below: Brook defied tradition with his Stratford production of *King Lear* in 1962; Paul Scofield is seen here with Alec McCowen as the Fool

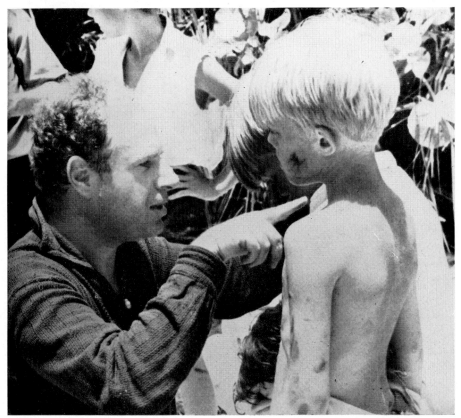

In *Lord of the Flies,* a group of tidy and well-behaved English schoolboys are stranded on an uninhabited tropical island, and in a horrifyingly short time revert to a state of primitive savagery. The two photographs on the left show the transformation, and the picture above shows Peter Brook working with one of his young cast

Left: Irene Worth as the hunch-backed asylum superintendent in *The Physicists,* by Dürrenmatt, at the Aldwych in 1963

In the spring of 1964 the Royal Shakespeare Company took Brook's production of *King Lear* on a tour of Eastern Europe. In the top picture Brook and his wife, Natasha, arrive in Moscow; below, Brook, Paul Scofield and Irene Worth are welcomed to Belgrade by the British Ambassador (*second from left*)

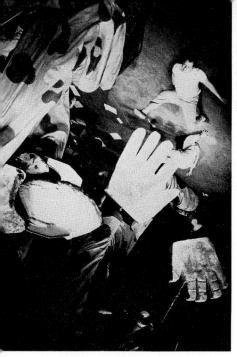

Above right: Glenda Jackson as Charlotte Corday in Brook's production of *The Marat/Sade* by Peter Weiss at the Aldwych, and in New York, in 1964

Above left and below: US explores the relationship between 'something called Vietnam and the man sitting in the stalls at the Aldwych'. The scene above shows the crash of the monstrous doll, a marine commando, on to the stage

Above: Brook's production of the *Oedipus* of Seneca for the
National Theatre Company at the Old Vic in the spring of 1968;
Irene Worth as Jocasta, Colin Blakely as Creon and John
Gielgud as Oedipus

Brook's famous and controversial production of *A Midsummer Night's Dream* at Stratford in 1970. *Opposite:* Sara Kestelman as Titania and David Waller as Bottom surrounded by Brook's idea of the fairies. *Above:* Alan Howard as Oberon and John Kane as Puck look down from their trapezes on Titania and Bottom, lying on the scarlet ostrich feather used for Titania's bower

Puck stilt-walking above
the baffled Demetrius in
one of the later Wood
scenes, and below, the four
lovers on the ladder (*top to
bottom*: Mary Rutherford as
Hermia, Christopher Gable
as Lysander, Frances de la
Tour as Helena and Ben
Kingsley as Demetrius)

Above: Paul Scofield as Lear in the film premiered in 1971, with Jack MacGowran as the Fool.
Below: One of the castles specially built for the film in the wintry wilds of North Jutland

Above: Lear riding with his attendant knights. *Below:* Peter Brook, swathed in furs, directs his *King Lear* company in the Danish snow

discovering the real Shakespeare theatre that had moved and excited an audience, terrified and dazzled it. Brook had presented his Romans as the Renaissance had seen and painted them; moreover, they were presented on a stage which in its essentials returned to the old Elizabethan tradition and achieved a remarkable unity and logic.

To an essay published in *Shakespeare Our Contemporary*, where he praised *Titus*, Kott gave the title, *King Lear; or, Endgame*. This examined the tragedy in terms of Samuel Beckett's play: the theme of *Lear* was the decay and fall of the world, Man destroyed by a universe without reason or interest in human fate. Gloucester was right when he said, 'This great world shall so wear out to nought'. Brook had read the essay soon after the publication of the French version in 1962. When he directed *Lear* at Stratford that autumn, his basis was existential; he regarded the play as the 'epic unfolding of the nature of the absurdity of the human condition.' His company underwent a rehearsal period of gritting intensity that Charles Marowitz, then Brook's assistant director, mapped in a journal that he called *Lear Log*.* Here he described how Brook saw the play as a mountain whose summit had never been reached, with the shattered bodies of other climbers strewn on every side. To him it was mainly about blindness and sight, sight that once acquired looks only into a void. The plot was Beckettian, the scene a metaphysical farce that ridiculed life, death, sanity and illusion. Marowitz summarized Brook's production approach as 'relentlessly (and at times, maddeningly) experimental. He believes that there is no such thing as the "right way". Every rehearsal dictates its own rhythm and its own state of completion. If what is wrong today is wrong tomorrow, tomorrow will reveal it, and it is through the constant elimination of possibilities that Brook finally arrives at interpretation.'

Slowly, the play was worked into its new theatre shape. In fact, by the time *Lear* reached the Stratford stage, Brook had been preparing it for more than a year; the production, because of Scofield's illness (and holiday in the Isle of Mull), had been postponed from earlier in the season, and after this he had scrapped the whole of his original set. One advantage: when it finally arrived, *Lear* had cost five thousand pounds less than planned. It was not until 6 November 1962, extremely late for a Festival première, that

---

* First printed in *Encore* (1963) and reprinted in *Theatre at Work*, edited by Charles Marowitz and Simon Trussler, London, 1967.

E

it opened before a Royal Shakespeare audience, unaware of the intense cerebral activity behind the night, the rigorous textual analysis, the method of the verse-speaking – no generalized rhythm, but each character with a rhythm as personal as his hand-writing – the experiments and improvisations, the awkward visual problem. That night, after Brook had at last left the actors to it – during the morning there had been a run-through hearteningly relaxed – *Lear* had the most blazing ovation in its modern history.

Playgoers' memories are often short; but many in the Stratford house had known the full mountain-range of Lears, from Ayrton to Laughton; such an audience as this is not given to easy applause.

Undeniably the union of Brook and Scofield was startling, though without a crib few could have said precisely what the director meant. Workers who have brooded over a production for many months believe that an audience must discern every shaving of the idea. It is not so; and after this première it took a little while for people to sort themselves out and for the general scheme of the production to shape itself. On the night we had simply to experience the event, to let the play wash over us, as Desmond MacCarthy put it in a note on drama criticism, and afterwards to examine the markings in the sand.

v

The Stratford stage was surrounded by tall, coarse-textured, subtly off-white screens against which were disposed various shapes of metal that looked as if they had been lifted, in their rust, from the sea depths. During the first scene and its deliberate hieratic pre-liminaries, Lear, more sinner than sinned against – 'a guttural upstart', said Alan Brien – was a figure of rigid arrogance, a pagan king set in tarnished gold, his hands clenched upon the arms of a crudely fashioned throne. This was established against a huge elliptical shield that seemed to act as a sounding-board for Scofield. A man not yet infirm, a ruler in command, never a stereotype of the pathetic old father, feeble or sentimental, the actor used a voice that made me think of a ground-swell, an intermittent surge beneath the vaulting of a sea-cave. Certain vowels had a strange rough nasality (more than once, and curiously, I was reminded of a record of Forbes-Robertson speaking Shakespeare in his last years). The forked beard and the fringe of whisker were grizzled, the eyes narrowed beneath their thatch of brow. We saw this Lear as a figure from a primeval, pagan world in a rusting Iron Age; an 'unameliorated world', as T. C. Worsley put it; one that, in its time, had blazed and smouldered, but that now, tried in the furnace, seemed to be flaking before our eyes. All was rough and primitive; a place of abstract symbols. Garments were shaped from worn, patched leather and heavy-textured wool. Not a primary colour was visible. Even the map appeared to be little more than a faded scroll. Later, with Lear among the riot of his drunken knights, his cropped head was bare, his eyes – in this sight-haunted tragedy – were wide and restless. As he strode the stage in leather coat and thigh-boots, his voice (said Alan Brien) 'sometimes like a rusty hammer', he resembled for a moment an ancient sea-captain commanding the bridge of his vessel, defying the cosmic fates as he drove unmanned towards death. Here I was reminded of a description by William Poel:*

After the first scene Lear should appear in hunting costume, big leather boots, leather jerkin, leather cap. Unless it is remembered that in appearance he is a big, burly fellow, interest in the dramatic action of the play will be considerably weakened. He should be able to show that he has as much physical strength as the youngest and strongest man on the stage. His face is purple from long exposure to the air in the hunting-field, and his close-cropped hair quite white, this being the only indication of his great age. On no account should his figure stoop until he is broken down with grief. His manners are brusque, impulsive and dominating. When moved his outburst of passion is titanic and uncontrollable, causing him to form decisions opposed to his own interest and even to his own safety.

The storm was raised, on a bare stage, by the appearance of men who crouched and huddled against the elements; by the slow descent of what resembled three black, rusted, rectangular metal guillotines that aided the thunder's reverberation; and by Scofield's Lear as he defied the apocalyptic storm with a mighty, sustained cry of 'Blow, winds!', the first vowel extended. During rehearsal one of the corroded thunder-sheets, each of them fitted with a small motor that enabled it to vibrate, was shaken from its moorings by a sudden motor failure, and sent with a crash to the stage only a few inches from Brook and his lighting team. Nobody heard about it until well after the première; but the actors' awareness of what had happened added to the scene a fresh spirit of apprehension.

As the night moved on, nothing was left but the environing screens, with the King and Gloucester ('a shrivelled walnut of a creature,' said Bamber Gascoigne), two old men who had reached

* In 1919; reprinted in *Monthly Letters,* London, 1929.

the common destiny deprived of everything, two lonely voices at the world's end, playing out their colloquy on a stark infinity of stage. Lear at first had had the strength of an ironbound winter. Arrogant age overthrown, cut to the brains, he passed at length from the fearful quietness of 'O, let me not be mad' to the bent head, the quadruple 'Howl!' and the quintuple 'Never!', the moment when death was lord of all and man could do no more than die. Besides Scofield we had the helpless agony of Alan Webb's Gloucester; a Regan and Goneril (Patience Collier and Irene Worth) with a certain early provocation; Alec McCowen as the Fool with a sight sharper than anyone; and a Kent (Tom Fleming) who shouted the last 'Vex not his ghost!' as guardian of a Lear who would not have wished to return to a life that bound him on a wheel of fire. There was little pity or sympathy in the production. Edmund was not allowed his line, 'But Edmund was beloved.' In the middle of the play, too, Brook had cut the two commiserating servants who take pity on Gloucester when he is thrust, blind, from the door. Instead, hustled and unaided, he made his groping exit upstage in the full glare of the suddenly raised house-lights. Earlier, Cornwall had blinded him with a pair of golden spurs, a grim scene for those unable to face this moment in performance. (Long ago, Lilian Baylis, at the Old Vic, insisted that it should always be played as the first scene after the interval, so that those playgoers who wished could remain in the coffee-bar until it was over: many did.)

Overnight at Stratford, no applauding critic – and practically everyone applauded – fully guessed the genesis of Brook's production, the intricacies of his approach: his insistence that *King Lear* is not primarily the tale of one individual, the rusting ironclad King; his view of the relationship of Edgar and Edmund; his belief that the 'whole play, besides being about sight and blindness – what sight amounts to, what blindness means – is also concerned with sclerosis opposing the flow of existence, cataracts that dissolve, rigid attitudes that yield, while at the same time obsessions form and positions harden'. Did anybody, uninstructed, realize on the first night the peculiar emphasis Brook gave to the last lines of Edgar (in the Quarto they are Albany's): 'We that are young Shall never see so much, nor live so long'? Did anyone realize immediately that the tragedy was a 'vast, complex, coherent poem designed to study the power and the emptiness of nothing – the positive and negative aspects latent in the zero'? The meaning, Brook had said, would be for the moment of performance. I think he asked too much of his first hearers, something, I agree, that is far better than asking too little.

Gradually, but after the première, we recognized that Brook had directed a Beckettian *Lear,* an end-game of the heath. He and his company had set out deliberately not to move their audience; at all costs to avoid a catharsis (an aspiration that in this play is near-impossible, however a director may try). Brook did not believe himself that being moved by *Lear* was as exciting as what really happened to the people, and what they meant; for that reason he kept the stage in a bright light so that romantic illusion was lost and something more considerable (at once Elizabethan and modern) gained. He had held that Olivier's Lear, much earlier, had failed because the actor, approaching the 'massive flood of energy' from a nineteenth-century point of view, had set out to paint a portrait as Sargent or Annigoni might have done. One would hardly have used those names at Stratford in November 1962.

The *Lear,* four hours of it – 'ample room the characters of Hell to trace' – went up to the Aldwych in December, more or less to critical unanimity. Soon afterwards, at a British Drama League meeting, Brook described Lear's situation as that of a man who has reached such a point of arterio-sclerosis, become so locked in his own world, that he cannot see beyond his nose. Shakespeare has brought several situations to this difficult question: 'As you impose yourself more and more on the world, are you getting somewhere, or is this making you worse and worse?' And Brook ended with Edgar's last lines. Lear, after dreadful torment, is dead, without hint that he is going to heaven or receiving reward; Edgar, no shining hero, says in effect: 'Is it worth it? Your reward is that you have been through it. Is the experience worth it at the price?'

Later, there would be some dissent, little from professional drama critics, though I doubt whether, like audiences in general, many of them responded precisely as Brook wished. I know that, while admiring the production's strength and consistency, I still found myself making the familiar responses to *Lear:* one cannot be changed entirely in an evening. Scholars continued to be troubled. Thus, in *King Lear in Our Time,** Professor Maynard Mack, of Yale, suggested that Brook had overlooked the fact that Goneril and Regan are paradigms of evil rather than – or as well as – spoilt children whose patience is exhausted. Professor Mack held that, in

* London, 1969.

an attempt to rationalize *Lear*, too much had been made of what the day's jargon called the 'subtext', or underlying 'reality' to which the text pointed: words could become expendable and a director totally subjective.

Robert Speaight, the Shakespearian actor and scholar, returned to the production in his Theodore Spencer Lecture at Harvard in October 1969.* He claimed that, though the value of the scene for the servants after Gloucester's blinding can hardly be overstressed, showing as it does the reaction of average humanity to conduct monstrously inhuman and preparing us for the nemesis of crime, it was omitted because it did not suit the director's *parti pris*. Further, Edmund's line in the last scene, countermanding the execution of Lear and Cordelia, 'Some good I mean to do despite of my own nature', was cut on the ground that it was a concession to sentiment. Further, though Shakespeare, having finished magnanimously with Edmund, carefully removed him from the stage, Brook removed everyone else, so that Edgar, with 'Let's exchange charity' hardly out of his mouth, might lug the body into the wings like a slaughtered pig. Speaight added:

Many directors have wondered why Shakespeare so inconveniently brought back the corpses of Regan and Goneril: there are always so many corpses littering the stage at the close of a Shakespearian tragedy that it seemed gratuitous to add to them. I thought this way myself until, on the second occasion of directing the play, I decided to see what would happen if I followed the stage directions. Two things happened – each extremely significant. Edmund lay dying in the middle of the stage with the bodies of Regan and Goneril, on their litters, to R. and L. of him. This enkindled one last flicker of vanity in that insatiable *coureur:*

> Yet Edmund was beloved:
> The one the other poisoned for my sake,
> And after slew herself.

A few moments later Lear entered with Cordelia in his arms, and we had the same picture at the end of the play that we had at the beginning: 'There was once an old king, and he had three daughters' – only now the old king was dying and the three daughters were dead. It was not difficult to see why Shakespeare had brought two of them back.

VI

Lear, that complex inter-action of people, events, and ideas, as Brook called it, had a steadily triumphant run in the Aldwych

* On 'The Cycle of Shakespeare Production'.

repertory. During May 1963 it went to the Théâtre des Nations in Paris and promptly caused a black market in tickets for the Théâtre Sarah-Bernhardt. Paul Scofield occupied Bernhardt's dressing-room; *Le Monde* was delighted to find that Stratford's official company could take *Lear* in an avant-garde spirit; and the company shared the Grand Prix with the Theatre Workshop Company from the other Stratford (atte-Bowe) in *Oh! What a Lovely War!* In the following spring, Shakespeare Quatercentenary Year, the production, with some cast changes – Ian Richardson instead of James Booth as Edmund, John Laurie instead of Alan Webb as Gloucester – began, with *The Comedy of Errors*, a long British Council tour of European capitals, particularly in Eastern Europe. Later the players visited the United States. Wherever they went in Europe, they were applauded. 'We must change our lives,' Iván Boldizsár editor of the *New Hungarian Quarterly*, said in Budapest, a city famed for its Shakespearian scholarship and possessing in Miklós Gábor one of the majestic actors of his time. In Belgrade President Tito came to talk to the cast. On the last Rumanian night riots developed in the streets of Bucharest; students trying to break into the theatre, and every part of the house, except the President's box, packed to its distant crevices. Critics in Moscow praised a performance in depth, the emergence of 'psychological and philosophical realities'; at the opening Sviatoslav Richter, the Russian pianist, led twenty minutes' applause from the front row. I like especially a brief news story published in a Czech paper after the first performance in the great green and gold Smetanova Divadlo in Prague:

Six minutes before *King Lear* was due to start, a man hailed a taxi far away in Strasnice. 'Can we get there in time?' The driver willingly gave it a try. One minute before the time the taxi stopped in front of the theatre. Neither the driver nor the passenger had small money. A banknote changed hands. 'I shall bring you the small change after the performance.' And he did. The name of the taxi-driver is Comrade Buldro, from the Trojická Street Garages. A truly exemplary service.

At length the company reached the United States. Brook remarked on the difference between audiences there and in Europe. European playgoers brought with them a love for the play, hunger for contact with foreigners, and an experience of life that took them directly to Shakespeare's painful themes. These things they expressed is silence, concentration, a sympathy that caused the actors to probe and illuminate the most obscure passages. But in America people came largely for the conventional reasons without real interest in the play; so the company found itself instinctively exploiting the louder, cruder moments and ignoring subtleties that Europe had relished.

Lear had been booked in New York during May at the costly State Theatre, less than a month old, in the Lincoln Centre. Unfortunately the acoustics were dire. Critics unfavourably placed had trouble in hearing; speakers had to fight a blurring echo. During the interval a horrified Brook, for the first time in his career, had to ask the players to face the house directly, to speak slower, to enunciate more precisely and, in the process, to 'throw away all that had become precious in their work'. He had ended *Lear* on a distant rumble that might presage another storm; and when the play was over that night, his own storm broke. He was angry that a dramatic company should have been invited to act in the building before the sound problems had been solved; even angrier that neither the architect nor the acoustical expert had come to listen. For all that, the company conquered. Howard Taubman, in the *New York Times,* said that the stage was like 'a vast, empty, heartless earth', and that Brook had produced a masterpiece with regard to the noble arch of its structure. Robert Brustein, in the *New Republic,* spoke of 'a work of admirable intelligence, carefully conceived, and beautifully executed; even its coldness, a quality which restrains one's enthusiasm, is part of a considered pattern. . . . The pacing is sluggish and numbed and full of pauses; the spiritual landscape is frozen and dead. . . . The actors appear less like characters than like dolmens – ancient, broken, irregular stones.' It was an extraordinary move from that shredded television *Lear* of nine years before. The last words can be Harold Clurman's: 'Cocteau once asked Sergei Diaghilev, his master, what that great impresario expected of him. "Astonish me" Diaghilev answered. Stagecraft cannot find a more brilliant summation. If Peter Brook's *Lear* could claim no further distinction, it would still be memorable because it is astonishing.'*

It was a word that Brook would have valued.

VII

That American visit was in the early summer of 1964. But a great deal had happened since Peter Brook had first begun to excavate *Lear*. In the spring of 1962 Natasha, in Paris, had given birth to

* *The Naked Image,* New York, 1966.

their first child, Irina Demetria, born on 5 April and christened in the Russian Church. Natasha had said, not long before this, that she and Peter travelled round so continuously that sometimes it was hard to know where she was: 'We came in hungry one evening to our Kensington cottage, and I said: "There are some sardines in a drawer in the kitchen." But there were not. They were in the drawer in the kitchen in our Paris flat. When you get muddled like that, it's time to settle down.'

Peter, not a born settler, moved from challenge to challenge, and when he was not directing he could always debate. 'Lack of discussion, lack of theorising, is a sort of pride among the English. Artistic talk has always been considered highly suspect.' He wrote in an *Encore* article about this time: 'I believe in the word in classical drama because the word was the dramatists' tool. I don't believe in the word much today because it has outlived its purpose. Words don't communicate, they don't express much, and much of the time they fail abysmally to define.' Reading this after revivals of such different dramatists as Eliot and O'Casey, I wonder a little; but the gospel is Artaudian, and at that stage Brook was growing more and more towards Artaud. He would write later in *The Empty Space*:

Is it that we are living in an age of images? Is it even that we must go through a period of image-saturation, for the need for language to re-emerge? This is very possible, for today writers seem unable to make ideas and images collide through words with Elizabethan force. The most influential of modern writers, Brecht, wrote full and rich texts, but the real conviction of his plays is inseparable from the imagery of his own productions. Yet in the desert one prophet raised his voice. Railing against the sterility of the theatre before the war, in France, an illuminated genius, Antonin Artaud, wrote tracts describing from his imagination and intuition another theatre – a Holy Theatre in which the blazing centre speaks through those forms closest to it. A theatre working like the plague, by intoxication, by infection, by analogy, by magic; a theatre in which the play, the event itself, stands in place of a text.

Almost immediately after Irina's birth, Brook accepted an invitation to join the directorate of the Royal Shakespeare Company, now under the artistic leadership of Peter Hall (who as a youth of sixteen had admired *Love's Labour's Lost* at Stratford): the third triumvir was Michel Saint-Denis. Brook told an American interviewer: 'In the RSC we shudder at the memory of our theatre's former name, the sepulchral, never-to-be-forgotten words, "Memorial Theatre". For us this is a living place; our purpose is to excite and concern

living people today.' *King Lear* was his first production as a director
of the RSC, and in the spring of 1963, with *Lear* in the London
repertory, he directed another production at the Aldwych. This was
a *comédie noire* by Friedrich Dürrenmatt, old friend of *The Visit*. It
was set in a lunatic asylum (that symbol of the modern world), and
John Bury's set at once reminded me of lines in quite another
context: 'Those the wall was to enclose alive, within the tomb.' A
murder had just been committed. Because the curtain was up when
the play began, the corpse, unhappy actress, had to get into place
with loyal fortitude half an hour before she was needed. We
gathered that she had been strangled by an apparently insane
nuclear physicist claiming to be Einstein. Two other patients, also
physicists, also stranglers, were a tall, wry figure – wearing a period
wig with a certain abandon – who called himself Sir Isaac Newton,
and another who was impelled, so he said, by King Solomon.
Throughout the first half, Dürrenmatt kept us unsure, Pirandello-
fashion, about the true mental condition of the three men, watched
by the asylum's hunchbacked psychotic superintendent (Irene
Worth); we suspected that she was herself trembling on the edge of
madness, and the end of the play, a theatrical grand slam, showed
how far we were justified in thinking so. Before then we had
realized that the trio (acted by Alan Webb, Michael Hordern, and
Cyril Cusack) had taken refuge from the world in order to keep
their fatal discoveries from it. While considering *The Physicists,* Peter
Brook may have thought of *Huis Clos* years earlier, and at the end he
could well have remembered two lines in *Lear:*

> The justice of the heavens, that makes us tremble,
> Touches us not with pity.

Violence at large had always fascinated Dürrenmatt. Here his play,
far better than *The Visit,* was like a growing thunderstorm, the
rising cloud-anvil, the deadly waiting, the release of violence
uncontrolled; the dramatist's questions about a nuclear scientist's
responsibility forked across the text like lightning. The play, and
Brook's concentrated precision, had a sequence of enviable notices.

Already Brook was collaborating in a production at Stratford; but
before this, in March 1963, he had returned for a night to his old job
as ballet critic, and on the same paper, the *Observer*. At the Covent
Garden première of *Marguerite and Armand,* he found himself
asking whether he was just bored with the romantic past. The
tradition of the English theatre that depended on manner, not

matter, had withered away; romance had turned to an empty
husk. 'I am confirmed in my belief that . . . the great red curtain
has not much left to hide.' Almost at once a production of *The
Tempest* – the exact phrase was 'Directed by Clifford Williams in
collaboration with Peter Brook' – opened the 1963 season at
Stratford. Clifford Williams said before it began:

The curious thing about the way Peter Brook and I discussed *The Tempest*
is how at first we skirted talking of what it's about. Our discussions were
almost purely in graphic terms, as if we had a tacit agreement on its
content. For the play is the whole world, and who can say what the world
is about? The play is termed a romance, but you can't present a romance
in romantic terms – the baroque, the rococo, we don't respond to them
any more. Romance in that sense is a lie about life; fairy-tales exclude all
the messy, inevitable facts of the world. The play is full of movement and
change, a flux of character in which only Ariel and perhaps Antonio are
stable; if there is any reconciliation at the end, there is infinitely more
irresolution.

It is this irresolution, which we believe is deliberate, that we have tried
to present. A man spends his life trying to perfect his responses to the
world, to control himself and nature; he still ends up senile. In this play,
Shakespeare includes all the themes from his earlier work – kingship,
inheritance, treachery, conscience, identity, love, music, God; he draws
them together as if to find the key to it all, but there is no such key. There
is no grand order, and Prospero returns to Milan not bathed in tranquillity,
but a wreck 'where every third thought shall be my grave'.

At one time we thought of lifting all the scenery away at the end (as
happens in one of Roland Petit's ballets), or of putting all the characters
of the finale in clown's costumes, to underline the derisory nature of the
play's 'resolution'.

However much exaltation there is towards the end of the play, there is
also a positive atmosphere of debasement. The masque may be 'heavenly',
but Prospero refers to its participants as 'rabble'. Caliban's grovelling
humility before the fine lords, his decision to 'seek for grace hereafter' is
shamefully ironic, and the shame touches all of us. Perhaps this needs a
stronger dose of de-sentimentalising if we, and the audience, are to cut
through the preconceptions which surround the play.

After *Lear* the production came as an anti-climax. Against a circular
galactic background, a translucent shell or skin, vague and brittle,
the bottom half of perspex, the top half of cinema-screen plastic lit
by four projectors on trolleys, all the enchantments of Prospero's
isle were those of *musique concrète* and abstract art. The people of the
imperilled vessel entered upon a moving strip, as if they were bound

from Waterloo to the Bank, appearing again presently on the fore-stage where they were duly swept under in the least persuasive of many *Tempest* wrecks. It was an island of trap-doors, blurred chameleon-like shadows, suddenly sprouting stools and clothes-lines, a 'black bombard' cloud like the nightmare of a pawnbroker's sign, and a masque where the three spirits were accompanied by what seemed to be immense, tottering 'corn-dollies', amorphous shapes, perhaps Artaudian 'effigies yards high'. Abd'Elkader Farrah, the designer, spoke of 'ethereal marionettes, blurred and soft like the shapes of the set'. Among all this the fantasy (with Tom Fleming as Prospero) struggled for existence. 'Of all the plays, none is so baffling and elusive as *The Tempest*,' Brook said later; he would return to it on his own.

VIII

At this time he was enmeshed with possibly the least-known of all his productions, a musical by Julian More and Monty Norman, his *Irma la Douce* associates. Entitled *The Perils of Scobie Prilt*, and under the James Bond influence, it opened among chaos at the New Theatre, Oxford, during the second week of June 1963: the sets were so big, and so full of technical complications, that the original date, a Tuesday, had to be abandoned, and the play opened on the following evening for what proved to be a four days' life. It was a medley of science fiction and secret agents: something about a young scientist (the 'pop' singer, Michael Sarne) who had dis-covered a method of turning people into robots. While he was on the way to a middle-European country with his large black box, a female spy (Nyree Dawn Porter) blew up his train; the musical went on from there. This chaotic business had everything in it between a rocket-launching and a film show; but in spite of Rolf Gérard's designs and Brook's gallantly inventive production – no longer the classical explorer, but for the last time the young man happy among his toys – nothing went right. Miss Porter played on only one night before a spinal accident obliged her to go into hospital in London; an understudy, book in hand, took over the part at three hours' notice. On the second night another leading member of the cast pulled a cartilage in his leg and had to limp through to the end of the play. After the Saturday night *Scobie Prilt* was withdrawn. Brook had known indeed, from the first ten minutes of working on it, that the thing – unlike *Irma* – was going wrong: it was as if he were pouring invention into a bottomless bucket.

While *Scobie* was still in rehearsal, Peter and Natasha had moved into a new London home in 50 Holland Street, Kensington. Once in, and after a Tunisian holiday and an appearance at an Edinburgh Festival discussion when he asked if we were present at 'the death of the word' – an obsession at the time – he turned once more to Paris and to an exciting production, at the Théâtre de l'Athénée, of *La Danse de Sergent Musgrave*. While filming *Lord of the Flies* in Puerto Rico, Brook had read the first half of John Arden's drama in *Plays and Players*. Deeply impressed, he got the second half, and now his Paris production had emerged, with the talented Laurent Terzieff as Musgrave and '*mise en scène, décors, et costumes de Peter Brook*'. This is the piece, harsh as an inexorable lava-flow, that Arden has set in a strike-bound, winter-clenched Northern mining town during the eighteen-eighties. During the last act the fanatical sergeant, 'Black Jack' Musgrave, produces in the town square his machine-gun and a uniformed skeleton to show what war can mean, and what revenge he proposes to take. Finally, in his desperate efforts to explain himself, he begins a rhythmic stamping out of which a savage dance and chant develop. The play had a poor Press in the powerful Right-Wing papers, and nobody came to the theatre. On the day after the major reviews, which had spoken of a hysterical and pretentious bore, only five people appeared, though there had been enthusiasm among the intellectual Left Wing critics. Brook was sure that somewhere there ought to be an audience, so they advertised a trio of free performances and immediately had to face swarming crowds and queues around the theatre. Police pulled iron grilles across the main doors. The company, stirred by a crowded and swiftly alert audience, had never acted better. It appeared to be a young, well-dressed house; when, after the play Arthur Adamov, the Left Wing dramatist, and the film directors, Alain Resnais and Jean-Luc Godard came upon the stage with Brook and the actors, a debate lasted for two hours, indeed until after the last Métro had gone; nobody left his seat. Françoise Spira, who ran the Athénée, asked if anyone was there who could not have afforded a ticket. One man held up his hand. Then why had the rest of them hung back until they could get free admission? The play had had a bad Press. True; but did they believe the Press? Cries of 'No'. Then what did it all mean? Answer: it was too great a risk to come to see for themselves; an expensive seat did not carry with it the guarantee of an enjoyable evening. Brook wrote to the *Sunday Times:* 'The essential point to be grasped, in my view, is that there are countless theatre enthusiasts who are perfectly content never to go to the theatre. Then subsidise the theatre. As other prices rise, the cost of theatre seats must begin to fall.' A sharp cut in prices brought some money to the Athénée box-office, and for a time the play was able to run.

Brook followed it by co-directing, with François Darbon, a production of *Le Vicaire,* acted in London as *The Representative*, Rolf Hochhuth's play about the dilemma of Pope Pius XII. During the war, should the Pope have broken the Concordat with Hitler and condemned the Nazi slaughter of the Jews, instead of regarding the Holy See as the spirit of neutrality, impartial mediation? Two scenes are masterly in a very long play that needs selective editing: the argument in a small throne-room at the Vatican, and the last duel in the abyss of Auschwitz between the spokesmen of Heaven and Hell, the Jesuit who has allowed himself to be taken to the camp, a voluntary martyr, and the devilish 'Doctor' (a war criminal still uncaught). In Paris the première of Brook's production, with Jean Topart as the 'Doctor', was interrupted several times by a few people who threw pamphlets and stink-bombs, and who were said to be members of a Catholic group representing a non-existent League for Liberty of Thought. It was an occasion for debate that ended peacefully, with members of the audience standing about outside the theatre into the cold midnight, discussing what they had seen. Though demonstrations of various kinds continued nightly at first, the play outlived them, and six months later, calmly now, it was still running at the Athénée. Brook had directed with complete simplicity, using no glib emotional effects and staging the play against a cycloramic setting that left the audience to concentrate on the argument.

Back in Stratford, as if he had not done so already, Brook had cut himself off sharply from his romantic youth in the theatre. To the Royal Shakespeare Company's pamphlet, *Crucial Years*, he contributed his statement that productions and sets must move away from romance, from fantasy, from decoration. 'Outer splendour can be exciting, but has little relation to modern life; on the inside lie themes and issues, rituals and conflicts which are as valid as ever. Any time the Shakespearian meaning is caught, it is "real" and so contemporary.' Brook had always been ready to experiment, to be capable of what T. C. Worsley had called 'splendid madnesses'.

Now he was outstripping some of his admirers who panted to keep up with him as he marched purposefully – and with a smile as ready as ever – further and further away from the theatre in which he had been bred. Who spoke now of a Watteau *fête-champêtre*? Where the 'great tent of Mediterranean blue'?

X

Theatricalities: 1964-1965

I

IT was a period when nearly everything had to have such a label as the Theatre of the Absurd, or the Theatre of Menace, or, ironically, the Theatre of the Opaque. So it was natural that there should be a revived Theatre of Cruelty, though Brook, using the title for his experimental workshop as a tribute to the inventor, Antonin Artaud, surrealist poet and avant-garde visionary of modern French drama, did not propose to create an Artaudian theatre, or to suggest that Artaud's phase could cover any drama of violence. Rather, it meant immediacy and intensity of expression, a theatre of nerves and senses, of non-verbal, physical means of expression; as many shocks as possible, 'theatricalities of all kinds'. (But not, it seemed, those 'forms of mystery and surprise' in the lost theatre of colour and movement during the late Forties). In the words of Patricia Louise Ryan, elements of the Theatre of Cruelty could be in any play or production from which the audience received a vital and instantaneous subjective experience.

Brook decided that Jean Genet's comment on the Algerian war, *Les Paravents (The Screens)* would be an important play to stage, but that a group would have to be intensively rehearsed for some time. The Royal Shakespeare subsidized the venture, amply and embracingly; and the London Academy of Music and Dramatic Art gave the use of its new and flexible experimental theatre in Earls Court. A company was recruited, with Charles Marowitz's aid, and after a bizarre audition period in which candidates were required to improvize and mime until their heads reeled. Those whose heads reeled least, became the first dozen members of a company for twelve weeks' exploration of acting and stagecraft problems in laboratory conditions without the commercial pressures of performance. Brook had resolved to break the rigidity of the one-dimensional approach to playing, and also to secure a special group rhythm and rapid adaptability to change. The company would seek to discover whether thoughts could live and communication exist without the medium of speech.

In January 1964 the workshop first revealed itself at the Lamda Theatre with an esoteric programme, a public work-in-progress session. Here were such things as Artaud's three-minute surrealist sketch, *A Spurt of Blood,* presented both in the original text and entirely in screams; various mimes and improvisations; two collages created by Brook; and Marowitz's brief and pointless *Hamlet* variation, the lines in a scrambled shake-up and the Prince as a stricken clown. Brook called the programme 'a form of surrealist revue composed of shots in the dark; shots at distant targets. We are exploring theatre language.' Again: 'We present the programme at a time when all conventions of the theatre have been challenged, and there are no rules any more. . . . Meanwhile the need to define a true experience in the theatre is as urgent as ever.' From one point of view, the devisers said, Artaud's 'cruelty' could be seen as an attempt to recover the Shakespearian variety of expression by other means; an experiment, employing Artaud's work as a springboard, rather than as a model for slavish reconstruction, could also be a search for theatre language as agile and penetrating as the Elizabethans'. The theatre had moved away from narrative and naturalism. Now this programme sought deliberately to get away from words. (I still do not know what the *Hamlet* paste-up tried to prove.)

Certain things went extremely well, especially the bath scene in which a girl (Glenda Jackson) was stripped, bathed, and dressed in a prison uniform to the words of a report on the recent Christine Keeler case; the same words were then used to transform her into Mrs Kennedy at the President's funeral. But, in sum, the directors and the players knew what they were doing more than the audiences that watched them. Brook certainly knew. He explained to an interviewer that he was eager to explore further a field he had entered long ago in *Salome,* and in different forms, in *Titus Andronicus* and *Lord of the Flies:* 'a field in which ritual and what one calls "outside reality" completely overlap; this is the world of Genet.' Bamber Gascoigne suggested in the *Observer:* 'There is a world of difference between doing something new and looking for something new to do. The Lamda experiment may be, I fear, little but a public love affair with the mere idea of newness, supported by woolly romantic notions about the crisis in theatre and society.'

Brook went cheerfully on, fortified by encouraging private comment. Martin Esslin, recalling the production two years later,*
wrote of *The Public Bath:*

Brook demonstrated that, through a mere rearrangement of figures in the
stage, a magical effect can actually be produced – the same girl in the same
raincoat can be transformed from an object of disgust into one of reverence,
a tin bathtub into a coffin, merely by a change of context not only in
space, but also in time. It was not merely the groupings that changed
(although not very much); it was that before the ritual cleansing the girl
was by implication unclean and, after it, cleansed and pure.

II

While the Lamda experiment was still being discussed, and while
Brook was preparing for his next effort, at the unexpected address
of a rehearsal room in Seven Dials, down by the Cambridge Theatre,
he found himself once more, for a single afternoon, in Birmingham.
A welcomed rebel among the academics, he had travelled up to
receive the University's honorary degree of Doctor of Letters at the
same time as Margaret Leighton, the actress, and the Shakespearian
scholars, Wolfgang Clemen and Louis Booker Wright.

It was the day after Shakespeare's Quatercentenary, an occasion
for which Brook had already expressed in the *Birmingham Post* part
of his creed as a director:

We have traditions of Shakespearian production, but these are not
Shakespearian traditions; they come from the Victorian theatre. Every
attempt to produce a play of Shakespeare in an orthodox post-Victorian
manner that claims to allow the play to speak for itself is a stifling of the
play. In Stratford we are all very much aware of a responsbility, through
bold experiment and the risk of failure, to create a new tradition, to put
into question the entire process of interpretation, to revivify Shakespeare's
meaning, moment for moment, with today's means for today's spectators.

(He might have added: Remember *Lear.*) There was no sign of
academic distaste on this sunny April afternoon at Edgbaston when
Peter Stephen Paul Brook became the University's youngest
Honorary Graduand. He heard the Public Orator, Professor
Douglas Hubble, recalling the past life of a man who must, at
times, have seemed only dimly like the Peter Brook on the University
platform. Where was the youth who had directed *King John* at Sir
Barry Jackson's theatre, and *Love's Labour's Lost* at Stratford? But

---

* *New York Times Magazine,* 6 March 1966.

Professor Hubble also had the audience cheering when he recalled *Titus* and the fresh thinking in *Lear:* 'Our interest must lie in the future of this great and still young producer.' Presently, Peter Brook, when he responded on behalf of his fellow graduands, wondered mischievously whether he could execute the 'piece of business' he had seen the Public Orator performing. There was room for experiment, so he turned directly to address the 'Most Honourable Vice-Chancellor', doffing his academic cap according to custom, and receiving from Sir Robert Aitken the traditional acknowledgment. It was the most agreeably theatrical part of the afternoon. Peter Brook, D.Litt. (Hon.), went back to his preparation of the first twelve scenes of the Genet play at the Donmar Rehearsal Theatre in Earlham Street, Seven Dials. He had chosen the play, he said – hopefully, if not persuasively – because Genet was among the few authors who tried all the time to make his meaning not from his text alone, but from 'a geometric structure in which words and action criss-crossed to produce deeper sense'. *The Screens*, a commentary on the Algerian conflict, with a central theme of redemption, had to be an acquired taste, even if somebody with a certain touch of humour likened it to the Cathedral of Chartres in 'its rigour of construction and richness of detail'. Whatever one thought of the play, one could appreciate the close subtleties of lighting and movement, Brook's use of moving screens, and the general fluency of a performance that showed the growth of the company since its workshop weeks; clearly it had been trained in the languages of sight, sound, and silence. The strongest passage was the burning of an orchard, symbolized by a headlong rush of incendiarists to paint red flames higher and higher upon the canvas screens. A rehearsal impressed Grigori Kozintsev, director of the Soviet film of *Hamlet:**

Upon opening the door I fell from a London street straight into our 1920s. It is a smallish room, with a steeply raked platform and unplastered walls. There is no curtain, just a platform with white screens. . . . During the course of the action, a capitalist, a French general who has come to Algeria for a while, and a prostitute . . . had an unhurried discussion. Meantime, far upstage, darkly tanned Algerians appeared in white burnooses. In a rapid-fire tempo, using pieces of red chalk, the latter scribbled tongues of flame on to the white screens. Towards the end of the episode, the white platform was covered from top to bottom with

---

* *Shakespeare: Time and Conscience,* translated from the Russian by Joyce Vining, London, 1967.

whirling, fiery spots; but the colonialists had not noticed anything, or, more accurately, had not understood any of the events around them, they merely continued their conversation.

The day before I had seen the movie, *Lawrence of Arabia*. Infinite caravans of camels passed by on the screen; though they had been filmed in a real desert, there was no feeling of heat. I felt heat in the combination of light and colour in Peter Brook's production. I understood why the experimental workshop was attached to the Shakespeare Theatre: here they are seeking the white heat of passion and the colour of folk theatre.

III

Back from the United States and the *Lear* opening, Brook got down to a project which put to better service the discoveries and the techniques evolved during the workshop months. Towards the end of August he staged at the Aldwych a play called, in English, *The Persecution and Murder of Marat as Performed by the Inmates of the Asylum of Charenton under the direction of the Marquis de Sade:** a title that would be shortened, inevitably, to *The Marat/Sade*. Its author was Peter Weiss who combined, as Brook said later, Jewish family, Czech upbringing, German language, Swedish home, and Marxist sympathies. One had to realize, as a beginning, that between 1787 and 1811, Monsieur Coulmier, liberal-minded, pre-Freudian director of the Charenton Asylum for lunatics on a ridge near the confluence of the Seine and Marne, established regular theatrical entertainments in his clinic: it was a part of his enlightened therapeutic treatment of the inmates. The Marquis de Sade, now over sixty and with a life of stormy excess behind him, was an inmate of Charenton from 1803 until he died in 1814; he wrote and directed many of its entertainments, and it became fashionable in Paris to visit the asylum, as much as to observe the *louche* behaviour of the lunatics as to watch the performance. The plays were acted on a specially built stage; facing this was a box reserved for the director and his friends; and on each side were stands for selected patients who had to bear the scrutiny of the fashionable Parisian crowd in the stalls. From this rose Peter Weiss's play, set within the communal bathhouse, the hydropathic department of the institution.

Brook had received the manuscript from Weiss, a name new to him, just before he was leaving for the European tour of *Lear* during the spring. He was immensely excited to find a complex of

---

* *Die Verfolgung und Ermordung Jean Paul Marats dargestellt durch die Schauspiel-truppe des Hospizes zu Charenton unter Anleitung des Herrn de Sade.*

people, sounds, and action, in which words were an essential element but not, except for notation, a separable one. Moreover, Weiss's ambition delighted him. The theatre had lacked ambition since its Elizabethan years at a time of new discovery and new hope: London, a city of feverish life, its mad blood stirring, its dramatists, each with a host of furious fancies, children of their day, wanting to know and possess their world and to understand themselves in relation to it. Now, in Weiss, Brook had encountered an author who restrained neither his ambition nor the exuberance of his demands. Obviously, they must join forces. They met during May when the play, without particular success, was staged in Berlin at the Schiller Theatre. Brook told Weiss that the two opposing tendencies, Artaudian (demanding the spectator's complete and intense involvement) and Brechtian (insisting on the spectator's alienation) must come together in performance.

Eventually the experimental group, numbering seventeen now, was fused with the larger company needed for *The Marat/Sade*. Certain ideas used in the Theatre of Cruelty workshop entered the Aldwych production, the bath-tub and guillotine imagery in particular. For most people it proved to be a tumultuous and stimulating spectacle; Brook, in the heat of his rehearsal methods, had had the cast with him for two strenuous months ('The work of rehearsal is looking for meaning, and making it meaningful'). He said at once that he had no time for traditional prettified or melo-dramatic stage madness. Personally he had expert advice from his brother Alexis, a consultant psychiatrist, and he also visited asylums in London and Paris. During a television programme that autumn 'in the course of talking about acting, he managed to say things about insanity that a qualified psychiatrist might have taken years to arrive at' (Jonathan Miller). He told the cast to study paintings by Breughel and Hogarth and etchings by Goya; articles on mental illness were read together; the company saw two French films (*Regard sur la Folie* and *Le Maitre-Fous*) that studied various aspects of madness; and, for two weeks before any script was disclosed, Brook worked with the players severally, trying to get them to 'dig out the madman' from themselves, and to find personal expressions of madness that – while remaining true to the piece – could be sustained for two and a half hours. At first he required the players to create ('We were all convinced that we were going loony,' Glenda Jackson said); then, when they tired, he produced his own ideas, never losing his temper, his eagerness, or his capacity for work. He believed that the only directing method to give results was a fusion of several different methods, all aimed at getting the actor to contribute more and more: every rehearsal became a living process.

As he told Weiss, he approached the play from the Artaudian and Brechtian angles. Herald (Ian Richardson), speaking in octosyllabics, was announcer and satirical commentator; there were signs and placards, and an expository singing chorus of four grotesques. On the other side, the production offered a frightening variety of Artaudian shocks, everything from hallucinations, paroxysms, executions, and whippings, to cries and moans, an infinity of sound variations, and a startling use of make-up. In a preface to the text when it was printed in America, Brook said:

Weiss not only uses total theatre, that time-honoured notion of getting all the elements of the stage to serve the play. His force is not only in the quantity of instruments he uses; it is above all in the jangle produced by the clash of styles. Everything is put in place by its neighbour – the serious by the comic, the noble by the popular, the literary by the crude, the intellectual by the physical: the abstraction is vivified by the stage image, the violence illuminated by the cool flow of thought. The strands of meaning of the play pass to and fro through its structure and the result is a very complex form: as in Genet, it is a hall of mirrors or a corridor of echoes – and one must keep looking front and back all the time to reach the author's sense.

Further:

Everything about this play is designed to crack the spectator on the jaw, then douse him with ice-cold water, then force him to assess intelligently what has happened to him, then give him a kick in the balls, then bring him back to his senses again. . . . It's not exactly Brecht and it's not Shakespearian either, but it's very Elizabethan and very much of our time.

Unwillingly released by Brook from rehearsal, the play reached the Aldwych on 20 August 1964: Geoffrey Skelton's English version adapted into free verse by Adrian Mitchell. Mild first-nighters discovered that they represented simultaneously an early nineteenth-century audience and their twentieth-century selves. In a few hours of punching, kicking, dousing and assessing, Weiss imagined Sade's presentation of a subversive play on Charlotte Corday's murder of the extreme social revolutionary, Jean Paul Marat, at the height of the Terror. Alan Brien described the setting in the *Sunday Telegraph* (23 August):

A towering windowless silo walled with tiny bricks and booby-trapped with sunken pits. Among the inmates with their padded clothes and sunken faces, the devil-worshipping priests and burned-out whores, the lecherous ex-aristos and the lethargic ex-rebels, the childish voluptuaries and the aged virgins, move the black-eyed nuns and the muscle-bound warders.

Bamber Gascoigne said in the *Observer* on the same day:

The lunatics in their shapeless white tunics and strait-jackets make a bustle and swirl somewhere between Breughel and Daumier. Probably the most stunning scene of all is a guillotine sequence, complete with metallic raspings, buckets of paint (red and blue), and other techniques which seemed self-conscious and false in the Theatre of Cruelty isolation at Lamda.

Dramatically, the play was a debate between the paranoiac Marat (Clive Revill), prophet of the totalitarian state, and Sade (Patrick Magee), the cold voluptuary, the anarch, apostle of unbridled individual liberty. But what most people remembered, shuddering, was the visual impact, the 'debris of souls from some private hell' (Milton Shulman), the chalky clothing, the writhing limbs, the hysteria, the grimacing, the lolling heads, the whirr and thud of the guillotine, the buckets of blood, the schizoids and cretins, eroto-maniacs and manic-depressives, the faces peering from the hidden baths, and Charlotte Corday's use of her hair to whip the naked Sade (Charlotte acted by a somnambulistic lunatic expressed agonizingly by Glenda Jackson). Then the end, for Brook saw that the close of a production crowned all: the moment when the entire company, advancing towards the edge of the stage, fell to fighting, and to smashing up the bath-house. On a signal, all went quiet. The audience applauded, whereupon the cast replied with the sudden irony of a slow hand-clap. 'If we had conventional curtain-calls,' said Brook, 'the audience would emerge relieved, and that's the last thing we want.' An Aldwych audience, shocked and bat-tered, never emerged relieved. According to a famous mental specialist: 'It was hard to credit that the actors had not been coached by someone who had worked in chronic mental wards for many years, so resolute was their acting.'

After such an experience, exhaustive and exhausting, some of us felt that we could never face again the conventionally stylized lunacies in the relevant scenes of *The Duchess of Malfi* or *Peer Gynt* (neither of them plays that Brook has yet directed). Weiss, Brook said, stated clearly that the stage image and the stage action should carry his meaning as much as the spoken lines. To separate the meanings would be as childish as it would be to try to separate image and text in, say, *Citizen Kane*.

Early in its run *The Marat/Sade* was caught in the boiling-over of an angry silly-season debate on 'dirty plays'. It came to nothing; but Brook spoke his mind in several interviews. He had had his share of the Theatre of Delight, pretty and pleasant; he was working towards a Theatre of Disturbance. If he could make people leave the theatre with their senses and intelligence jolted and disturbed – here spoke Artaud – then he felt he was getting somewhere. To a *Daily Mail* man* he spoke in his softest, almost soothing tones: 'Violence is the natural artistic language of the times. A play must leave you in a more receptive mood than you were before. It isn't there to "move" people.† That's a ghastly idea. You cry, you have a bath of sentiment. You come out saying you've had a lovely time. I prefer the notion of disturbance which leaves you in a greater state of disturbance.'

In October it was like gliding into a lagoon after a hurricane to reproduce *The Physicists* in New York, at the Martin Beck: Robert Shaw, Hume Cronyn and George Voskovec as the three men, and Jessica Tandy as the hunch-backed matron. It was received appreciatively; but after *The Marat/Sade,* Brook might have said, with Milton: 'All our lives turned to jollity and game.'

IV

He woke on New Year's Day, 1965, to his appointment as a CBE in the New Year Honours. At first, this spring, he was writing and lecturing. Since school debating nights he had been a ready talker. In the late autumn of 1964, when he had spoken at Unesco's Shakespeare Quatercentenary celebration in Paris, calling Shakespeare 'experimental, popular, revolutionary,' his eloquence so exhilarated a Frenchwoman that she cried out: '*Il est formidable, ce gars!*' Now in February 1965, Granada Television invited him to give the first of an annual set of lectures on art and communication: talks in the four Universities of Hull, Keele, Manchester and Shef-

---

* 26 August 1964.
† Robert Brustein on *King Lear* in New York (1964): 'Scofield's first scene with the Fool (played with ethereal sadness by Alec McCowen) is surely one of the most affecting moments in the modern theatre . . . but most of the play is oddly unmoving.'

field, on 'The Theatre Today'. These, when revised a few years later, would be published as *The Empty Space,* with its four definitions of 'Theatre' – Rough, Holy, Deadly, Immediate. In 1965 itself Brook appeared as the introducer of the English version of *Shakespeare Our Contemporary* by the Polish professor, Jan Kott, who treated the plays as black fables for our time, and who had led him into *Lear:* 'Kott is an Elizabethan . . . Shakespeare is a contemporary of Kott, Kott is a contemporary of Shakespeare – he talks about him simply, first-hand, and his book has the freshness of the writing by an eye-witness at the Globe or the immediacy of a page of criticism of a current film.' Already deep in the thickets of the future – for *US* was in mind, untitled and amorphous – Brook returned to the Aldwych on the night of 19 October 1965 to direct, with David Jones, a Royal Shakespeare reading of Peter Weiss's Auschwitz, document, *The Investigation:* nothing could have been more relevant to the time. That night the same text was being played simulta-neously on thirteen stages in East and West Germany, and the Berliner Ensemble, like the Royal Shakespeare, was presenting it as a public reading. Weiss had prepared what he called 'an oratorio-stage documentary', a selective record of the concentration-camp trials that, after a two-year hearing, had ended at Frankfurt in the previous March: it was divided into eleven 'cantos' with such names as 'The Possibility of Survival', 'The Black Wall', 'Cyclone B', and 'The Fire-Ovens'. Brook wrote a terse foreword to a duplicated Aldwych programme:

It's the German's business not ours teutonic guilt complex it's all over it's buried a thing of the past what good will it do let's forget bygones be bygones no muck raking we know it by heart sick of it
     What label can we put on Peter Weiss' script to make it respectable as theatre?
     How can we defend it against the predictable attacks?
     I don't know.
     I only know that hearing that 13 German theatres and also the Berliner Ensemble were making a collective manifestation with this play we felt this to be right and we wished to stand with them. We share their belief that the ingredients of the camps have not vanished from this world and that the topic of man's indifference is not yet out of date.
     I suppose I've never got over hearing Alain Resnais' film about the concentration camps described as 'beautiful'.
     With more time we could have prepared a more polished performance, built a set, made music. What for?
     We feel our job is to transmit this text at once – to whom it may concern.

It concerned everyone that midnight at the Aldwych where twenty-five chairs in scarlet leather were ranged as for a board meeting. With entire simplicity the Royal Shakespeare cast uttered a requiem for the Auschwitz dead. The mechanics of play-reading, the intermittent shuffling of positions, the rustle of scripts, ceased within a moment to obtrude; at once we identified the readers with the people of an investigation that in little over two hours held all conceivable horror. No sentences were pronounced. The narrative merely stopped; the readers dispersed. I had not known a quieter audience, either in the theatre or as it came into the hush of an early-morning London.

v

In the ebb of the year, immediately after Christmas, the Royal Shakespeare production of *The Marat/Sade,* under David Merrick's management, reached the Martin Beck in New York. Brook, with one of his sudden decisions, felt, as he listened, that the audience for a New York première must be the worst ever: a brick wall of unresponsiveness: whole sections rose to leave before the end as if they were hurrying to get the best restaurant table. But notices were a relief: soon both Brook and his actors found the play more rewarding in New York, where people accepted and believed the proposition that man is a potential lunatic, than in London where it was not so much a play about revolution, war, and madness as an exhibition of theatricality. Artaud's term, yes; but Brook held that though the opposing words, 'literary' and 'theatrical' have many meanings, they are dangerous in the English theatre. There, too, often, when used as praise, they do nothing but ward off a disturbing theme.

From 27 December to 16 March *The Marat/Sade* (Ian Richardson now as Marat, Michael Williams as the Herald) crowded every house, becoming in Broadway jargon 'the hardest ticket in town'. Possibly the most eloquent tribute, even though he suspected the quality of the play, was Walter Kerr's in the *New York Herald-Tribune* (28 December:)

One by one the untormented faces beneath matted hair, with mismatched eyes or with skulls cracked open like reddened eggs mesmerise us. Together they are a chorus of universally condemned mankind, the mankind that continues to perpetuate its follies today, and when their voices mass they make a singing sound of doom, due tomorrow, not the day after.

The management of human forms that are both less and more than human forms – an ex-priest, strait-jacketed, tossing himself like a cannon-ball at a spindly-legged courtier who goes down like a rotted campanile – could not be more graphic, more meticulous, in its very turbulence.

The Brechtian songs that interrupt the savage action so sweetly come from the lips of kewpie-doll harlots and mop-wigged clowns, then most sweetly from the virginal throat of that Charlotte Corday who is to knife Marat in his bath. The clash of tones is instantly evocative. It is a child's rhyme that begins the war that kills him. A violin sobs from the balcony while an execution is dreamed of, a bleated trumpet cuts across speech whenever a fool in the balcony opposite chooses to drape one leg over the balcony and blow. In a chalky smoke, a dance of white sheets prepares a nightmare for Marat. And while the Marquis de Sade sensuously arranges for the plunge of a dagger, an orchestrated stageful of collaborators beat out rhythms with wooden spoons against their knees, their ankles, their thighs.

Kerr had been excited; but in a later article (16 January 1966) he took care to say that Peter Brook had been left to do all the work, and the fact that he delighted in it did not give us a playwright. 'Unless the stage games are informed, fed, moved forward by a self-sustaining, inherently commanding text, all the lovely tools of total theatre will in the end produce little more than the equivalent of sober-sided revue sketches.'

To this Brook replied loyally:

The author had an extraordinarily complex and daring vision, and one that was very hard for him to put down on paper. The nearest he could get was a title which reflects a complex stage machine we had to recapture. And I think that what we do on the stage, for better or worse, is exactly what the author was seeing on the stage of his mind, seeing in his vision. This is why I am very jealous of any attempt to divide his work from mine. I feel that any criticism of the production is a criticism of the play, and that any praise of the production is a praise of his vision.

The argument about the value of the text went on. Robert Brustein was for it; Harold Clurman, against; Susan Sontag, for; but it was Brook's work that, in the words of Stanley Kaufmann (*New York Times*), not hitherto an admirer, held most of the reviewers: 'The production surges, opens and narrows like the iris of a camera, using its members in mad, stuttering, but carefully composed movement.' One can get lost sometimes in a theatre of abstractions, in a fuzz of theory, a two-in-the-morning eloquence that seems eccentric in the first sunlight. What matters to stage history is whether the event was an excitement. *The Marat/Sade* was. Its memory endures.

XI

US: 1966-1967

I

PETER BROOK was now forty-one: questioning insistently, diving for coral in the deepest seas. It was just twenty years since the Watteau *Love's Labour's Lost* which had trailed him through his life in the theatre and which he would grow as tired of hearing about as Belloc did of 'Balliol Men'. He was directing today's theatre in terms of the day after tomorrow, terms often fiercely cerebral; reading between everyone's lines from Shakespeare to Genet and Weiss; working for his own ideal playgoer (too many could still admire without comprehending); arguing everything in depth – 'the Grand Canyon is nothing to it,' said an American critic – and never forgetting Artaud on actors and audiences, 'victims burnt at the stake, signalling through the flames'. He lived in a world of experiment where nothing at all could be taken for granted, and he could have said, with Dr Johnson, 'I never think I have hit hard unless it rebounds'.

He had never sat on a fence, and he would not camp on its sunnily fashionable side. He could not write without asking questions, as in a foreword to a book on design* by Michael Warre: 'I believe today that design means creating possibilities for a continually moving and evolving set of images that need have no consistency, no stability, no architecture, but which spin out of the actors' themes and play on the audience just at the moment when they unfold. They should parallel the rich and formless impressions of the world we live in. Yet behind this is the call to classicism, the constant wish to give form, to impose order again. But what form? Whose order?'

What form? Whose order . . . ? In October 1966 he directed at the Aldwych a work named *US* (which could imply either ourselves, our consciences corporate or individual, or simply the United States).

* *Designing and Making Stage Scenery.*

It sought to explore the relationship between 'something called Vietnam and the man sitting in the stalls at the Aldwych': it contained fold upon fold of meaning, far beyond the bare Euripidean line, 'Would you be wise, you cities, fly from war'. Prepared for a year, this work was rehearsed for fifteen weeks: a collective search* by a group of people, led by Brook, who wanted to say something honest about Vietnam, a situation 'more powerful, more acute, more insistent, than any drama that already existed between covers.' What, in London today, did it all mean? Brook's question at the end of a first meeting was, simply: 'If I say I care about Vietnam, how does that influence the way I spend my time?' (Someone, in current jargon, would translate this as a study of 'the elusiveness of genuine commitment in the British social context').

From the first questions rose the long period of improvisation and analysis, the evolution of the ideas and their rehearsal; a period described in a composite book† intensely sincere but inevitably self-conscious. A record of this type of laboratory research, work in progress, must be for the committed specialist: it is the narrative of the quest for a truth that, though it can reveal itself to the players, cannot always be brought home to a random audience during three hours in a theatre. Still, the need to attempt this is the force that drives Peter Brook; we know very well that he will continue striving and searching while he has a work to direct, details to alter, contention to raise, arguments to answer, and players to encourage. He wrote in a preface to the published *US* (immediately after doing *Oedipus*): 'The contemporary event touches raw nerves but creates an immediate refusal to listen. The myth and the formally stated work has power, but is insulated in exact proportion. So which in fact is more likely to the spectator? I want to find the answer.'

II

In the nature of its theme, *US* could hardly expect continued existence, revival in repertory: a point Brook would make in later years when he wrote of it, in *The Empty Space*, as a 'group-happening-collaborative spectacle', every element of which had come into being for the particular cross-section of London that sat during

---

* On the programme it was ascribed to Peter Brook (director), Sally Jacobs (designer), Richard Peaslee (music), Adrian Mitchell (lyrics), Denis Cannan (original text), Geoffrey Reeves and Albert Hunt (associate directors), Michael Kustow and Michael Stott (adaptors of documentary material).

† *US*, London, 1968.

1966 in the Aldwych Theatre. 'The fact that we had no text wrought and set by a dramatist was the condition of this particular experiment. Contact through the audience, through shared references, became the substance of the evening.' Inevitably, much had to be lost in keeping *US* in the repertory, even through a five months' London season. A single performance would have been the true product, but, according to the rules of the game, the play had to be 'fixed' for repetition. Liveliness decreased as the actors lost the first immediacy of their relations with the public and their theme.

All of them, inspired by Brook, had felt deeply about the terrors, cruelties, and deceptions of a weary war; some did not find until the rigour of rehearsal just how much they did care. The production that finally came alive on the stage of the Aldwych had a concentrated, fanatical fierceness of self-examination as (in the words of the *Morning Star* critic) it sought to shock its audience into a respect for man and a consciousness of what was happening in the world. The Bishop of Woolwich, in a *Guardian* article later in the year, summarized the night as, at first, 'an anamnesis of Vietnam history, a representation of it, partly by recitation, partly by re-enactment, in which the central figure is a half-naked man representing his people in their sufferings, torn apart, daubed and despised of men. There follows a kaleidoscopic succession of readings, songs, refrains, antiphons, dialogue, preaching, confession, intercession, ritual movements, and recurring symbolic actions and images, particularly of fire and burning.' And he said: 'The whole thing reminded me more than anything else of a Holy Week liturgy. It is not specifically Christian: far from that. It spoke of confession, but not of absolution, of fraction but not of communion. It judged, but it did not pretend to save.'

The tale of the making of *US* was of an intricate struggle to find the right language of communication: debates, exercises, sustained improvisations, a search for disciplined control, as the company gradually developed its statement of the war, the reaction it could not avoid. One of Brook's actors, in a familiar love-hate relationship, said bewildered: 'Three people I can't begin to understand – a madman, a drunk and Peter!'

In the middle of it all, having conducted – as Michael Kustow put it – a first foray into the players' knowledge and images of America, Vietnam and Asia, the company settled to work for ten days with Jerzy Grotowski, Director of the Polish Teatr Laboratorium at Wroclaw, for whom Brook had a great admiration: the only man in the world, he said, since Stanislavski, who had so closely investigated the nature of acting, 'its phenomenon, its meaning, the nature and science of its mental-emotional-physical processes'. Grotowski rejects all forms of theatre except his own: he calls it the Poor Theatre, and its purpose is 'to cross our frontiers, exceed our limitations, fill our emptiness, fulfil ourselves'. He aims – and one can see the affinity with Brook – at disturbing the spectator, getting the audience to join in act of collective self-analysis. The actor needs an intense discipline, an act of self-presentation: 'One must give totally in one's deepest intimacy with confidence, as when one gives oneself in love.' I have seen only one of Grotowski's works, his version of Wyspianski's *Akropolis*, re-conceived as a poetic paraphrase of an extermination camp – metaphor and literal interpretation mixed as in a day-dream. Technique apart, I found it far too deliberately contrived to be moving; but Grotowski is clearly a ferocious figure among the abstractions of the avant-garde. Behind closed doors, and aided by his colleague Riszard Cieslak, he brought to the Royal Shakespeare Company his most gruelling methods, demanding 'a fiery commitment', giving to the players (said Brook) 'the shock of seeing that somewhere in the world acting is an art of absolute dedication, monastic and total'. Not all of them responded willingly to Grotowski's uncompromising demands.

This was bound to be a period of pressure. At home Peter had the happiness of knowing that Natasha had given birth, on 27 September 1966, to a second child, a boy named Simon after his paternal grandfather. A few days afterwards, and a fortnight before the end of the fifteen weeks of rehearsal – everyone staggering a little from Grotowski – the Lord Chamberlain telephoned L.T.G. Farmer, Chairman of the Governors of the Royal Shakespeare Company. In Lord Cobbold's view, *US* was 'bestial, anti-American, and communist', and would Mr Farmer exercise his influence to stop it? Next day the Chairman flew down from Scotland, where he was on a fishing holiday, to see, with Peter Hall, a run-through at the Donmar rehearsal rooms. When it was over, he, Hall, and Brook went straight to St James's Palace where Farmer insisted that it was a performance of integrity, with a definite point, and in no sense easily propagandist. Lord Cobbold asked if he thought that the show was anti-American.

'No. It criticises Britain as much as the USA.'

'But if the American Ambassador should come to the first night. Would he walk out?'

'No,' replied George Farmer in what someone called afterwards a perfect theatre-of-the-absurd answer: 'No. Not if he stayed until the end.'

What more could be said? Lord Cobbold agreed to issue a licence, but he demanded at the same time that the company should abide by the cuts of certain adjectives, a proviso that, though Brook at once objected strongly to it, had to stand. Two days later Brook told the company: 'The crisis with the Lord Chamberlain is an image of the whole war itself, the corridors of power, the power of rumour. Remember, if this crisis had taken place in Vietnam, some of us would be dead by now.'

III

The première was on 13 October 1966. Playgoers saw a stage covered with the detritus of war. In their programme they read two important notes. One was by Peter Brook:

This performance is a collaboration. We have attempted together to understand a situation too vast to encompass alone, and too painful to ignore. A programme is the place in which, conventionally, credit must be given where it is due. In this case, any division of responsibilities is conventional, not precise.

Another note was by L. T. G. Farmer, Chairman of the Executive Council of the RSC:

The Executive Council of the Royal Shakespeare Theatre firmly believes that it has a duty to support the company's presentation of serious experimental work, however controversial, whilst, of course, not agreeing individually or collectively with all the views expressed.

Documentary drama, as yet in its infancy, may well prove able to challenge people to serious thought over burning topical problems more forcefully than newspapers, radio or television.

US is an attempt by a body of dedicated people – directors, writers, actors and designers – to pass balanced comment in a responsible way on a current problem of vital concern to all.

It was a time when news-plays were in fashion; the National Theatre had contemplated one on the Cuban crisis, a project mercifully stillborn. Brook repeated firmly that *US* did not belong to any Theatre of Fact (which he called a silly title): the point of any interpretation of current events was that one never reached the facts: he would prefer to speak of a theatre of myth. The house that night was strongly held, though the moment before the interval, when players, their heads enveloped in paper bags, groped and scrambled blindly from stage to auditorium, had no real impact and would soon be cut. Otherwise the play, peopled by actors in casual clothes and without make-up, moved unfalteringly forward, a study of metropolitan attitudes to the war and a sermon without hint of self-righteousness. One critic would speak of 'sheer theatricality' (the word recurs in this Brook period), but how many it influenced we do not know.

I have to admit that after a battering night I was thinking less of the actual problems of Vietnam than of the theatrical attack of the stage-play; of such moments as the self-immolation of the Buddhist monk in Saigon and of the Quaker on the Pentagon steps; the crashing to the ground of a monstrous uniformed doll – 'a trophy of arms' according to one critic – a rubberoid marine commando with a napalm fireshell in his belly, which hung on wires over the stage; a corrosive speech by Glenda Jackson as she imagined the coming of napalm to an English suburban lawn; and the ritual burning of a white butterfly which ended the night, and was perhaps its most dismaying effect. I found myself recalling, again and again, a passage from a Granville-Barker lecture in which he spoke of Sean O'Casey, breaking from Dublin realism 'under the spell of a greater theme and his own deeper passion', into the symbolic second act of *The Silver Tassie:* an endeavour to give us, 'seated in our comfortable little theatre, some sense of the chaos of war'. At the last the entire company remained on the stage, another of Brook's challenging silences, a 'confrontation' (he used the modish word) between the United States and us, Vietnam and London. There the players stood, frozen, the house lights on, the audience uncertain whether or not to leave the theatre. Actually, so we were told later, they were 'switching their attention to a private task in which they evaluated their own personal views in the light of the day's event and the evening's performance'.* But spectators were not to know this; it was an uneasy moment for the first audience, and Kenneth Tynan, literary manager of the National Theatre, shattered the silence with a peevish query, 'Are you waiting for us, or are we waiting for you?'

Brook was happy that, instead of what he called the normal

* Peter Brook in *The Times,* 17 February 1968.

glazed brightness of a first-night performance, the house had indeed seen something rock-solid, authentic. Notices varied between the excited, the respectful, and the exasperated. Irving Wardle (*The Times*) had never experienced more fully a breaking-down of detachment in the theatre. B. A. Young (*Financial Times*) said: 'Let no one be discouraged by any existing opinions they may hold on the subject. Mr Brook and his collaborators put their case with great brilliance. Disagreement makes it no less remarkable.' Alan Brien (*Sunday Telegraph*) thought it was 'the case for the prosecution, in the absence of the defence, with the judge bemused and blinded by some brilliant courtroom tricks.' For Bryan Magee, in the *Listener,* it succeeded because it was 'art and not animated documentation; it transfigures fact (and, for that matter, half-truths, propaganda, and downright lies) into something else; it becomes the theatre of com- passionate involvement.' Hilary Spurling (*Spectator*) attacked the 'cheap, facile ambivalence' of the company's attitude to Vietnam. The *Universe* admired 'a brave attempt to pierce the easy aloofness and non-involvement of the man-in-the-street. Jeremy Kingston, the young drama critic of *Punch*, put it in a few words: 'The aim of this stark, complex, fair, emotional and rational play is to encourage us to think what we suffer by not thinking. . . . A valuable and noble piece of art.' And a word from France: 'Les Londoniens se ruent a l'un des spectacles les plus violents et les plus engagés de l'histoire du théâtre. . . . Un extraordinaire boomerange artistique' (*Le Nouvel Observateur*).

   US had defined again our attitude to war. The trouble was that it had to lose its original impact. After the first flare in the papers when (this is always dangerous) it had reddened into a news story, it smouldered on into the Aldwych repertoire. Many visitors were impressed; sometimes, during the ultimate silence which could last for as long as ten or fifteen minutes on a good night, total strangers would begin to talk to each other and would leave the theatre together. Even so, it could not be the *US* of those last rehearsals with the company in mounting fever. It did start one crackling television row during a BBC programme called 'The Look of the Week'. In this Professor Patrick Honey criticized what he said were factual inaccuracies, whereupon Brook answered that the RSC had written twice to the accepted expert on Vietnam affairs, asking for advice; the expert, who was Professor Honey himself, had not replied, presumably because Brook and others had signed a plea for 'mediation and peace'. (This was a telegram, urging mediation, sent to the Prime Minister by two hundred leading intellectuals.) When the Professor retorted that from this he had been afraid it would be a pro-Communist production, Denis Cannan, one of Brook's nearest collaborators, and Brook himself, protested angrily. Until Robert · Robinson, the chairman, intervened, it seemed likely that television sets everywhere might be incinerated.

Not long after this there was a question and answer in the House of Commons. Sir Knox Cunningham, calling *US* 'the anti-American play recently produced by the Royal Shakespeare Company', put a question to the Secretary for Education and Social Science. Would he withhold payment of the Company's £90,000 subsidy from public funds so long as it remained Government policy to support the policy of the United States in Vietnam? The Under-Secretary of State (Jennie Lee) replied: 'I have no intention of interfering with the discretion of the Arts Council in making grants.' She added, after another question: 'It would be a very bad day for this country when our theatre and arts simply begin to reflect whatever happens to be the policy of the Government, of either the hon. and learned gentleman's party, or my own.'

Here, perhaps, the last word should be with the critic, Irving Wardle. He wrote in *New Society*:

Once again, the evil is in the eye of the beholder, and if you turn up simply to support a piece of theatrical high fashion, that will be your reason for condemning the show. One can get a salacious kick from reading Martha Gelhorn's and James Cameron's reports on Vietnam; the only difference in *US* is that it drags this motive out into the open. It is vicarious psychodrama, aiming to uncover what we want to forget rather than tell us anything new. . . . *US* contains elements of every type of theatre you care to name, including documentary, but what they add up to is a vastly magnified image of the fears and confusions of British society.

IV

Brook had by no means finished with *US*. Within two years it would have become the basis of a film entitled *Tell Me Lies*, from the song, 'Tell me lies about Vietnam'. Before this we have to return transiently to *The Marat/Sade* which Brook – during the long preparation of *US* – had filmed in a brief and turbulent period at Pinewood. United Artists had put up the money for a two and a quarter hours' film: it was just enough to cover eighteen days' shooting, and in that period it was completed, with what was called an eerie colour-palette, livid and ghostly, and with the company (led by Glenda Jackson, Ian Richardson and Patrick Magee) that had acted it in the United States.* It was not intended to be a record of the stage performance, but a film of the play as Weiss wrote it; in fact, it could involve spectators even more closely than in the theatre, especially during the final deadly pandemonium. But in both film and play one had to observe again what Brook said, in his preface to the play-text, about bringing together two apparently irreconcilable styles, those of Brecht and Artaud: 'Brecht's use of "distance" has long been considered in opposition to Artaud's conception of theatre as immediate and violent subjective experience. I have never believed this to be true. I believe that theatre, like life, is made up of the unbroken conflict between impressions and judgments – illusion and disillusion co-habit painfully and are inseparable.'

He had, he explained, to disperse one form of staginess to create a new theatricality for his film. This he managed with ease, having watched filmed and televised boxing matches where the long shots would give the general view while, a moment later, one was right in the thick of things, as involved as the referee himself. Now in *The Marat/Sade* he worked simultaneously with two cameras and sometimes more, one of them photographing the entire scene from the front, looking dispassionately on the bathhouse, the barred cage, and the audience viewed in silhouette, and the others deployed, almost at random, to hit on close-ups and bits of ensemble playing that could be inserted into the master-shots.

From the première at the Odeon, Haymarket, in March 1967, there rose the kind of dispute that meant critics had been made to think. Thus, though the *Observer* said, 'It seems more sensitive to human suffering than the stage production could be', *The Times*, while agreeing about the boldness of the colour photography, thought the asylum inmates false and actorish. For Dilys Powell (*Sunday Times*) the argument was clearer and more powerful on the screen. For Alexander Walker (*Evening Standard*): 'Brook uses his camera like a stock-whip, making faces flinch as it passes over them.' The film was simultaneously a success in America where the *New Yorker* said: 'His camera moves in great random-seeming

* *The Marat/Sade*, as a play, had had several New York awards: both the Drama Critics' and the 'Tony' for the best play and best director; the critics chose Glenda Jackson as the most promising new actress, and there were 'Tony' awards to Patrick Magee as the best supporting actor and to Gunilla Palmstierna-Weiss as the best costume designer.

sweeps, now against a harsh, sun-struck window, now in steaming shadows, and, by its fluent restlessness, convinces us that we are roaming at will not only inside the four walls of that suffocating bath-house but inside the lost minds of the patients as well. It is a scary sensation.'

In the summer of 1967, while Peter was engaged on his next film, *Tell Me Lies,* Natasha was having an experience that could have reminded her husband of battles long ago: the contentious *Romeo and Juliet* at Stratford in 1947, the torrid heat of Verona within and the damp spring night outside, and an audience waiting to pounce on any of a young man's misdeeds. Not that Natasha, in 1967, had much to worry her. She had gone to Italy with the children, and for three months that summer she was playing Lady Capulet in Franco Zeffirelli's film. Zeffirelli had made her fall in love with Tybalt; and a correspondent wrote to the *Evening Standard* about one of the scenes he saw in production at Fienza:

When Tybalt (Michael York's) death scene and Lady Capulet's violent reaction to it was being filmed, Natasha Parry reduced even the most blasé and uncooperative onlooker to silence, by her extraordinary and moving performance. Her screams rang out over the old square, and spines chilled. More impressive, she repeated this innumerable times, for take after take, until Zeffirelli was satisfied with the rest of the action in the scene. Surrounded by make-believe, the lights, lamps, lorries and cameras, she made the city panic each time at the death of Tybalt.

'To have more talk of these sad things . . .' Peter Brook's *Tell Me Lies*, 'a film about London,' shot during 1967 and shown in February of the following year, could not well be a straight film of *US*. Only the songs remained in a script elaborately re-devised for the camera. Here, after pictures of napalm-burned children had stirred his conscience, one saw an ordinary man about London re-examining the Vietnam problem as it was seen through many eyes: it was, indeed, an anxious record of personal conscience: talks with writers, students, members of Parliament, a Mao-ist, a Buddhist monk, a leader of Black Power. There were demonstrations and a protest meeting (with Paul Scofield)*; and documentary insertions from the Far East. Brook had been determined that *Tell Me Lies* should be made. After various commercial companies had turned

* 'Nothing in the film,' said Alan Dent (*Illustrated London News*), 'moved me quite as much as that beautiful actor, Paul Scofield's subtle little pause before uttering the name of the human quality in which the human race would seem to be so tragically deficient these days, that of – kindness.'

the project down, seventy separate Americans joined to finance it, not the rich, but professional people, doctors and business men who believed it to be essential. It took four weeks to complete; the response again, was most varied, angrier in America than in London where the *Evening Standard*'s 'a sour, sardonic, inventive, and totally biased film about Vietnam' was a typical notice, and Ian Wright said in the *Guardian:* 'It might have been called a film about what actors of the Royal Shakespeare Company think of Vietnam.' Boleslaw Sulik wrote in *Tribune* that though, cinematically, it did not always work, its cumulative impact was 'quite strong and lasting. It does seem to portray, with considerable accuracy and a sense of urgency, the current plight of a British radical. . . . The most disturbing feature of this film, intentional or not, is that it shows orthodox pacifist feelings, the finest public expression of middle-class decency, as impotent in the face of an issue like Vietnam. Peter Brook goes no further, offers no solutions. Perhaps he doesn't believe in solutions.'

The film's young man had begun his inquiry after seeing a pamphlet with photographs of the burned children, that had been pushed through his door. At the end of his search the camera paused for a long time at the same open door. What might be coming through it? Brook said that in the moments of blank white screen at the last he faced his audience with the impossibility of Vietnam. On that screen they could write any message they wished. In a sense, I think, it was like the low, premonitory roll of thunder at the end of the Stratford *Lear*.

XII

Grand National: 1968-1969

I

DURING the bitter spring of 1968 Peter Brook found himself directing at the Old Vic, now the first home of the English National Theatre, established, very properly, not far from Bankside. So far it was his only professional association with a building that for more than half a century had meant so much to the record of the classical stage: until 1963 London's home of Shakespeare, though by no means Shakespeare in Brook's own terms. The Vic had been governed for many years by the legend that was Lilian Baylis, single-minded, demanding, and tactless, whose passion for her theatre and her cause transcended all the profession's jokes about her. Before her death, and during an ensuing twenty-five years, the name of the Old Vic had stood by proxy for a National Theatre; but it was not until the autumn of 1963 that, with Laurence Olivier to administer it, the National Theatre – an institution about which Brook had been dubious – moved fully into being.

In the summer of 1967 Olivier invited John Gielgud – who had made on the Vic stage his first classical reputation – to appear in two National plays. The first, as directed by Tyrone Guthrie, an American version of *Tartuffe* in couplets, proved to be curiously unprofitable. Molière in English had seldom held a stage except in the cheerfully free and theatrical texts of Miles Malleson. Now, though Guthrie sustained the pace, a steady rhyming through two hours or so could be difficult for speaker and listener. One naturally jumped forward to the end of each couplet: 'hear' must follow 'fear', 'spell' must follow 'fell'. Inevitably one went to the sound of the dialogue, not the sense; there were times – a pause, perhaps, on 'reprehensible' (the partner was 'sensible') or on 'hocus-pocus' (which went with 'focus') – when the translator's ingenuity blurred one attention to Molière. Here, too, Gielgud was cast not as Tartuffe, but as the dupe, Orgon, a part that, for all its length, had to be subsidiary. Everyone heard with relief that his next part would be Oedipus Rex. But whose Oedipus? Not that of Sophocles in which Olivier had triumphed in the middle of the forties. It was to be the unacted, and long considered unactable, *Oedipus* of Seneca, directed by Peter Brook: in a sense, for those who remembered, it would be the full turn of the wheel from the sub-Oedipean nights in the last spring of the war: Cocteau's *The Infernal Machine* in that little theatre behind Gloucester Road.

Originally, Olivier had planned to direct the production himself in a version by David Anthony Turner. But after his illness in the summer of 1967 he chose towards the end of the year to invite Peter Brook (who would observe typically, in an interview a few weeks later, 'The Greeks and Romans embody everything I detest'*). Whatever Olivier might have done, his work could not have been remotely like the production we saw on 19 March 1968 upon the Old Vic stage, in the Old Vic auditorium, and in our own burdened imaginations. First, the translation worried Brook: he wanted a text that, as Ted Hughes, who finally did the work, has said, 'could release whatever inner power this story, in its plainest, bluntest form, still has, and to unearth if we could the ritual possibilities within it'. Hughes, returning to the original Latin, began work only three weeks before rehearsal, and David Anthony Turner (who had made the earlier translation) has chivalrously praised the result: 'In place of good serviceable prose, there was inspiration, elegance, fire, poetry. It was all magic.'† Actually, it was the style of the production, rather than the text, that startled the first-night audience at the Vic.

Why Seneca? ('Seneca cannot be too heavy, nor Plautus too light.') Though the plays by Nero's tutor, the only surviving Latin tragedies, were left severely to the books, their rhetoric, their lurid invention, their whole apparatus of death and doom, powerfully influenced the Elizabethan dramatists. Ted Hughes had a fine analogy for the tortured Senecan figures. 'They are Greek only by convention; by nature they are more primitive than aboriginals. They are a spider people scuttling among hot stones. The radiant moral world of Sophocles is simply not present here.' Peter Brook, in his production of *Titus Andronicus,* had shown what impact the neo-Senecan drama could have. Now, clearly, he was the man for

* *Observer,* 21 January 1968.
† 'A word about *Oedipus*' in *Seneca's Oedipus,* adapted by Ted Hughes, Faber, 1969.

the master himself, more particularly because, at this time, he was concerned deeply with ritual: 'It is foolish to allow a revulsion from bourgeois forms to turn into a revulsion from needs that are common to all men. If the need for a true contact with a sacred invisibility through the theatre still exists, then all possible vehicles must be re-examined.' This passage would appear, later in 1968, in *The Empty Space*. What he says in this richly idiosyncratic book (published in many countries) is implicit in his work. I need quote only a few passages from it to show its manner:

There is always a deadly spectator, who for special reasons enjoys a lack of intensity and even a lack of entertainment, such as the scholar who emerges from routine performances of the classics smiling because nothing has distracted him from trying over and confirming his pet theories to himself.

In the theatre, every form once born is mortal; every form must be reconceived, and its new conception will bear the marks of all the influences that surround it. In this sense, the theatre is relativity.

It is a strange role, that of the director: he does not ask to be God and yet his role implies it. He wants to be fallible, and yet an instinctive conspiracy of the actors is to make him the arbiter, because an arbiter is so desperately wanted all the time.

When I took a tour of *Titus Andronicus* through Europe this obscure work of Shakespeare touched audiences directly because we had tapped in it a ritual of bloodshed which was recognised as true.

A 'holy theatre' not only presents the invisible but also offers conditions that make its perception possible.

The theatre needs its perpetual revolution. Yet wanton destruction is criminal; it produces violent reaction and still greater confusion.

The theatre can only advance crabwise in a world whose moving forward is as often sideways as backwards.

II

Brook spent weeks of single-minded concentration upon Seneca and the response of an initially startled National Theatre company. He searched for ways of presenting the inner power of the remorseless text through words by Ted Hughes that seemed to him to be 'miraculously powerful'. To do this he almost eliminated physical movement, stripped scenery and costumes to a form in which heads and hands would emerge most sharply, and sought, by various means, to focus attention on the spoken words, their tones and rhythms. A cast of thirty-six worked as it has never worked before. Irene Worth, who had joined the National to play Jocasta, has described* how, in her death scene, she and Brook endeavoured to get the ultimate vocal resonance, which had to come from her stomach. The company listened to many anthropological recordings – of primitive tribes and Buddhist and Tibetan monks who could resonate through every part of the body. Players, as Irene Worth added, are never asked as a rule to do an eighth of what they are capable of doing. It required a Brook to bring out their latent resources. Freda Dowie has remembered elsewhere how, in the Theatre of Cruelty, they would explore everything in every way; once she was asked to learn and to act the opening scene of *King Lear,* herself as Lear, and then to convey it all, using nothing but grunts.

The première of *Oedipus* on 19 March had to be a highly-strung experience for all concerned, not least the audience through an unbroken two hours. As late as six o'clock that night, Brook, who had been in intense artistic disagreement with Olivier, was still threatening not to let the production open. But it did. The audience, as it entered, saw that already, round the house in stalls, circle, and gallery, men and women of the chorus stood sombrely waiting, each by a spotlit pillar or perch, human caryatids. Upon the shadowed stage some of the company had taken up their places as they would nightly, half an hour before the play began. A great sheet-metal cube, silver in the half darkness, revolved slowly. It flashed and opened out into gold as the lights intensified; the walls of the cube spread apart to create stage platforms; and a pitiless sun blazed upon plague-ridden Thebes. Ronald Bryden would say in the *Observer*† that Brook had turned the Old Vic into 'a kind of cathedral laboratory of the 21st century, a wind-tunnel designed to contain a hurricane of human emotions', with the chorus as 'a many-headed respiratory machine'.

In the early moments we were conscious first of sounds, a humming and chanting, and of a quick, harsh tattoo that changed to a crescendo of angry drumming. We heard the sibilance of many voices; around us the theatre seemed to speak ('Show us a simple riddle'), and we were part of the stricken city in its outcry and its torment. John Gielgud, the Oedipus, visually a weary eagle and

---

* In an interview with Charles Lefeaux, BBC Third Programme, February 1970.
† 24 March 1968.

using the majesty of utterance that contemporary mumblers scorned, said early in the night: 'Fear came with me, my shadow, into this kingdom, to this throne, and it grew till now it surrounds me. Fear. I stand in it like a blind man in darkness.' These words lingered throughout the play. Fear did surround us, heightened by the vocal devices, Richard Peaslee's spoken *musique concrète*, as players on stage and in the auditorium joined in droning and humming, deep breathing, hissing whispers, speeches sometimes echoed *sotto voce*, and mocking laughter ('The gods are dead of the plague'), a commentary in sound upon the agony of the Oedipean fable. Seneca left little unsaid in his narrative of the sacrifice and the raising of the dead man. The night moved inexorably forward in its terrors, its incantation, its complex orchestration of voices (especially in the second chorus to Bacchus), its pause when the shepherd in the dazzling light made his slow progress through the house towards the king, and its charged moment when the tale of Icarus wavered in unearthly aerial cadences ('stars loaded with his crazy dream').

At length a slave brought news of the blinding. Ronald Pickup's hands were contorted into claws as he spoke the most fearful of the Senecan narratives.* Then, from blind Tiresias, Gielgud received, ritually, the eye-patches that denoted the empty sockets of Oedipus, and the play reached its ghastly end with Jocasta's self-impaling – mimed by Irene Worth, on the golden spike which stood for the king's sword – and Gielgud's stumbling movement from the stage: 'Pestilence, ulcerous agony, blasting consumption, plague terror, plague blackness, welcome. Come with me. You are my guides. Lead me.' There, I think, the night should have ended. Instead, and not at first according to the rubric, 'The chorus celebrate the departure of Oedipus with a dance', attendants brought in ceremoniously, and unveiled, a great gold phallus ten feet high; a drum-beat rose insistently, and we were left – certainly at the première – wondering whether all was over, whether or not to applaud. On later evenings I gather that there was a band to parade to the tune of 'Yes, we have no bananas', while through the house the players, some masked, all gold-cloaked, streamed towards the stage to perform a kind of bacchanal round the unveiled phallus, shedding their cloaks as they did so.

I presumed that Brook sought to symbolize rejoicing after terror. Darkness had been lifted from the city of Thebes; here now was the

---

* 'Ten weeks of tortured work' (*Guardian* interview, 2 October 1970). But 'when you're totally committed to an idea, it breeds relaxation and confidence'.

symbol venerated in the Dionysiac festivals. Still, without aid (and
for once a programme note might have been useful) the scene could
be all too easily misunderstood. I did realize – and here the programme did help – that Brook was asking not for 'the feel and sound
of celebrating through applause', but for 'the climax of silence –
another form of recognition, and appreciation for an experience
shared. We have largely forgotten silence, it even embarrasses us,
we clap our hands mechanically because we do not know what else
to do, and we are unaware that silence is also permitted, that
silence is also good.'* Even so, at the première, the house was
puzzled, in two minds, uncertain what to do; a superbly exciting
theatrical experience ended in indecision, accompanied by the kind
of noise Alice heard when the lion and the unicorn were drummed
out of town. Until then the production had been a feat of the
haunted imagination. We forgot what the cast was wearing, its
anonymous black or brown uniform, sweaters and slacks. We were
aware only of the strong assault upon the nerves and senses, and
of some of the individual playing and speaking, Gielgud's voice,
for example, enunciating the name 'Tiresias'. Notices, in general,
were immensely appreciative, though few critics could accept the
climax. Some, in discussing the production, suggested that Brook
was fusing Artaud and Brecht; it was recorded, too, as significant,
that he had gone five times during the World Theatre season of 1967
to the performances of the Japanese Noh actors at the Aldwych.
Influences, no doubt; but he had assimilated them and produced
something entirely personal. If the end seemed to be perverse, no
matter: he would have been entitled to say of this *Oedipus*, in a
phrase from a modern poet, 'You see, I do not hate the splendour'.†
It has always been better to experience the splendour that Brook
can produce than to hear him explain why and how he has contrived
it.

One unexpected audience responded: children from London
schools at a special matinee. These were regular events in the
National repertory; but the management, belatedly realizing what
the end of *Oedipus* contained, took fright at the twelfth hour.
Wearily, Brook said the company would stop after the fourth act,
and he would describe the rest of the narrative. When he and
Geoffrey Reeves had done so, they heard a noise like the swarming
of locusts; the children were crying out for the end to be performed.

* A quotation from *The Empty Space*.
† In Jonathan Griffin's play, *The Hidden King*.

Brook invited the teachers to decide; they went into conference and only two of them, with about twenty children, left. Then the players were summoned from the wings and the rest of *Oedipus* was acted to a silent house and to ultimate storming enthusiasm.

III

That spring, Jean-Louis Barrault, controller of the Théâtre des Nations in Paris, invited Brook and the Royal Shakespeare Company to open an international centre of research where actors from different countries – England, the United States, France, Japan – could work on a common project: to explore the possibilities of performance in a place without theatrical associations. The French Ministry of Culture offered a vast, bare gallery at the Mobilier National; other directors, writers, musicians, and designers joined in, examining methods of making mystery plays come directly to life in these surroundings, and using as a basis material from Calderon and from *The Tempest*. Then French politics exploded: the Government closed the Théâtre des Nations, but in July, thanks to many sponsors, the group moved to London for a few public performances at the Round House, Chalk Farm, a converted engine shed – still less fashionable than it would be – in a north-western inner suburb. There Brook conducted a theatrical exercise as far from orthodox Shakespeare as the planet Neptune from the earth.

The workshop project, confined here to *The Tempest,* inquired into the nature of a theatre and a play, an actor and a spectator, and the relationship between them. Visitors allowed to see the exercise, and accommodated upon scaffolding in either 'safe' or 'dangerous' areas, were watching an adventure in theatrical dynamics, a testing of ideas, a sequence of experiments in movement, vocal orchestration, non-verbalized sound, that would not startle anybody familiar with Brook's method, but that might seem to a newcomer totally anarchic: alarming as well if one were suddenly pulled off upon the mobile scaffolding into the very heart of the arena. In many ways it was an engrossing night, from the first moment when lights blazed upon the inner ring and paired players strove to outface each other in mime, right up to the dying fall and variations upon phrases from Prospero's epilogue. I think now of an hour of urgent vocal and physical experiment, poised between drama and mime and again doing with the words what the chorus did in *Oedipus*. The company was in surge round its girdered scaffolds and planked catwalks; reeling, writhing, and fainting in coils among the spectators; evolving personal rituals, or joining in concerted set-pieces. Best, I remember a potent suggestion of shipwreck and thunderous storm.

Brook would probably reject any elaborate attempt to analyse what he and his players did that night; but I kept reverting to a line from *The Tempest* about Claribel of Tunis, 'she that dwells ten leagues beyond man's life'. The Round House devotees, who included Natasha Parry and a Japanese Ariel, were living ten leagues beyond their normal stage lives in a thrust at techniques yet to be perfected. We were conscious as never before, of Miranda's brave new world – a phrase, rubbed now, that needs to be re-minted – and of Prospero, figure of harsh power, teaching his master-slave language to Caliban (whose birth from Sycorax we had witnessed). Any report must be tentative: call it an evening of unlooked-for excitement, especially for spectators who became involved, swept upon their scaffolds into mid-arena while the actors swarmed over, across, and round, and the isle was full of noises.

It was not *The Tempest,* but we could respect the force of this workshop-effort to get nearer to the heart of a prodigious poem that has so baffled the theatre across 350 years. Sovereign as it is in its own high and strangely secret place, little is harder to raise from the text; the penetration of what a critic has called the phosphorescent veils of its verse, the release of its compelling ritual. Sometimes that conflict between the flesh and the spirit, the arts of air and earth, can move us exceedingly; but *The Tempest* must always be frightening to translate into action on any level,* as a poem arcane and eternal or as a epithalamic masque devised for the English Princess who became the 'Winter Queen'. Peter Brook says he has not got it right yet. One day he will, just as a Japanese Noh actor, searching for what he speaks of as the 'flower' – the true moment of communication – must one day succeed in his task.

IV

Now, again, the snow-peak of *King Lear* loomed icily. Indeed it had been looming for some time, since Brook's resolve to make a film

---

* Lady Pitts, in James Bridie's *Daphne Laureola,* remembers her nine-year-old self thinking of it as a terrible nightmare: 'It was about an old scientist on an island. He had a daughter who was almost an imbecile. He had a slave called Caliban. He tortured poor Caliban with rheumatism and frightened him with spangled spooks. After twenty years on the island he sailed away and left it worse than it was before. No books, no spooks, nothing but the rheumatism and Caliban in a bad temper . . .'

of the tragedy that had possessed him a few years before. He and Paul Scofield resolved then to come back to it. They did so with formidable concentration.

More than half a century earlier, *Lear* had been made into an American silent film, advertised as 'a drama of powerful heart interest staged in barbaric splendour'. This was not exactly Brook's view of the play. He and the producer, Lord Birkett, who were limited at first in capital and scope, had to decide upon a legendary world that was totally persuasive, its landscape as unobtrusive and as visually acceptable as a landscape in a modern film, but corresponding to the nature of the society in *Lear*. 'As Lear's castle is built in a cold country for protection,' Brook told an interviewer,* 'and it is the place where life goes on closed to the elements, so Lear to be a great king shut himself out from all that was terrifying and all that was marvellous in the outside world. If a man shuts himself off, he does not get out to the heath, he can never find his way or see his way straight. It is so much a story of our time.'

The right location – it could be the set of an Icelandic saga – they found at last in Denmark. There in the extreme North of Jutland, on a disused mink farm upon the drifting sand dunes of the Raabjerg Mile, the unit came to rest. The nearest small town, Skagen, was fifteen miles away. There was no house within four miles. 'Nobody', said the assistant Danish producer, 'would ever go there in winter unless it was an absolute necessity', a view that would have appealed to Brook at once. In this inhospitable world between two frozen seas, the North Sea and the Kattegat, the unit† worked between January and April 1969 in a freezing east wind at sub-zero temperatures, down to twenty degrees below; one day, when it registered minus two, the players called it a heat-wave.

Snow-bound during most of the filming, the area was a vast, flat saucer with patches of heath and heather, and without a road, a path, or a building, in fact a thoroughly plausible scene for *Lear*. Huge, monolithic castles were built, as well as three costly miles of road. (The total budget was just over a million dollars, some of it supplied by a grant from the Danish Film Fund.) Immediately work was over, buildings and road had to be demolished at the authorities' demand; today the dunes are as forsaken and primitive as ever they were.

During the production of *Lear,* not a straight version but

---

* Sydney Edwards in the *Evening Standard,* 7 March 1969.
† Filmways, in cooperation with the Danish film companies, Athena and Laterna.

adapted, and made in sombre black and white – Brook rejected all
suggestions of colour as incongruous – the Raabjerg Mile became
an extraordinary place, with Scofield at its centre after his daily
make-up session which took four hours. Peter Brook rode round in
the furs and leather that all the players* had to wear to enable them
to live in Lear's world (and in North Jutland); and Lear's attendant
knights were numbers of weatherbeaten fishermen and farmers, and
old cavalrymen, aged up to eighty, who had answered an advertisement for 'men able to fight from the saddle, drill with halberds, grow
a full beard, and do all kinds of work outside for three months in the
worst of winter'. Their horses and tough, shaggy ponies were
carefully chosen. Nothing was permitted that would jar: even a
ceremonial coach, from the National Museum at Copenhagen, was
felt to be too elegant and light for primitive service.

It was a long wrestle with *Lear* in that cold country, on the dunes
by the northern sea; and there would be a far longer wrestle in the
Paris cutting-rooms, and among the intricacies of film finance,
before the final work could reach the cinema. ('Search every acre in
the high-grown field, and bring him to our eye.') The task had not
long been finished, and the film had still not arrived, when Brook,
after an absence of seven seasons from Stratford-upon-Avon,
returned there to direct – of all plays – the tripartite fantasy of *A
Midsummer Night's Dream,* his tenth Shakespeare production since
the Birmingham Repertory *King John* in the autumn of 1945. 'I had
a very strong wish,' he said, 'to go as deeply as possible into a work
of pure celebration.' One could understand it.

---

* Besides Scofield, the principals were: Duke of Cornwall, Patrick Magee;
Duke of Albany, Cyril Cusack; Earl of Kent, Tom Fleming; Earl of Glouces-
ter, Alan Webb; Edgar, Robert Lloyd; Edmund, Ian Hogg; Oswald, Barry
Stanton; Fool, Jack MacGowran; Goneril, Irene Worth; Regan, Susan
Engel; Cordelia, Annelise Gabold (a Danish actress).

XIII

A Most Rare Vision: 1970

WRITING during the autumn of 1968 in the Royal Shakespeare Company's newspaper, *Flourish*, Peter Brook said simply:

If a well-known play is pulled to pieces and reconstructed, it is an attempt to understand more fully how certain structures work at certain times. If an audience is put in strange positions in unusual surroundings, it is to help both actors and audiences to discover what is gained and what is lost if certain apparently accepted conventions are broken. No experiment can succeed or fail, because every experiment is a potential success. Potential because success depends upon the observer. Does he wish to know?

Answers would have been widely varied if Brook had asked that question of his Stratford-upon-Avon audience on the night of 27 August 1970. He had just directed *A Midsummer Night's Dream*, and we need to know something of the play's background in the theatre before we can understand why Brook's production so astonished the critics and, with them in time, most of the Shakespearian world.

Where *Titus Andronicus* had scarcely any stage history, *A Midsummer Night's Dream* had far too much, symbolized by a clot of fairies in butter-muslin and by a sequence of venerable gags for the artisan actors, the amateur dramatic society of Athens-by-Arden, in the interlude of 'Pyramus and Thisbe'. For all the efforts to shed visual and verbal clichés, the *Dream* had been smothered. As late as the mid-nineteen-fifties we found at Edinburgh Festival for export to America, the kind of production, lush and balletic, that took the stage as smugly as if Granville-Barker and his followers had never breathed.

We must assume that, at first, the Mechanicals were the most valued figures in the triune comedy with its mingling of three worlds, the intellect, the flesh and the spirit. During the Puritan interregnum, when plays were allowed only 'by stealth', there was a so-called droll, its text entirely Shakespearian, labelled *The Merry Conceited Humours of Bottom the Weaver:* its principal figures were Peter Quince's amateurs; Oberon and Titania who – it should be noticed, in the light of the Brook revival – were doubled with Theseus and Hippolyta; and 'Pugg', or Puck. Pepys saw and recorded a performance of presumably the full *Midsummer Night's Dream* by Killigrew's company in September 1662: 'I had never seen [it] before, nor shall ever again, for it is the most insipid ridiculous play that ever I saw in my life. I saw, I confess, some good dancing and some handsome women, which was all my pleasure.' The adjective 'insipid' – though this was the diarist's own – seems, at any rate, to be a Restoration denial of Jan Kott's belief, strongly debated in the nineteen-sixties, that the *Dream* is just an erotic nightmare. By no means a children's play, the common simplification, it can hardly be reduced to the uncompromising terms of Kott. Quiller-Couch may be out of fashion, but here he spoke wisely of Shakespeare's 'trust in an imaginative world which he understands'.

About three decades after the production Pepys saw, Thomas Betterton put on *The Fairy Queen,* that exuberant business, with Purcell's music, in which the last act was devoted not to 'Pyramus and Thisbe' (this came earlier) but to a near-demented efflorescence of spectacle with a dance of six monkeys and a chorus of 'Chineses' in a Chinese garden. During the eighteenth century the play was a helpless sacrifice to the operatic stage, sometimes with the Romantics omitted and sometimes, remarkably, without the Mechanicals, though these as a rule had better luck than the other characters. Garrick used twenty-seven songs in his version. They were still turning the play to an opera during the late Regency, and this brought Hazlitt to his exasperated attack on spectacle at the expense of Shakespeare. It should be quoted:

We have found to our cost, once for all, that the regions of fancy, and the boards of Covent-Garden, are not the same thing. All that is fine in the play was lost in the representation. The spirit was evaporated, the genius was fled; but the spectacle was fine; it was that which saved the play. Oh, ye scene-shifters, ye scene-painters, ye machinists and dressmakers, ye manufacturers of moon and stars that give no light, ye musical composers, ye men in the orchestra, fiddlers and trumpeters and players on the double drum and loud bassoon, rejoice! This is your triumph; it is not ours. . . .

Hazlitt was talking about Frederick Reynolds's preposterous operatic spectacle, 'with alterations and additions', which ended with a tableau of the Triumph of Theseus, introducing 'the Cretans, the Amazons, the Centaurs, the Minotaur, Ariadne, the Labyrinth, the Mysterious Peplum or Veil of Minerva, the Ship Argo, and the Golden Fleece'.

It was 1840 before Madame Vestris and Charles Mathews restored the play to London, in J. R. Planché's reasonable Shakespearian version, and with 'Mendelssohn's celebrated overture'. Thenceforward Shakespeare was allowed to speak through a pictorial fantasy, often cut for the scenery's sake (old oaks, massive pillars), but at least with a certain amount of the original text. Samuel Phelps, who was Bottom, kept the dream-feeling at Sadler's Wells in 1853, more than Charles Kean did in his comically archaeological effort at the Princess's three years later. John William Cole, the sturdy sycophant who wrote Kean's life, regretted that in the *Dream* there was hardly 'any scope for that illustrative and historical accuracy, or for that classical research so peculiarly identified with Mr Kean's system of management'. Nevertheless, he did his best:

So little is known of Greek manners and architecture in the time of Theseus, twelve hundred years before the Christian era, and so probable is it that the buildings were of the rudest form, that any attempt to represent them on the stage would have failed in the intended object of profitable instruction. Holding himself, for these reasons, 'unfettered with regard to chronology', Mr Kean presented ancient Athens to us, in the opening scene, at the culminating period of its magnificence, 'as it would have appeared to one of its own inhabitants at a time when it had attained its greatest splendour in literature and art'.

His scholastic taste took advantage of the specified scene of action, to place before the eyes of the spectators, on the rising of the curtain, a restored view of that famous city, 'standing in its pride and glory', which excited the spontaneous sympathy and called up some of the earliest and deepest impressions of every educated mind. We saw, on the hill of the Acropolis, the far-famed Parthenon, the Erichtheum, and the statue of the tutelary godess Minerva, or Athena; by its side the theatre of Bacchus; in advance, the temple of Jupiter Olympus, partially hiding the hall of the Museum; and on the right, the temple of Theseus. The view also included the summit of that memorable eminence 'from whence the words of sacred truth were first promulgated to the Athenian citizens by apostolic inspiration'.

That was a useful beginning; and Kean, said Cole, went on to present the Wood, a 'haunt of supernatural beings', the noiseless footsteps of the dance on the moonlit greensward, with the 'shadowy reflection of every rapid and graceful movement' (very odd, this), the 'innumerable fairy legions', the 'shifting diorama; the beams of the rising sun glittering on the leaves; the gradual dispersion of the mist, discovering the fairy guardians, light and brilliant as gossamer, grouped round the unconsciously sleeping mortals'; and 'the dazzling magnificence of the palace of Theseus at the close, thronged on every staircase, balustrade and corridor, with myriads of aerial beings'. All of this brought a run of 150 performances, and Cole remarked on 'the precocious talent of Miss Ellen Terry, a child of eight years [actually she was nine] who played the merry goblin Puck'.

Thence forward the *Dream* belonged to its fairy legions and merry goblins, through a variety of revivals that included Frank Benson's (provinces, 1887; London 1889), intensely of the period in a moss-rose-and-velvet manner, with the most congested of Athenian woods, scampering coveys of elves and fairies to mingle with the trees, plants and flowers (many of them after Walter Crane's flower-books); a protracted fight between a spider and a wasp; an 'Indian boy' who would be a drag on Titania; Titania herself, 'all gauze and huge butterfly wings'; the full Mendelssohn score; and the entire atmosphere of moonbeams and mist. In 1895 Shaw went to Augustin Daly's revival at Daly's Theatre where all the fairies were fitted up with 'portable batteries and incandescent lights which they switch on and off from time to time, like children with a new toy'. Oberon was a woman; Puck behaved 'like a page-boy earnestly training himself for the post of footman'; and a 'panoramic illusion of the passage of Theseus's barge to Athens' was 'more absurd than anything that occurs in the tragedy of Pyramus and Thisbe in the last act'.

Presently, Tree (His Majesty's, January 1900) had a programme note that spoke of 'a picture of pure love unsullied by any grossness of sensual passion'; and, on stage, a Wood of cushioned moss, bluebell thickets, and scurrying rabbits; Julia Neilson, wearing electric coronal and breastplate', and looking like 'some gorgeous bird', to play Oberon and to sing 'I know a bank'. The *Dream* would remain densely arboreal until Granville-Barker, at the Savoy in the spring of 1914, made the first strong break with the Decorated manner, keeping Shakespeare's music but replacing the Mendelssohn by English folk-tunes, stylizing the midnight Wood, and offering fairies in gold and bronze like Cambodian idols. Shakespearians

came away, arguing desperately. The Wood was nothing Tree
might have recognized. Above a rough green velvet mound,
dappled with white flowers, there hung an immense terra-cotta
floral wreath from which depended a gauze canopy where fireflies
and glow-worms flickered. Behind were curtains lighted in changing
tones of green, blue, violet and purple, with a green backcloth rising
to a star-spangled purplish-blue. The fairies, so long stereotyped as
what Kipling's Puck called 'a painty-winged, wand-waving,
sugar-and-shake-your-head set of impostors', now had their hands
and faces gilded, wore bronze tights, and moved like marionettes.
The Mechanicals were simply a charmingly earnest group, working
against fate. Granville-Barker, moreover, had a note: 'In this play
I can visualize neither a beginning nor an end to realism of either
scenery or animals.' And again: 'What else was Shakespeare's
chief delight in this play but the word-music to be spoken by
Oberon, Titania, and Puck. At every possible and impossible
moment he is at it.'

At Drury Lane in 1924 Basil Dean would make one of the last
returns to Tree's full-dress method, but without rabbits: it was also
one of the last occasions when a director allowed us to laugh at the
romantic lovers (Edith Evans was Helena). Granville-Barker had
believed that Shakespeare meant the lovers' poetry to be spoken
'with a meticulous regard to its every beauty', but the hour for this
had gone. There followed productions in several degrees of stylization; and at the Old Vic in 1929, that place of 'acanthus leaves,
Prince of Wales's feathers, and gas-bracket rococo', as Alan Pryce-
Jones called it affectionately, Harcourt Williams directed the *Dream*
as a Jacobean masque, with the Cecil Sharp folk-tunes Granville-
Barker had used, and, instead of wispy fairies, attendants in seaweed costumes deriving from Inigo Jones. At Christmas 1937
Tyrone Guthrie tried an Early Victorian production, 'one more
attempt to make a union between the words of Shakespeare, the
music of Mendelssohn, and the architecture of the Old Vic'. For
Guthrie the Mendelssohn, though a classic in its own right, was
'inescapably Early Victorian, redolent of crimson and gold opera
houses, and of operatic fairies in white muslin flying through
groves of emerald canvas'.

When I wrote in 1964 on the history of Shakespeare production,*
I noted how in the revivals of *A Midsummer Night's Dream*, one
had almost a graph of the changes in stage taste: Tree's 1900

---

* *Shakespeare on the English Stage 1900–1964*, Barrie and Rockliff, 1964.

production, 'every available atom of Mendelssohn's entrancing sounds' included; Granville-Barker's gold fairies; a touring company of the Twenties ready to play in what served also as 'our *Hansel and Gretel* wood'; the quiet patrician courtliness of Bridges-Adams's productions at Stratford; a spacious pastoral treatment on summer nights in Regent's Park; Reinhardt's grandiose film; Guthrie's album of Victoriana in 1937 and his sparse 1951 revival; and the steady improvement of Peter Hall's Stratford *Dream* from noisy steeplechasing to the Tudor mansion that melted to a glimmering wood in the Aldwych production of 1963. There was also an Old Vic production that went in 1954 from Edinburgh Festival to a surprising home in New York, the Metropolitan Opera House. It had been planned for the prairie of that vast stage; but Walter Kerr, in the *New York Herald-Tribune* showed how the old manner had faded:

Some thirteen tons of painted scenery have been flown across the sea. There are slow and languid fade-ins through greenish gauze to slow and languid figures uncurling themselves from tree-trunks. Acres and acres of receding arches, in the best ruined-classic manner, rise stodgily into the heavens. Trumpeters in gold hoist their trumpets, fairies in gossamer flutter their hands, kneeling maidens toss actual rose-petals as Titania and Oberon mark off Mendelssohn's 'Wedding March'. The boys wear laurel wreaths, the girls tiaras; when Bottom puts on his donkey's head it has pronounced eyelashes, ears that prick up, and lips that would do credit to Francis the Mule. An elaborate love-chase is staged behind a scrim of spider's webs, with the wily Puck nestling neatly at the centre of one . . . There is an orchestra of sixty playing like sixty . . . The spectacle is lush, and the rose-petals may make your evening. But Shakespeare's own 'rare vision' is not really in evidence; there is no life in the lines.

II

Here roughly, then, was the position round Athens-by-Arden when Peter Brook faced *A Midsummer Night's Dream* during the late summer of 1970. Many remembered his partisanship of the controversial Jan Kott, whose essay on the Beckett *Lear* had influenced him in 1962. Kott had written contentiously about *A Midsummer Night's Dream*.* ('In no other tragedy or comedy of his, except *Troilus and Cressida,* is the eroticism expressed so brutally'; 'the pungency of the dialogue, the brutality of the situations'; 'in the universal madness of Nature and History, brief are the moments of

* 'Titania and the Ass's Head' in *Shakespeare Our Contemporary.*

happiness'.) Would Brook mirror this? Pundits suggested that he
might; but pundits should have known better. Peter Brook had
never done anything he was expected to do, and he did not now.

On the programme that Stratford night, a much less congested
programme than usual, there were simply a few quotations: the
first from Brook's own book, *The Empty Space:*

Once, the theatre could begin as magic: magic at the sacred festival, or
magic as the footlights came up. Today, it is the other way round. . . . We
must open our empty hands and show that there is really nothing up our
sleeves. Only then can we begin.

One from the Russian, Meyerhold:

There is a fourth *creator* in addition to the author, the director, the actor –
namely, the spectator. . . . From the friction between the actor's creativity
and the spectator's imagination, a clear flame is kindled.

And two from the play, itself, most notably:

> Hippolyta: This is the silliest stuff that ever I heard.
> Theseus: The best in this kind are but shadows; and
>   the worst are no worse, if imagination
>   amend them.
> Hippolyta: It must be your imagination then, and not
>   theirs.

Here it was. Brook proposed to show at once that there was
nothing up his sleeve. He would have no flower-wreaths, Indian
boy, emerald canvas, electric coronal and breastplate, fairies 'like
shadowy, ethereal, bright, elastic essences' (Cole), Mendelssohn's
'entrancing sounds', Erichtheum, Parthenon, borrowings from
The Two Noble Kinsmen (the bridal lyric, 'Roses, their sharp spines
being gone'), butter-muslin, Chineses, moonshine, six monkeys,
encrusted gags; even the theories of Kott, though he did agree
that the play contained – even if it was one aspect only – a darker,
more sinister exploration of love than usually suggested. What, for
example, of Oberon's deliberate, cool intention to degrade as a
woman the wife he loved totally? 'The play is about something very
mysterious, and only to be understood by the complexity of human
love.'*

On the hot August night we knew nothing of Brook's intentions.
Nearly eight weeks of rehearsal, from 1 July, with those now insistent group exercises – mainly physical – and continual handling

* *Plays and Players,* October 1970.

of odd props the actors called 'toys', had been as tense, testing, and complex as ever. John Kane, who played Puck and Philostrate, has described them in an essay* that begins, months before, on a Sunday afternoon in January when, among other improvisations, some members of the company – casting not then completed – were asked to read the Bottom/Pyramus 'death' speech as if they had never seen it before; as if, indeed, it had no past or future. During a meeting of the full *Dream* company a few weeks later, Brook talked for the first time about the 'secret play' discoverable only in rehearsals; in preparation for these he asked the company to work on verse that would encourage mental and vocal dexterity. At another preparatory rehearsal during the summer, the company tried to hold conversations without words, using only the gymnastics of the circus tumbler as their vocabulary. Further:

The stage management produced a bundle of short sticks and these were distributed among the company. We were encouraged to twirl or bounce them as they were passed round the ring from hand to hand. Peter asked us to experiment with them among ourselves in the three weeks before rehearsals in order that we might acquire a basic dexterity. But their real value lay in the equation of them with words. As we passed the sticks from hand to hand, to the rhythm of drums, over long distances or from great heights, so we were to learn to handle words and speeches, sharing and experiencing them as a united group.

Later the players saw their costume sketches. Brook explained that recently both he and the designer, Sally Jacobs, while watching a Chinese circus in Paris, had been struck by the difference between our own performers and theirs:

When the occidental acrobat performs, his costume emphasises his physique. You not only see the trick being performed, you see the mechanism ticking over. If we applaud, we applaud their expertise but rejoice in the perfection of the human body. Peter's Chinese acrobats hid the shape of their bodies with long flowing silk robes and performed their tricks with delicacy and speed, so that it seemed the most natural thing in the world for them to spin plates or walk on stilts. When Peter applauded them he was appreciating their skill while celebrating the existence of this particular group of people who seemed to perform in a rarefied atmosphere far removed from the physical reality of their audiences. Sally's costumes were an attempt to give this uniqueness to the magical elements of the play. It was up to us to fill them with the required degree of assurance.

* Kindly lent to the author.

From the end of June an eight-week rehearsal period began, and a ring of cushions on the floor of the studio building became a familiar setting for company debate. Kane describes how, in times of confusion, Brook would take things very slowly, looking at the ceiling or at the floor, his hands soft pink pincers that moulded like pie-crust, his head thrust forward as if to propel his thought across the distance that separated him from the players trying in silence to sift his unfinished sentences – trying to supply the missing magic word and to re-establish communication. There would be physical exercises as well; and the studio was filled with trapezes, ropes, plastic rods, spinning plates, tennis-balls, hoops, paper, string, and a variety of musical instruments: 'toys' with which the players worked for at least half an hour daily until the things became extensions of themselves.

Reporting how the performance gradually grew, Kane says:

We had many hours of black despair when we tried unsuccessfully to recapture the sensations we had first felt when we knew that a moment of the play had been 'experienced' properly. Peter could drive us to distraction by his demands for an increase in our self-awareness. He would sit down with us and shake his great head in disbelief that we could have gone so far forward in one direction while taking so many steps back in another. And then painfully he would, step by step, recover the ground we had travelled and we would once more all nod our heads in agreement, believing honestly and truthfully that we understood exactly what he was talking about and where we were going wrong. And then, even as we walked through the door of the studio at the end of the rehearsal, our certainty would fade like cigarette smoke, leaving the conjecture to rattle round inside our heads for the rest of the day.

Though he knew it was not really a piece for children, Brook invited children between eight and twelve to an early rehearsal to observe their reactions: he wanted people who could concentrate, and who had a virginal approach. Though the results here simply confirmed what he knew, he had made what he believed to be an essential experiment. Some months earlier, in preparing an announcement for the new International Centre of Theatre Research (of which more would be heard) he had written, in effect:

The freest of all spectators is the child. Playing for children is becoming vitally important today. The classic division between grown-up theatre (playing ocasional children's matinees) and a special children's theatre is no longer valid. What is needed is a theatre in which working for children takes its natural place in an adult's working day. In the healthy use of a free space the same adult actors and writers, directors and designers, would continually be moving through different spheres. At one time of the day the challenge would be to satisfy the needs of the very young. At another the workers would probe an adult situation with all the intensity and integrity they possessed. And at still another moment they would be opening themselves to all ages in the expression of a simple joy.

Most of the children at the *Dream* rehearsal, though they enjoyed the experience, really could not understand what was going on half the time. Still, Kane relates a conversation with one little girl at the end of the performance:

> *He:* Did you enjoy the play?
> *She:* Oh yes, very much.
> *He:* Did you understand what was happening?
> *She:* Oh yes.
> *He:* How did you like the fairies?
> *She:* Very much.
> *He:* Would you have liked them better if they had worn wings and things?
> *She:* Oh no. I liked them best when they were wearing their ordinary clothes. Wings and things don't matter.
> *He:* Have you been to the theatre before?
> *She:* Oh yes. Lots of times.
> *He:* Does your daddy work in the theatre?
> *She:* Yes.
> *He:* What does he do?
> *She:* He's a director.
> *He:* What's his name?
> *She:* Peter Brook.
> *He:* Oh!

Just before the première of *A Midsummer Night's Dream* – there had been a private performance (for adults) at the Midland Arts Centre in Birmingham, as well as the usual theatre previews – Brook told an interviewer* that one had to begin with the simple belief that the play was entirely fresh. Naturally there would be memories and echoes from the text and from other productions. But what one sought was 'the hidden play behind the text. Our effort is to bring the hidden play into daylight.' The first effort in the theatre, at a Royal Shakespeare Club preview, was technically a disaster; at a second preview the company was far more in key, though the audience was often uncomprehending. Next, the pre-

* John Barber's article appeared in the *Daily Telegraph,* 14 September 1970.

mière itself, an especially dangerous enterprise on a night when the audience contained a core of Stratford playgoers to whom traditions were paramount. Nearly all of Brook's major successes at Stratford had been with plays less strong in accumulated tradition – *Love's Labour's Lost, Measure for Measure, Titus Andronicus*. *King Lear* got through the barrier because memories of what Komisarjevsky had done with it still lingered round Waterside. But in *Romeo and Juliet*, during his earliest days, Brook had ignored tradition, and he suffered. With the *Dream*, too, he was environed by powerful ghosts; older Stratford, contentedly haunted, waited in anxiety. Brook did not mind: 'After a long series of dark, violent, black plays, I had a very strong wish to go as deeply as possible into a work of pure celebration. *A Midsummer Night's Dream* is, among other things, a celebration of the arts of the theatre.'*

III

The stage for his celebration, when the hard white light, almost unvaried during the evening, shone dazzlingly upon it, was a bare, white-walled, bevelled cube – an empty space fit for the rigour of the game. Designed by Sally Jacobs, close collaborator from Lamda, through the *Marat/Sade* and *US*, it looked, as watchers testified variously, like a clinic, a gymnasium, a scientific research station, a squash court, an operating theatre. A few white cushions were scattered on the floor. Upon the back wall blazed a great scarlet ostrich feather that would become a mattress or a trampoline. Above, on three sides, was a railed gallery, or catwalk, where the musicians were placed and from which, throughout the play, actors observed the goings-on below. Ropes and circus trapezes dangled.† At each side of the stage were vertical iron ladders. In effect, a book was open, its pages blank: the sheet upon which Brook would write the play as it rose to him from the text, apparently for the first time, while he asked himself: 'In what circumstances can a true love take place? How can three couples find their way to a true marriage that makes sense?' He pursued his questions with the utmost invention and vigour, though it seemed to us afterwards that, in a phrase from another context, he had been crossing a current roaring loud, upon the perilous footing of a spear.

* *Plays and Players*.
† 'A way of lifting the Immortals off the dank and dirty ground' (Wendy Monk in the *Stage*, 3 September 1970.)

The company, without wigs or make-up, swept on in a whirl of white silk cloaks; and into a startled theatre Brook brought the comedy of *A Midsummer Night's Dream*. Soon we realized what he was doing with it; that he and his cast were employing the techniques of the circus, and that the more closely we watched the actors' unexpected virtuosity, the more we heard of the play, better spoken than most people had ever known. The stage grew enchanted in movement and sound. Ten months earlier, in Budapest, I had watched a brilliant Hungarian director's attempt to stage *Timon of Athens* circus-fashion. Here the manifold ingenuities merely harmed the play, a dubious choice in any event: one ceased to listen. With Brook at Stratford one barely missed a comma. As soon as we had accepted that this was Shakespeare's play, approached by a new road through country hitherto unexplored, and with no need for a flutter of *tutus*, a superfluity of foliage, or an attendant moon, the night slipped magically into the theatre of the future. Though it may have horrified an older Stratford as much as Granville-Barker's stylization once shocked contemporary traditionalists, most people, in spite of what Brook called 'the artificial, critical tension' of a première, were genuinely excited – none more so than the critics who could express themselves next day.

We had, as Brook desired, to look at the *Dream* as if it had never been acted. The stage, in the eye of the beholder, became a terrifying Wood when coils and tendrils of helical steel wire, swung down on fishing rods from the catwalk, turned immediately to the glades where Oberon and Titania were ill met by moonlight, or the Mechanicals rehearsed by the Duke's oak, or Hermia was bedabbled with the dew and torn with briers. It was not much like the intricate forests of an older stage, or even the austere, moon-silvered thickets of a newer invention, but it was assuredly the Wood near Athens. Here Puck, riding a trapeze high over the stage, tossed down a silver plate, or flying saucer, to stand for the 'little Western flower', love-in-idleness. Oberon, in billowing purple, on another trapeze below him, caught and spun the plate upon a juggler's wand in the most alert of circus routines. This was magic responding to magic; and it was so again when, the plate still spinning, Oberon spoke 'I know a bank where the wild thyme blows' (words Julia Neilson used to sing as an operatic aria). Puck, in clown's billowing yellow breeches, managed to look like a genial Oriental djinn (one of the 'Chineses', perhaps?) but with the moonlight-blue skull-cap of Harlequin. In the scene our imaginations made readily 'as black as Acheron', he stalked above the scurrying lovers on a monstrous pair of stilts.*

The stage was never quiet while the lovers joined in probably the most athletic racing and chasing on record, up the ladders, round the gallery, through the doors. Hermia spat her challenge to Helena ('You canker-blossom, you thief of love!') while hanging by both arms from a trapeze: earthbound, maybe, but ready at any moment to take flight. The Mechanicals wore grubby string vests, braces and corduroys, and yellow boots, and carried planks and tea-mugs. The British-workman Bottom, when 'translated', had simply ass's ears, blocked shoes for hooves, and the nose-blob of a clown, no muffling mask. The fairies were bulky, hearty young men (and one woman) who wore what looked like grey pyjamas, or track-suits: one had, for a fleeting moment, to think of Hazlitt ('Ye full-grown, well-fed, substantial, real fairies'). As they carried off Bottom – now on the scarlet ostrich-feather mattress – to Titania's bower, and Oberon swung above the stage on his trapeze, we heard the amplified roar of the Wedding March, Mendelssohn matched by a whirling storm of plate-size confetti that, when the stage was empty for the interval, the fairies, as circus attendants, obligingly swept up with rakes. Fifteen minutes later, again with the set bare and a furious noise of drumming from above, Oberon, on trapeze, swung in with the mildly questioning 'I wonder if Titania be awaked?'

Certainly the audience never drowsed. None could surmise what might happen next, or how it would happen. Every sense was sharpened. The verse, especially as spoken in the grave incantatory method of Alan Howard, the Oberon,† reached us as new. Familiarity had clouded it for us; now, where nothing was familiar, Shakespeare's voice could be heard in all its moods and tenses. Not a word was cut; but sometimes, once or twice mock-operatically, Brook let the players modulate into song, Lysander and Hermia in 'Fair love, you faint with wandering in the wood', Demetrius in 'So sorrow's heaviness doth heavier grow', Helena in 'O weary

* John Kane, who read a great many detective novels during the rehearsal period, says: 'If you want to find one of the sources for the "stilt sequence" during the Lysander-Demetrius quarrel, I direct your attention to the chapter called "The Scissor Man" in Nicholas Blake's *The Deadly Joker*.'

† Alan Howard and Sara Kestelman were Oberon and Theseus, Titania and Hippolyta; John Kane was Puck; the Mechanicals were David Waller (Bottom), Philip Locke (Quince), Glynne Lewis (Flute). Terrence Hardiman (Starveling), Norman Rodway (Snout), and Barry Stanton (Snug); the lovers, Mary Rutherford (Hermia), Frances de la Tour (Helena), Ben Kingsley (Demetrius), and Christopher Gable (Lysander). John Kane was also Philostrate; and Philip Locke, Egeus.

night'; Puck had a barbaric 'Up and down', the Mechanicals a dirge, 'Sixpence a day'. Noises from the watchful musicians were like nothing we had heard in the *Dream* before: Richard Peaslee supplied them with such things as autoharps, bongo-drums, a guitar, the coil spring from a car suspension unit, and a corrugated plastic hose which threw out notes as it was swung. 'The passage of air through the hose produces what is reportedly a mixture of notes in the harmonic series with a C fundamental. The harder you swing the higher the pitch rises.'*

Brook did not minimize the agony implicit in the lovers' tangle. Nor did he minimize the 'translated' Bottom's sexual response to Titania: something that would bring correspondence to the Midland newspapers. But he lost nothing of the play's gaiety or ultimate healing gentleness. He refused to mock the interlude by Quince's dramatic society; for once the courtiers were compassionate, no longer insolently condescending. Like Granville-Barker, Brook presented the Mechanicals as a group of charming earnestness, a company of reasonable human beings, not a repository for a hundred gags, the myriad accretions of the years: no piping treble for Flute, no anxious mispronunciation. Earlier, a touchingly anxious Quince had wept for joy at Bottom's twelfth-hour return. In the Court the audience was so carried away by the lamentable comedy of Pyramus and Thisbe that it joined in song with the actors. At the end of the night, after Oberon had given his solemn blessing, Puck spoke, as usual, the epilogue. Crying 'Give me your hands if we be friends', he jumped into the house and caught the nearest member of the audience by the hand while the rest of the company, again in white, the wedding cloaks thrown off, followed him closely. It was a world of utter harmony, 'sweet peace', the end of a festival. As a critic would say, the whole of the night had seemed to be like a preparation for that final act of stretching out to greet the audience: the playgoers who must be active participants.

In this *Midsummer Night's Dream,* as in *The Merry Conceited Humours of Bottom the Weaver* three centuries before – but not for the same reason – Oberon and Titania doubled with Theseus and Hippolyta, possibly their other selves released in dream and night; it was a haunted moment in the pause before sunrise and the glory of daybreak, when the Immortals become mortal simply by the assumption of cloaks. There were other doubles: Egeus with Quince, two forms of paternalism, and Puck, a natural master of

* *Music and Musicians,* November 1970. The Free-Ka is an American invention.

the ceremonies, with Philostrate. Throughout, the worlds were interwoven, interdependent; in the fantasy of the night's fears we saw what was hidden by day: there was no division now between 'the outer man whose behaviour is bound by the photographic rules of everyday life and the inner man whose anarchy and poetry is usually expressed only in his words'.* In a space of plain, unsullied colours, lemon, emerald-green, blue, startling against the dazzle of white,† the three-levelled fantasy was re-thought: Brook's dream. However, he had illustrated Shakespeare, the play was Shakespeare's own: Brook had simply polished the mirror. I have always remembered Shaw's words about Daly in 1895: 'He swings Puck away on a clumsy trapeze, with a ridiculous clash of cymbals in the orchestra, in the fullest belief that he is thereby completing instead of destroying the effect of Puck's lines.' I would like Shaw, who appreciated inspiration and what he called 'the march of music' as much as any man, to know what might be done with a trapeze and with circus legerdemain when magic meets magic. I do not say that there is no other way of presenting the *Dream*. Moonlight will be silver again, and the Duke's oak will rise. But at Stratford Peter Brook demolished thoughtless convention. We had to hope that he had not created a form that would be botched in admiring imitation. Only two months after Stratford I saw the first signs of his influence in a Birmingham Repertory production – by no means botched, but without his daybreak quality – in which substantial fairies swung themselves round on a stage framed in rigging (almost I expected to see St Elmo's fire at the masthead) and the Wood was simulated by tangles of what looked like coloured plastic knitting.

IV

Brook had never had a stronger critical response, even for *Titus*. Because, on the day after the première, he left with Natasha for the Shiraz-Persepolis Festival in Iran, he saw only the first few of the notices that showered applause. The one full-scale objector, Benedict Nightingale (*New Statesman*) came a week later: 'Brook's most dispiriting production', 'Shakespeare as he might be conceived by a science-fiction addict, or, indeed, performed by enthusiastic Vegans: the *Dream* 2001 AD'. Rosemary Say in the

* Quoted by John Barber, *Daily Telegraph*, 14 September 1970.
† The play was designed by Sally Jacobs; the music was 'by Richard Peaslee, with the actors and Felix Mendelssohn'.

Sunday Telegraph had thought wistfully of Regent's Park. Otherwise, Brook had notices such as these:

The Times (Irving Wardle): 'A masterpiece. . . . It brings Brook himself to a new point of rest. You could not have predicted what he would do with the play; but after seeing the production, you feel you ought to have known, as it is a simple and inevitable crystallisation of what has gone before.'

Daily Telegraph (John Barber): 'A new way of making Shakespeare eloquent to this generation.'

Observer (Helen Dawson): 'Radical, full of thought, and theatrically a triumph.'

Sunday Times (Harold Hobson): 'The sort of thing one sees only once in a generation, and then only from a man of genius.'

Evening News (Felix Barker): 'It is Brook's triumph as ringmaster of this circus that he has taken an idea which seemingly can't possibly work and made it constantly entertaining and valid.'

New York Times (Clive Barnes): 'Brook gives us new eyes.'

Time (Christopher Porterfield): 'By not ridiculing Titania or patronising Bottom, Brook deftly amplifies one of Shakespeare's theories: the harsh comedy of human shortcomings is only bearable when tempered by tenderness and generosity of spirit.'

Most notably, I think, the actor-scholar, Robert Speaight, wrote in the *Tablet*: 'Mr Brook takes his cue from nothing but his own artistic conscience and from no one but Shakespeare himself. This production will be applauded as an invention of genius; more exactly, it should be seen as a response. It leaves the impression, for all its breath-taking virtuosity, not of a man who has asked himself what he can do with a play grown too familiar, but of what the play can do with him – stranded as he is, without magical beliefs, in the middle of the twentieth century.' Mr Speaight would fortify this later (*Shakespeare Quarterly*: Autumn 1970): 'He commanded you into a frame of mind when the very notion of magic, of supernatural agency, had to be created afresh. . . . The French have a phrase which communicates the peculiar, the explosively original, quality of this production. They speak of a *mystère en pleine lumière*, and this suggests the brilliant white light that Mr Brook threw upon his staring white stage, with only Titania's bright red feather-bed to relieve it.'

Criticism aside, *The Times* gave the full accolade in a leading article two days after the production opened:*

* 29 August 1970.

A good Shakespeare production is true to the original in a sense other than the textual accuracy or resemblance to how it might have been at the Globe. One begins to see why Plato needed his doctrine of Forms. The question is easily resolved if one is allowed to have a Form of the *Dream* laid up in heaven. Productions of the play to be good would have to resemble the Form of it, the resemblance being not one of copying but of congruence. So it would come about that for all the trapezes, juggling, helical wire trees, and general non-Elizabethanism, the Stratford production is not just good theatre but a true production of the *Dream*.

When, some weeks later, Brook was over at Stratford to re-work certain scenes, he was talking to a few of the players after a performance that had not gone too well: the company had felt depressed and the audience was not exhilarated. Brook (John Kane writes) said:

It surprises me that in a company working full-time on Shakespeare, this sort of depression can still take hold of its actors. If only we could all fully realize that the man and his works are so far beyond our capabilities as actors and directors that we can never do justice to them, a healthier attitude to performance would surely develop. No matter how long we worked on a play, we could never come to the end of the work. There could never be any complacency or boredom because we would be starting on a journey that has no end, and surely for the creative artist the journey itself is the reward. The moment you arrive anywhere, you limit the distance you might have travelled.

(Kane adds: 'At least, that's what I think he said'.)

Early in December 1970, on a visit to London for a single night, the *Dream* had what Brook considered to be a grand performance* in the Roundhouse at Chalk Farm, a theatre progressively popular with young people. Remarkably, it was the first time the Royal Shakespeare Company had worked in something like Elizabethan intimacy, in the middle of eight hundred people who were sitting on the floor. There were neither costumes nor sets. At once the mood was right. Nobody seemed to feel any of the usual embarrassment when an actor came down from the stage. In their chase the lovers darted in and out of the colonnade that runs round the house, or they hid and skirmished among the nearest playgoers. During the Pyramus interlude the watchers became instinctively the court

---

* But Ronald Bryden (*Observer*, 13 December 1970), who had greatly admired the full-dress production at Stratford, found the studio version 'an unnecessary step backward from perfection'. He excepted the last scene, 'a moment of magical gain' that 'could not have happened behind a proscenium arch'.

of Theseus, realizing that nothing could be amiss when simpleness and duty tendered it.

v

The official theme of the Shiraz-Persepolis Festival, to which he flew from Britain after the Stratford opening, was very much in the Brook mood: 'ritual drama'. Thus there were Persian mystery plays; a production by Grotowski; the American Bread and Puppet Theatre; and a variety of other rituals. Brook had been impressed especially by what he called 'an ideal theatrical experience' that he had met a few months before in a village of north-east Iran: a performance of the Persian folk-drama-cum-religious observance, the *ta'zieh*, a 'total communal event' in what the drama critic of *The Times,* Irving Wardle, described as a mood of sustained lamentation (the word *ta'zieh* means mourning). The plays are all performed by villagers, and they deal with the martyrdom of followers of the prophet: 'a bit like Oberammergau,' Brook said, 'but without the commercialism.' Several of his films were shown in Shiraz, and he shared a vigorous four hours' discussion with other directors (Grotowski among them) and Iranian writers and students.

He had arranged to return to Iran in the following year. After a gap of eighteen months and more, he was resuming the experimental work in Paris that he had had to drop so suddenly: now as head of an international centre of theatre research, not itself a theatre, not an academy, not an institution. It would occupy a vast warehouse of the Mobilier National (roughly Ministry of Works) that was owned by the firm of Gobelin and designed for tapestry-weaving. 'Like a large white box,' he said, 'which can be used as a single space, or into which we can fit smaller boxes, according to the play.' Measuring 130 feet by 35 feet, the Centre was to be the home of a group of international actors 'evolving original material', but not playing in repertory. Brook explained:* 'We shall give performances of different lengths, at different times, and at different places. We shall change the entire structure of the piece as we go along. All sorts of international groups and foundations have given backing; they are trusting us as they would trust research workers, and – strictly speaking – we don't have to show an actual product.'

A preliminary statement, some time earlier, had expressed the intentions of the Centre with stern clarity. It began:

* In an interview with Philip Oakes, *Sunday Times,* 5 July 1970.

The world's theatre has rarely been in so grave a crisis.

With few exceptions, it can be divided into two unsatisfactory categories: those theatres that remain faithful to traditions in which they have lost confidence, and those that wish to create a new and revolutionary theatre, but have not the skills that this requires. And yet theatre in the deepest sense of the word is no anachronism in the 20th century; it has never been needed so urgently.

The special virtue of the theatre as an art form is that it is inseparable from the community. This could mean that the only way to make possible a healthy theatre is by first of all changing the society around it. It can also mean the opposite. It can mean that although the world cannot be reformed in a day, in the theatre it is always possible to wipe the slate clean and to start again from zero.

What, then, was required? First, that all the elements should be equally fresh. For years experiments had been made with a new acting style on old texts, on new plays in old surroundings. Now, boldly and at the same time, all the parts had to be renewed. To begin with, there would have to be a group of actors* of many nationalities and different backgrounds, with every skill and no prejudices. Belonging to no particular school, they would master the arts of them all. Moving like dancers and acrobats, they would be equally dexterous with words. Any actor, however young in attitude, must bring something of his own to exchange with the others; together they should have great suppleness and flexibility. Their work, unremittingly educational, would involve constant research, experiment, training and discipline, for only a disciplined actor could escape from the confinement of clumsy and incoherent attempts at free expression.

Then a passage that Brook alone could have signed:

A group of actors must also be a community: it needs to be conceived not as a 'company' for certain hours during a day, but as a social experiment, in which the actor seeks to assume a mature adult responsibility. Only in this way can an actor truly know what he is doing when he makes contact with an audience without the protection of conventional ways – in conditions that are new and free.

Next, the theatre itself: no conventional building with its familiar associations but a neutral place: one that became a theatre simply as the living event unfolded, one where the same group could present many different sorts of work – intimate, popular, serious – in a free space that continually redefined itself. So to the author who

* There were sixteen at first.

would find by direct experience what was truly needed of him; and to the audience, 'all those members of a community who see theatre as a possibility for themselves of renewal'. This is the road that can bridge the false and sterile separation between popular entertainment and the *avant-garde*. Finally:

The Centre cannot accomplish its aims if it has to operate like a theatre that depends even partly upon a box-office for its livelihood. The essential basis of its activity as a community of creation and research must be a subsidy adequate for all its physical needs.

With this before them the workers of the International Centre – Irene Worth would be one – began their task in the autumn of 1970. Already they knew what their first engagement would be: a visit to Persia in 1971. There, after three months as guests of the Iranian authorities, they could perform whatever in their experiments had seemed to be valuable. Another new book; another empty space ready for inscription. And what would the inscription be? The future would tell; for Peter Brook it was always the future.

XIV

Last Words: 1971—

I

'In me' (so goes the Siegfried Sassoon poem), 'in me, past, present, future meet.' Peter Brook has sifted what he needs from the past; it is very little. Ceaselessly questioning the present, he has already entered the future: *A Midsummer Night's Dream*, which one alarmed traditionalist called science fiction, spoke to a world of the theatre yet to be. New York in January 1971* received it with the excitement of Stratford audiences in the previous summer and autumn. On Broadway, and during a brief American tour, box-office receipts totalled 1,161,000 dollars, or £483,000. No doubt Brook would have described his production in a few words he wrote for the RSC journal, *Flourish*, during 1967: 'Our aim is a new Elizabethan relationship – linking the private and the public, the intimate and the crowded, the secret and the open, the vulgar and the magical. For this we need both a crowd on stage and a crowd watching – and within that crowded stage individuals offering their most intimate truths to individuals within that crowded audience, sharing a collective experience with them.' He might also still recognize what he wrote during 1953 in an introduction to *As You Like It*:† 'In *As You Like It*'s neighbour, *A Midsummer Night's Dream*, the more attractive the scenery, the more it takes away from the magic of the words, for they make their greatest effect only in the simplest of settings.' (None of Walter Kerr's 'acres and acres of receding arches . . . rising stodgily into the heavens.')

Stray influences apart, we may not see another comparable revival of the *Dream*, for inspiration cannot be begged or borrowed. But at least, when we meet another Shakespeare play magically recreated, without theft from past history, nothing brashly or modishly defiant, then we shall know that Peter Brook has already

---

* The RSC staged the play at the Billy Rose Theatre, Broadway, where that spring Peter Brook was given the 'Tony' Award for the Best Stage Director.
† For the Folio Society.

passed that way. Compact, watchful, his eyes an unflickering blue, he is probably the most insistent inquirer in the century's theatre, the Grand Inquisitor of the stage: his interrogation of himself and his authors leads him further and further from the theatre as we have known it, and as he knew it when he went to the rehearsal room of the Birmingham Repertory and then to Stratford in the immediate post-war awakening. Precociously he was worried even then. In 1948 he wrote:*

Shakespeare production today is based on a number of axioms whose presence no one even troubles to question. It seems inevitable that *A Midsummer Night's Dream* should have gauzes, ballets, and Mendelssohn, that Romeo and Juliet should be middle-aged, that the histories should be played in front of tapestry curtains, red for England, blue for France. . . .

Like other young men, he was being cavalier with stage history: it would have been easy to tell him – and, no doubt, somebody did – about former questioners, former Shakespeare revivals, within his own brief lifetime. Certainly, even in the pre-war shallows at Stratford, Romeo and Juliet were not middle-aged, and Graham Robertson had written of the Old Vic pair (Eric Portman and Jean Forbes-Robertson) in the early spring of 1928: 'The two *very* young lovers made the whole thing so poignant and real that you longed to wait for them at the stage door with a double perambulator and wheel them home to bed.'† True; but Peter Brook would never be outfaced by a handful of dates and facts; he had evolved his beliefs for himself, and in any event he was still fighting back against the condescending criticisms of his Stratford *Romeo and Juliet* as a work of youthful exaggeration, of a marvellous boy who perished in his pride.

He believed then that 'to communicate any of Shakespeare's plays to a present-day audience, the producer must be prepared to set every resource of the modern theatre at the disposal of his cast.' Again (from the same *Orpheus* article): 'There is no perfect production of any play, nor is there any final one; like a musician's interpretaion, its existence is inseparable from its performance. . . . The theatre deals with living material and is in an endless state of flux.' In effect, he was still enlarging that final sentence when he wrote in the autumn of 1961:‡

* *Orpheus I*, John Lehmann, 1948.
† *Letters from Graham Robertson,* edited by Kerrison Preston, Hamish Hamilton, 1948.
‡ 'A Search for a Hunger' in *Mademoiselle,* November 1961.

I want to see characters behaving out of character, in the lies, inconsistency, and total confusion of daily life. I want to see outer realism as something in endless flux, with barriers and boundaries that come and go, people and situations forming, unforming before my eyes. I want to see identities changing, not as clothes are changed, but as scenes dissolve on a film, as paint drops off a brush. Then I want to see inner realism as another state of movement and flux. I want to sense the energies which, the deeper one goes, become true forces that impel our false identities. I want to sense what truly binds us, what truly separates us. I want to hold a mirror, not up to nature, but up to human nature, and by this I mean that interwoven within-and-without world as we understand it in 1961 – not as people defined it in 1900. I want to understand this not with my reason, but with the flash of recognition that tells me it is true, because it is also in me.

Then, in *The Empty Space* seven years later:

Deadliness always brings us back to repetition: the deadly director uses old formulae, old methods, old jokes, old effects; stock beginnings and scenes, stock ends; and this applies equally to his partners, the designers and composers, if they do not start each time afresh from the void, the desert, and the true questions – why clothes at all, why music, what for? A deadly director is a director who brings no challenge to the conditional reflexes that every department must contain.

Through the years he has been the most sagaciously articulate of directors, never afraid to alter course at the twelfth hour even if it means shoal-water. It might be said of him in the day's jargon: 'He re-thinks too much; such men are dangerous.' But Brook has always had something to show for his questioning, his listening – somebody has said that he listens like a tape-recorder – his sway of mind, his quick intuitions, his progressively longer rehearsals, his insistence on taking his actors through a maze of exercises, his resolve that a director (however long it takes) must reach 'a genuine point of communion with the author's intention', and his absolute refusal to accept anything as the last word. A theatre-man said to me: 'If Brook were putting on the Day of Judgment, there'd be no official opening night. He would go on rehearsing into eternity, and he'd compose the Last Trump himself.'

II

No director in this century has been more fertile, readier to reply to his own questions, though these lead inevitably to another inquisition. He can himself remind us of the David Lindsay passage* that, as we have seen, Barry Jackson would quote about *Love's Labour's Lost:*

It looked as if life-forms were being coined so fast by Nature, that there was not physical room for all. Nevertheless it was not as on Earth where a hundred seeds are scattered in order that one may be sown. Here the young forms seemed to survive, while, to find accommodation for them, the old ones perished . . . without any ostensible cause – they were sinply being killed by new life.

A natural iconoclast, he has long ceased to cherish tradition, which means little more to him than throttling ivy; at heart, as the most probing of intellectuals, he cannot understand why playgoers can still be moved – and deeply – by a straight classical performance in an older mode. For him, yesterday in the regular theatre is always dead except as a post-mortem subject: what was the cause of death? There would be no more alarming member for the Society for Theatre Research. He says, too, precisely what he feels at the moment, which is the one moment that matters. In 1953 he was speaking of the 'magic of the words'. In 1964 he was worried, as Artaud had been, about 'the unhealthy dominance of words in the theatre'. Early in 1970 he was saying of Shakespeare: 'What holds you in the theatre is the movement of sound that never really stops because of the structure of a very free verse beat.' Later that year critics were praising him for the 'most beautifully spoken' *Midsummer Night's Dream* they had heard.

Henry Brandon, introducing a tape-recorded conversation with Brook in 1966, said:† 'I noticed that he was not only completely unaware of the presence of the microphone, but that he went almost into something of a trance to develop his ideas.' Actors and interviewers know those trances and what has come from them during the years. Quotations from them can be misleading because last week's pronouncement is already hidden under the files. *The Empty Space* nears its end with the words, 'As you read this book it is already moving out of date. It is for me an exercise now frozen on the page.' But he goes on: 'Unlike a book the theatre has one special characteristic. It is always possible to start again. In life this is a myth: we ourselves can never go back on anything. . . . In the theatre the slate is wiped clean all the time.'

* In *A Voyage to Arcturus.*
† *Conversations with Henry Brandon,* Andre Deutsch, 1966.

We have seen this happening throughout the present book. We have seen him as a child of his period, that neo-romantic world immediately after the war; we have watched him learning the dynamics of theatrical expression and seeking to rationalize the production of grand opera (his one defeat, for he fought the campaign too early); we have watched him turning to stripped and austere Shakespeare at an hour when people, with gum-brush and label, were trying to fix him as a director too lavishly overblown; we have watched him trying to re-vitalize commercial comedy, and enjoying such a musical as *Irma la Douce* as if he were a veteran of show-business; we have seen him making startling theatrical experiences of, first, a despised tragedy, and then a great one; admiring Kott, learning from Artaud, considering Grotowski; observing a new race of actors, pondering on ritual, becoming involved in the Theatre of Cruelty and the drama of protest – such terms as these proliferated in the Sixties – and at length, having declared that the theatre of illusion was dead, finding his own celebration of Shakespeare and the arts of the stage in the mysterious magic of *A Midsummer Night's Dream*.

There is no glib description for him. He voyages through strange seas of thought. As in the theatre, so in the cinema: he condemns the casual cliché. It is not an easy life: to those with him he offers incessant toil, whether on the high trapeze, in the snow-winds of north Jutland, or in the rigours of an experimental laboratory. Already he has entered the future, though if his past, as a virtuoso director, has ceased to exist for him, it exists for us in all its mutations and surprises. There have been matters to question (the denial of the cathartic quality in *Lear*, the end of *Oedipus*); there have been odd utterances in trance; there have been too many explanations, too easy a dismissal of the Deadly Theatre, too esoteric a statement of the Holy Theatre. But behind him are things ineffaceable in mid-century record. Today he may have forgotten his early searches for the stinging theatrical effect: the sustained pauses, as in *The Lady from the Sea, Love's Labour's Lost, Vicious Circle,* and *Measure for Measure*; the sudden blaze of the Italian sun upon the market-place of Verona; the elaborated procession of the prisoners in *Measure for Measure*. We think of them still, just as we remember the rhythms of his early productions, their unity, the knowledge that a young director, possessed by the play, could possess his actors, and, through them, his audience.

For some of us the name of Peter Brook means the close of

Love's Labour's Lost, its fall of frost in the summer night; the terrible laughter that ended *Vicious Circle*; Romeo and Juliet isolated at their first meeting, the world forgot; the ripple of *Ring Round the Moon*; a sultry night in medieval Vienna; the Statue scene of *The Winter's Tale*, reconciliation in utter simplicity; the pressing weight of the conspiracy in *Venice Preserv'd*; the transition at the end of *The Lark* from the prisoner at Rouen to the splendour of Rheims; *Titus Andronicus* as a terrifying ritual without parade of terror; the pulsating wave-light at Wishwood that announced the Furies; the transformation of the boys in *Lord of the Flies* to a horde of screaming, painted devils; the crowd converging on its victim in *The Visit*; Lear and Gloucester, two lost old men at the world's end, on a vast empty stage; the ferocious guillotine sequence in the *Marat/Sade*; the burning of the butterfly in *US*; the orchestration of that Senecan chorus, environing its audience at the Old Vic, and the last moment in *A Midsummer Night's Dream* when the company ('Give me your hands, if we be friends') came up through a dazzled house. Much else (marked, too, by the voices of Scofield, Olivier, and Gielgud, Thorndike and Evans, the Lunts, Irene Worth, Ian Richardson, Alan Howard), but these things remain indelibly, many of them, I notice now, from the end of a play; with Brook no play has ever wavered into nothing, though now and then – as in *US* and, particularly, in *Oedipus* where even he could not explain away his climax – he has left an audience uncertain what to do: to applaud, to stay, to go.

More and more, his later effects have been wrought by his devoted attention to ensemble playing, to the work of a small group (as in the *Dream* where doubling reduced the numbers), and to his determination to break what has been called 'the rigidity of the one-dimensional approach to acting'. He has said:* 'I believe the only directing method that can bring results is a great number of different methods, all of which aim at enabling the actor to concentrate more and more, so that rehearsing becomes a living process, not a rational one.' Further:†

The aim of improvisation is training actors in rehearsal, and the aim of exercises is always the same, it is to get away from Deadly Theatre. It is not just a matter of splashing about in self-indulgent euphoria as outsiders often suspect; for it aims at bringing the actor again and again to his own barriers, to the points where in place of new-found truth he normally

* Interview in *New York Times*, 9 January 1966.
† *The Empty Space*.

substitutes a lie . . . The purpose of an exercise is to reduce and return: to narrow the area down and down until the birth of a lie is revealed and caught. If the actor can find and see this moment he can perhaps open himself to a deeper, more creative impulse.

III

Finally now, hear Peter Brook speak through the Sixties:

'The true snobbery and the true barriers today are the mental ones that separate playwrights from the abstract and frightening themes of the world they live in' (1962).

'If a play does not make us lose our balance, the evening is unbalanced' (1965).

'I have tried desperately in Shakespeare to avoid style simply because style is the way to anticipate the performance' (1966).

'The theatre has one precise social function – to disturb the spectator' (1967).

'Why do we applaud, and what? Has the stage a real place in our lives? What function can it have? What could it serve? What could it explore?' (1968).

'The one thing that distinguishes the theatre from all other arts is that it has no permanence' (1970).

Here, at the end of the book, is the place for Paul Scofield's tribute* to the director and friend with whom he has worked, off and on, for a quarter of a century (eleven plays and two films), and for whom he has a whole-hearted admiration:

It always seemed to me at first that Peter's main strength was an immense singleness of purpose; that he had a vision of what he wanted, and cut through obstacles and redundancies like some sort of electronic light beam until he got it. I now see, and have for some time, that this is an over-simplification of a very complex working mechanism; indeed all that I say can only be an over-simplification.

At the moment I can best express this complexity as a duality: a gift of being able, as a director, to be at once open and closed. Open to a multiplicity of influences, seeming to collect them through the pores of his skin, like a water-creature taking invisible nourishment from the sea – while at the same moment his eyes are fixed on the final objective and closed to anything irrelevant to its demands.

The eyes and the hands seem to provide the best metaphor for this duality. Astonishingly steady eyes, seeing through a beyond; and the

* In a letter to the author.

hands moving and picking. A stillness and a mobility together, and entirely natural to him.

This dual impression was less noticeable in the earlier years – perhaps, I think, because he relies more and more on his own nature, and less and less on his intellectual judgment which is considerable. If he has shifted position as an artist it is from spectatorship to participation, from remote control to a more sensual involvement. I think he would like the experience of being a director to be closer to that of the performer.

I don't want to pay easy tribute to Peter, or say that he is the most 'this or that' director in the world; he is quite unique and I am lucky to have worked with him so often.

Today, moving between Paris (home and workshop), London, New York, Iran – where you will – Peter Brook's life is a prolonged and peripatetic experiment. There must be a new form of theatre, a new kind of play, new forms of acting, a new response from a new audience. It is, as he sees it, a most rare vision. The young man who knew, so long ago, what he desired, is still creatively in search. It is wrong to call this chapter *Last Words,* for Peter Brook is beginning again; he is always beginning again. What he does in the workshop matters less than what finally appears on the stage. If he gets the right answer, the calculations should be his own affair. We know what he thinks is the right answer. He gave it as far back as 1961 in his own urgent, headlong phrasing:

I want to see a flood of people and events that echo my inner battlefield. I want to see behind this desperate and ravishing confusion an order, a structure, that will relate to my deepest and truest longings for structure and law. I want through this to find the new forms, and through the new forms the new architecture, and through the new architecture the new patterns and the new rituals of the age that is swirling around us.

The age that is always ahead.

Postscript: *The Empty Space,* p. 139: 'A representation is the occasion when something of the past is shown again – something that once was, now is . . . a representation denies time. It abolishes the difference between yesterday and today. A representation is . . . a making present.' Peter Brook is searching for a right representation. This will make not only yesterday present, but tomorrow as well. Then the age that is always ahead will be here and now.

Appendices

PLAYS DIRECTED BY PETER BROOK

1942   *Dr Faustus* by Christopher Marlowe, Torch Theatre, London (with an amateur cast).

1945   *The Infernal Machine* by Jean Cocteau, Chanticleer Theatre Club, London (with Sigrid Landstad and Frederick Horrey).

       The Barretts of Wimpole Street by Rudolf Besier, 'Q' Theatre, Kew Bridge, London.

       Pygmalion by Bernard Shaw, directed for an ENSA tour (with Mary Grew as Eliza).

       Man and Superman by Bernard Shaw, Birmingham Repertory Theatre (with Paul Scofield as John Tanner).

       King John by William Shakespeare, Birmingham Repertory Theatre (with Paul Scofield as Philip Faulconbridge, the Bastard).

       The Lady from the Sea by Henrik Ibsen, Birmingham Repertory Theatre (with Paul Scofield as Doctor Wangel; Eileen Beldon as Ellida).

1946   *Love's Labour's Lost* by William Shakespeare, Shakespeare Memorial Theatre, Stratford-upon-Avon (with Paul Scofield as Don Adriano de Armado; David King-Wood as Berowne).

       The Brothers Karamazov, adapted by Alec Guinness from the novel by Dostoevsky, Lyric Theatre, Hammersmith (with Alec Guinness as Mitya).

       Vicious Circle by Jean-Paul Sartre; translated by Marjorie Gabain and Joan Swinstead, Arts Theatre, London (with Alec Guinness as Garcin; Beatrix Lehmann as Inès; Betty Ann Davies as Estelle).

1947   *Romeo and Juliet* by William Shakespeare, Shakespeare Memorial Theatre, Stratford-upon-Avon (with Laurence Payne as Romeo; Daphne Slater as Juliet).

       Double bill of *Men Without Shadows* and *The Respectable Prostitute* by Jean-Paul Sartre, translated and adapted by Kitty Black, Lyric Theatre, Hammersmith (with Mary

Morris as Lucie in *Men Without Shadows*; Betty Ann Davies as Lizzie in *The Respectable Prostitute*).

Romeo and Juliet, His Majesty's, London (Stratford production in short autumn repertory season by Stratford company).

1949 *Dark of the Moon* by Howard Richardson and William Berney, Lyric Theatre, Hammersmith; later transferred to Ambassadors Theatre, London (with William Sylvester as John; Sheila Burrell as Barbara Allen).

1950 *Ring Round the Moon*, a 'charade with music' by Jean Anouilh, adapted by Christopher Fry, Globe Theatre, London (with Paul Scofield as Hugo and Frédéric, Claire Bloom as Isabelle; Margaret Rutherford as Mme Desmortes).

Measure for Measure by William Shakespeare, Shakespeare Memorial Theatre, Stratford-upon-Avon (with John Gielgud as Angelo; Barbara Jefford as Isabella).

The Little Hut by André Roussin, adapted by Nancy Mitford, Lyric Theatre, London (with Robert Morley as Philip; Joan Tetzel as Susan; David Tomlinson as Henry).

1951 *La Mort d'un Commis Voyageur* (*Death of a Salesman*) by Arthur Miller, Brussels (Belgian National Theatre).

A Penny for a Song by John Whiting, Haymarket Theatre, London (with Alan Webb as Sir Timothy Bellboys; Denys Blakelock as Lamprett Bellboys; Marie Löhr as Hester Bellboys; Virginia McKenna as Dorcas Bellboys; Ronald Squire as Hallam Matthews).

The Winter's Tale by William Shakespeare, at the Phoenix Theatre, London (later at Edinburgh Festival before resuming London run, with John Gielgud as Leontes; Diana Wynyard as Hermione; Flora Robson as Paulina).

Colombe by Jean Anouilh, adapted by Denis Cannan, New Theatre, London (with Yvonne Arnaud as Mme Alexandra; Joyce Redman as Colombe).

1953 *Venice Preserv'd or, A Plot Discovered* by Thomas Otway, Lyric Theatre, Hammersmith (with John Gielgud as Jaffier; Paul Scofield as Pierre; Eileen Herlie as Belvidera).

The Little Hut Coronet Theatre, New York (with Anne Vernon as Susan).

1954 *The Dark is Light Enough* by Christopher Fry, Aldwych Theatre, London (with Edith Evans as Countess Rosmarin Ostenburg).

Both Ends Meet by Arthur Macrae, Apollo Theatre, London

(with Brenda Bruce as Margaret; Arthur Macrae as Tom; Alan Webb as Sir George Treherne; Miles Malleson as Lord Minster).

House of Flowers by Truman Capote, music by Harold Arlen, Alvin, New York (with Pearl Bailey).

1955 *The Lark* by Jean Anouilh, translated by Christopher Fry, Lyric Theatre, Hammersmith (with Dorothy Tutin as Joan; Richard Johnson as the Earl of Warwick; Donald Pleasance as the Dauphin).

Titus Andronicus by William Shakespeare, Shakespeare Memorial Theatre, Stratford-upon-Avon; brought to London in 1957 (with Laurence Olivier as Titus; Anthony Quayle as Aaron; Vivien Leigh as Lavinia).

Hamlet by William Shakespeare, Phoenix Theatre, London (with Paul Scofield as Hamlet; Diana Wynyard as Gertrude; Alec Clunes as Claudius, Mary Ure as Ophelia).

1956 *The Power and the Glory* adapted from Graham Greene's novel by Denis Cannan and Pierre Bost, Phoenix Theatre, London (with Paul Scofield as Priest; Harry H. Corbett as Lieutenant of Police).

The Family Reunion by T. S. Eliot, Phoenix Theatre, London (with Paul Scofield as Harry; Sybil Thorndike as Amy; Gwen Ffrangcon-Davies as Agatha).

A View from the Bridge by Arthur Miller, Comedy Theatre, London (with Anthony Quayle as Eddie; Mary Ure as Catherine).

La Chatte sur un Toit Brûlant, translated by André Obey from Tennessee William's *A Cat on a Hot Tin Roof,* Théâtre Antoine, Paris (with Jeanne Moreau as Maggie).

Titus Andronicus by William Shakespeare, Stoll Theatre, London (Stratford company, with Laurence Olivier).

1957 *The Tempest* by William Shakespeare, Shakespeare Memorial Theatre, Stratford-upon-Avon, and afterwards at Theatre Royal, Drury Lane, London (with John Gielgud as Prospero).

1958 *Vu du Pont,* translated by Marcel Aymé from Arthur Miller's *A View from the Bridge,* Théâtre Antoine, Paris (with Raf Vallone as Eddie; Lila Kedrova as Beatrice).

The Visit by Friedrich Dürrenmatt, adapted by Maurice Valency (staged previously in English provinces as *Time and Again*), Lynn Fontanne Theatre, New York (with Lynn Fontanne as Claire Zachanassian and Alfred Lunt as Anton Schill).

Irma la Douce, musical comedy, with original book and lyrics by Alexander Breffort, and English book and lyrics by Julian More, David Heneker and Monty Norman; music by Marguerite Monnot; Lyric Theatre, London (with Keith Michell as Nestor-le-Fripe; Elizabeth Seal as Irma).

1959 *The Fighting Cock* translated by Lucienne Hill from Jean Anouilh's *L'Hurluberlu,* ANTA Theatre, New York (with Rex Harrison as the General; Natasha Parry as Sophie).

1960 *Le Balcon* by Jean Genet, Théâtre de Gymnase, Paris (with Marie Bell).

The Visit by Friedrich Dürrenmatt, Royalty Theatre, London (with Alfred Lunt and Lynn Fontanne).

Irma la Douce, Plymouth Theatre, New York (with Keith Michell and Elizabeth Seal).

1962 *King Lear* by William Shakespeare, Royal Shakespeare Theatre, Stratford-upon-Avon, and later at Aldwych Theatre, London (with Paul Scofield as Lear; Tom Fleming as Kent; Irene Worth, Patience Collier, and Diana Rigg as Goneril, Regan, and Cordelia).

1963 *The Physicists* by Friedrich Dürrenmatt, translated by James Kirkup, Aldwych Theatre, London (with Irene Worth as Mathilde von Zaund; Alan Webb as Ernesti; Michael Hordern as Beutler; Cyril Cusack as Möbius).

The Tempest by William Shakespeare, Royal Shakespeare Theatre, Stratford-upon-Avon: directed in collaboration with Clifford Williams (with Tom Fleming as Prospero).

The Perils of Scobie Prilt, musical by Julian More and Monty Norman; staged for a week at New Theatre, Oxford (with Michael Sarne and Nyree Dawn Porter).

La Danse de Sergent Musgrave, translated from John Arden's *Sergeant Musgrave's Dance,* Théâtre de l'Athénée, Paris (with Laurent Terzieff as Musgrave).

Le Vicaire by Rolf Hochhuth, Théâtre de l'Athénée, Paris: co-director with François Darbon (with Jean Topart as the Doctor).

1964 'Theatre of Cruelty' season, Lamda Theatre, London; Royal Shakespeare Company.

Scenes from *The Screens* by Jean Genet, translated by Bernard Frechtman, Donmar Rehearsal Rooms, Seven Dials, London; Royal Shakespeare Company.

The Persecution and Assassination of Marat as Performed by the

Inmates of the Asylum of Clarenton under the Direction of the Marquis de Sade by Peter Weiss, English version by Geoffrey Skelton, verse adaptation by Adrian Mitchell, Aldwych Theatre, London (with Patrick Magee as the Marquis de Sade; Clive Revill as Jean-Paul Marat; Glenda Jackson as Charlotte Corday).

The Physicists by Friedrich Dürrenmatt, Martin Beck Theatre, New York (with Jessica Tandy as Mathilde von Zaund; Robert Shaw, Hume Cronyn, George Voskovec as the physicists).

1965 *The Investigation* by Peter Weiss, translated by Alexander Gross, Aldwych Theatre, London. Reading by members of the Royal Shakespeare Company, prepared by Peter Brook and David Jones.

The Marat/Sade, Martin Beck, New York (Royal Shakespeare Company; Ian Richardson now as Marat).

1966 *US*, ascribed to Peter Brook (director), Sally Jacobs (designer) Richard Peaslee (music), Adrian Mitchell (lyrics), Denis Cannan (original text), Geoffrey Reeves and Albert Hunt (associate directors), Michael Kustow and Michael Stott (adapters of documentary material), and acted by the Royal Shakespeare Company, Aldwych Theatre, London.

1968 *Oedipus* by Seneca, adapted by Ted Hughes, Old Vic Theatre, London (National Theatre Company) (with John Gielgud as Oedipus; Irene Worth as Jocasta; Colin Blakely as Creon).

1970 *A Midsummer Night's Dream* by William Shakespeare, Royal Shakespeare Theatre, Stratford-upon-Avon (with Alan Howard as Oberon and Theseus; Sara Kestelman as Titania and Hippolyta; David Waller as Bottom; John Kane as Puck and Philostrate).

II

SHAKESPEARE OVERSEAS

Five of Peter Brook's Shakespeare productions were also staged overseas:

1950 *Measure For Measure:* (Shakespeare Memorial Theatre Company) in West Germany at Berlin, Hamburg, Wiesbaden, and Dusseldorf.

1955 *Hamlet:* (with Paul Scofield) Moscow.

1957 *Titus Andronicus:* (Shakespeare Memorial Theatre Company)
Paris, Venice, Vienna, Warsaw, Belgrade, Zagreb.

1963 *King Lear:* (Royal Shakespeare Company) Paris.

1964 *King Lear:* (Royal Shakespeare Company) Berlin, Budapest,
Belgrade, Prague, Bucharest, Warsaw, Helsinki, Moscow,
Leningrad, Washington, Boston, Philadelphia, New York.

1971 *A Midsummer Night's Dream:* (Royal Shakespeare Company)
Billy Rose Theatre, New York; also Boston, Philadelphia,
Chicago, Toronto.

III

OPERA PRODUCTIONS

Royal Opera House, Covent Garden, London

1948 *Boris Godunov* (Mussorgsky).
La Bohème (Puccini).

1949 *The Marriage of Figaro* (Mozart).
The Olympians (Bliss).
Salome (Richard Strauss).

Metropolitan Opera, New York

1953 *Faust* (Gounod).

1957 *Eugene Onegin* (Tchaikovsky).

IV

FILMS

1944 *A Sentimental Journey* (amateur).

1953 *The Beggar's Opera* (with Laurence Olivier as Macheath).

1960 *Moderato Cantabile* (with Jeanne Moreau and Jean-Paul
Belmondo).

1963 *Lord of the Flies.*

1967 *Marat/Sade.*

1968 *Tell Me Lies.*

1971 *King Lear* (with Paul Scofield as Lear).

V

TELEVISION DIRECTION

New York

1953 *King Lear* (with Orson Welles).

London

1953 *Box For One.*

1955   *The Birthday Present.*
1955   *Report From Moscow.*
       (The three foregoing written by Peter Brook.)
1957   *Heaven and Earth* (by Peter Brook and Denis Cannan).

VI

BIBLIOGRAPHY

(Including work by Peter Brook; all published in London unless otherwise stated.)

AGATE, JAMES, *Ego 9*, Harrap, 1948.

BEATON, CECIL, and TYNAN, KENNETH, *Persona Grata*, Wingate, 1953.

BENTLEY, ERIC, *What is Theatre?*, Methuen, 1969.

BLAKELOCK, DENYS, *Round the Next Corner*, Gollancz, 1967.

BRANDON, HENRY (Editor), *Conversations with Henry Brandon* (including one with Peter Brook), Andre Deutsch, 1966.

BROOK, PETER, *The Empty Space*, MacGibbon and Kee, 1968.

BROOK, PETER (and others), *US: The Book of the Royal Shakespeare Production*, Calder and Boyars, 1968.

BROWN, IVOR, *Theatre 1954–5*, Max Reinhardt, 1955.
       Theatre 1955–6, Max Reinhardt, 1956.

BRUSTEIN, ROBERT, *Seasons of Discontent: Dramatic Opinions 1959–1965*, Cape, 1966.

BULL, PETER, *I Know The Face, But . . .*, Peter Davies, 1959.

BURTON, HAL (Editor) *Great Acting*, British Broadcasting Corporation, 1967.

CLURMAN, HAROLD, *The Naked Image*, Macmillan Company, New York, 1966.

CRAIG, EDWARD GORDON, *Gordon Craig*, Gollancz, 1970.

ESSLIN, MARTIN, *The Theatre of The Absurd*, revised and enlarged edition, Pelican Books, 1968.

FRY, CHRISTOPHER, *The Dark is Light Enough*, Oxford, 1954.

GENET, JEAN, *The Screens*, translated by Bernard Frechtman, Faber, 1963.

GIELGUD, (Sir) JOHN, *Stage Directions*, Heinemann, 1963.

GROTOWSKI, JERZY, *Towards a Poor Theatre*, Preface by Peter Brook, Methuen, 1969.

HAYMAN, RONALD, *Techniques of Acting*, Methuen, 1969.

KITCHIN, LAURENCE, *Drama in the Sixties; Form and Interpretation*, Faber, 1966.

KOTT, JAN, *Shakespeare Our Contemporary,* Preface by Peter Brook, Methuen, 1965.

KOZINTSEV, GRIGORI, *Shakespeare: Time and Conscience,* Dobson, 1967.

LEHMANN, JOHN (Editor), *Orpheus I* (contains Peter Brook's 'Style in Shakespeare Production'), Lehmann, 1948.

(Editor), *The Penguin New Writing,* Penguin, 1947.

LINGS, MARTIN, *Shakespeare in the Light of Sacred Art,* Allen and Unwin, 1964.

LUMLEY, FREDERICK, *New Trends in Twentieth-Century Drama,* Rockliff, 1957.

MACK, MAYNARD, *King Lear in Our Time,* Methuen, 1964.

MAROWITZ, CHARLES, MILNE, TOM, and HALE, OWEN (Editors), *The Encore Reader: A Chronicle of the New Drama* (contains Brook's 'Oh for Empty Seats', 'Happy Days and Marienbad', and 'From Zero to the Infinite'), Methuen, 1965.

MAROWITZ, CHARLES, and TRUSSLER, SIMON (Editors), *Theatre at Work* (contains Marowitz's 'Lear Log'), Methuen, 1967.

MARSHALL, NORMAN, *The Producer and the Play,* second edition, Macdonald, 1962.

ROSENTHAL, HAROLD, *Opera at Covent Garden: A Short History,* Gollancz, 1967.

RYAN, PATRICIA LOUISE, *Peter Brook: A Survey of his Directorial Achievement,* MS Thesis (unpublished), Wayne State University, Detroit, Michigan, USA.

SELLIN, ERIC, *The Dramatic Concepts of Antonin Artaud,* University of Chicago Press, 1968.

SENECA, *Oedipus,* adapted by Ted Hughes, Faber, 1968.

SHAKESPEARE, WILLIAM, *As You Like It,* Designs by Salvador Dali and Introduction by Peter Brook, Folio Society, 1963.

TREWIN, J. C., *Shakespeare on the English Stage 1900–1964,* Barrie and Rockliff, 1964.

The Birmingham Repertory Theatre 1913–1963, Barrie and Rockliff, 1963.

TYNAN, KENNETH, *He That Plays The King,* Longmans, 1950.

Curtains, Longmans, 1961.

WARRE, MICHAEL, *Designing and Making Stage Scenery,* Foreword by Peter Brook, Studio Vista, 1968.

WEISS, PETER, *The Marat/Sade,* translated by Geoffrey Skelton, Introduction by Peter Brook, Calder, 1965.

ZOLOTOW, MAURICE, *Stagestruck: Alfred Lunt and Lynn Fontanne,* Heinemann, 1965.

Index